MERMAN

by Ethel Merman

with George Eells

SIMON AND SCHUSTER
NEW YORK

Published by Simon and Schuster
A Division of Gulf & Western Corporation
Simon & Schuster Building
Rockefeller Center
1230 Avenue of the Americas
New York, New York 10020

Designed by Irving Perkins
Manufactured in the United States of America
1   2   3   4   5   6   7   8   9   10

Library of Congress Cataloging in Publication Data

Merman, Ethel.
    Merman.

    1.   Merman, Ethel.   2.   Singers—United States—
Biography.   I.   Eells, George, joint author.
ML420.M39A32   782.8'1'0924 [B]   78-92

ISBN 0-671-22712-2
The authors gratefully acknowledge Ira Gershwin, for permission to reproduce his letters in part; Walter Kerr and *The New York Times*, for permission to quote from a review by Mr. Kerr; Joshua Logan, for permission to quote from *Josh: My Up and Down, In and Out Life;* Mrs. Sylvia Lyons, for permission to reprint portions of a Leonard Lyons column; and for permission to reproduce letters by Cole Porter, © 1978, Robert H. Montgomery, Jr., as Trustee of the Cole Porter museum and Literary Property Trusts, all rights reserved.
    "I Get a Kick Out of You" (Cole Porter) © 1934 Warner Bros. Inc. Copyright Renewed. All Rights Reserved. Used by Permission.
    "He's Me Pal" (Vincent Bryan, Gus Edwards) © 1905 Warner Bros. Inc. Copyright Renewed. All Rights Reserved. Used by Permission.
    "Sam and Delilah" (George and Ira Gershwin) © 1930 New World Music Corporation. Copyright Renewed. All Rights Reserved. Used by Permission.

Photo editor: Vincent Virga

To Mom and Pop
To My Daughter
and My Son

Grateful acknowledgment is made for the generous help given by many individuals, including Josie Traeger, Russell Nype, Madeleine Gaxton, Tom Hendee, Martha Neubert, Gus Schirmer, Dick Kieling, Frank Liberman, Temple Texas, Aurand Harris, Ona Lucille Hill, Kathryn Shreve, Morty Sussman, R. E. Finley, Krysella Brose and the late Jack Penninger.

To Ted Fetter, Dr. Mary Henderson, Marian Spritzer Thompson, Bill Richards, Wendy Warnken and Mary Merrell of the Museum of the City of New York.

Paul Myers, Betty Wharton, Maxwell Silverman, Roderick Bladel, Brigitte Kueppers, Don Fowle, Monty Arnold and David Bartholomew of the Theatre Collection at the Lincoln Center Library for the Performing Arts.

John Knutson and Mrs. Alvista Perkins, Special Collections, Doheny Library, University of Southern California.

To our literary agent Gloria Safier; editors John Dodds, Larry Ashmead and Delfina Rattazzi.

To Vincent Virga for his pictorial conception and photo research.

Special thanks to Samuel Stark for indexing the book.

And to all others who helped in any way.

E.M. and G.E.

"DO YOU CRY EASILY?"

The hostess of a television talk show hit me with that question out of the blue.

"No, not particularly," I said.

The implication was that iron-lungs Merman never experienced any of the finer emotions. I told her that there was something about Christmas carols that always brought tears to my eyes. I added that I also cry at weddings. To me weddings are very solemn occasions. But then I said, "I should have cried at a couple of my own."

That remark broke up the studio audience and reinforced my public image as tough and brassy, funny and sassy. Great. For almost fifty years I've made a wonderful living playing that theatrical character—the *professional* brassy dame.

Thanks to newspapermen, magazine writers, talk-show hosts and me, legend has it that when God created me, he gave me a big distinctive voice, a lot of boldness and no heart.

I am also known to be able to take care of myself when I become angry. I don't mince words. If somebody needs telling off, he'll get it with both barrels. A friend can double-cross me once—then, fing! Maybe that's one of my problems. I'm too honest. One fellow told a reporter, "What I like about Ethel is that she'll give it to you to your face and not in your back. She has, I might add, a rather extensive grasp of the language."

Guilty! It's true that I use a few four-letter words when I'm riled or with close friends. In other words, I choose my spots. You won't find many in this book, for instance. I know when to use them and I don't use them on a tape recorder. If that's what you're looking for, you can reread Jackie Susann or Joyce Haber.

But probably the thing that contributed most to my public image is the fact that I've never suffered stage fright. That fascinates people. In almost everything that's ever been written about me, the reporter has eventually gotten around to some variation of the old chestnut about the opening night Betty Garrett confessed she was nervous, and I said, "Just remember if anyone out front could do as well as you, they would be up here doing it. They're the ones who ought to be worried."

You'll also read that I asked my husband Bob Levitt just before the out-of-town opening of *Annie Get Your Gun*, "Why should I be nervous? I know my lines."

And in 1975, when Alice Faye was coming out of retirement to appear in a revival of *Good News*, I told her approximately what I'd told Betty Garrett. When Alice said she still felt frightened, columnist Radie Harris comforted her by saying that I was the only star she had ever known who didn't experience stage fright.

Once I did feel a bit apprehensive. I was to sing "I Got Rhythm" in front of the 120-man Philharmonic at Guggenheim Stadium. For me, that was the ritzy side of the tracks. I wasn't nervous, but I felt that Rosa Ponselle or Lily Pons belonged there, not Ethel Merman from Broadway. When I finished, the audience of 20,000 longhairs stood up for me. So I bowed to them, then I turned and curtsied to the orchestra. The players rose and the violinists tapped their violins with their bows—the ultimate tribute. That's the only occasion I ever came close to stage fright, and look how well it turned out.

Maybe I'm one of a kind in that respect. But otherwise I am a reasonably normal human being. When I'm mistreated, I feel pain. When I'm hit, I bruise. And when I'm cut, I bleed like anyone else.

In my telling you about my life, you will find both the professionally brassy Ethel Merman *and* Ethel Agnes Zimmermann. This book will intertwine the two main thrusts of my life. My collaborator wanted to call it *MErman*. I thought the *ME* was a little too pushy, but he argued that it implied I was signaling the reader that this was not only going to tell the story of a girl with a big voice who came along at a time when musical comedy was becoming recognized as America's most original contribution to theatrical art and had the good luck to be at the right place at the right time, but also of Ethel Zimmermann, the girl from Astoria, who still survives.

As Ethel Merman, I have appeared in thirteen Broadway musicals—none ran less than six months. I was lucky enough to have the songs in my first show written by George and Ira Gershwin. Then Cole Porter wrote five shows for me. Irving Berlin? Two of my greatest. And Jule Styne and Steve Sondheim provided the capper for my career with *Gypsy*.

My favorite compliment over the years came from Cole Porter, who said, "I'd rather write songs for Ethel Merman than anyone else in the world." Maybe that's because I never change a word. I also try when possible to include the verse as well as the choruses. I don't tamper with the melodies or rhythms. Toscanini once remarked I was like another instrument in the band. In other words, I sing honest. Loud, but honest.

I was surprised to be told that the great German playwright Bertolt Brecht admired me. After *Gypsy* closed, his widow Helene Weigel of the Berliner Ensemble wanted me to play the title role in *Mother Courage* in New York. In fact, Madame Weigel was also kind enough to say that I was the only actress who influenced her acclaimed performance of the role. In the scene where Mother Courage refused to identify her dead son, Madame Weigel said she allowed her jaw to drop in silent horror. She said she had seen me use the same pantomime to achieve my "goon" effect when I fell in love with Frank Butler in *Annie Get Your Gun*.

As Ethel Merman, I've been called, among other things, "Miss," or more recently, "Ms. Musical Comedy." I've met and chummed with such people as Bea Lillie, Perle Mesta, Irving and Ellin Berlin, Cole and Linda Porter, Eleanor Holm and Billy Rose, and the Duke and Duchess of Windsor, to name-drop only a few.

That is part of the story. But truthfully, even though I have been ambitious to be a somebody from the time I was five years old, I never wanted to escape my past. My best friends are still Josie Traeger, who worked as a secretary with me at the B-K Vacuum Booster Brake Company in Long Island City, and Martha Neubert and Alice Welch, both of whom went through school with me. Sure, I made a lot of friends in later years, but the early ones are for keeps. As John Van Druten said in his play *Old Acquaintance*, we remember the same things.

On our noon hours, for instance, Josie and I used to hitch a ride to Bloomingdale's for a sandwich and some shopping. In those days it never occurred to us it wasn't safe. One day a black open barouche with a liveried chauffeur stopped and we hopped into the back and gave the driver our destination. I felt like Mrs. Astor and could just picture people asking, Who are those girls in that private limousine? The chauffeur marred the effect by lighting up a cigar. But my trip was really ruined when I noticed leaves and flowers scattered around the floor. We were in the open car that precedes the hearse in a funeral procession. In the blink of an eyelash, Ethel Astor was plain Zimmermann again.

Not long ago, Martha Neubert reminded me of the time that she had somehow gotten hold of a banned copy of James Joyce's *Ulysses*, but before either of us could read it, Mom tipped off Pop, who confiscated it.

Maybe that's why I don't like to read. I used to have books on the shelves in my home. People thought it was quaint when I called them props. But I was telling the truth, that's what they were. The only things I read are gossip columns.

If I read three pages of a book, I'm out like a light. When I pick up the book again, I've forgotten what I've read and have to start over again. By page three, even if I've just awakened from a nine-hour nap, I fall asleep again. So if anyone gives me a book, it had better have lots of pictures.

But if Mom and Pop had a terrible effect on my reading, it's one of the few ways they failed me. They always came first with me and I with them. I loved them both very dearly from earliest childhood. My relationship with my mom and pop remained the same as it was when I was a little girl. I was the apple of their eyes and they were of mine. Nothing could change that as long as I draw a breath.

Not that they were stage parents. After Pop stopped going to business, he used to stroll over to the theater and watch part of a performance, but he would leave before the show ended. Neither he nor Mom ever came backstage unless I invited them. I mentioned that to Mom once. She said, "Well, I never went to your father's office unless he invited me either."

That was her way. She never dominated me. I think maybe if I'd listened to her—especially about men—I wouldn't have made some of the mistakes in my personal life. But she was never insistent. She'd say, "I'll advise you, Ethel, but you don't have to take my advice." I didn't and I lived to regret it.

Once I began making money, Mom used to say to me, "Don't deprive yourself of anything. Whatever you want, you get it." She didn't care whether I had three cloth coats or twenty. If I wanted a piece of jewelry, she wanted me to have it. If I came in wearing something new, she'd say, "Oh, it's wonderful! Can you afford it?" She was a great lady.

Mom and Pop always came first with me, not because they demanded it, but because I appreciated their love and support and tried to return it. One of the things friends often comment on is how kind I have always been not only to Mom and Pop but also to all older people. Well, the way I look at it is they've earned my respect.

I suppose some people interpret my failed marriages as a result of my devotion to my parents. But nothing could be further from the truth. Nor have I ever let my career interfere with my marriages. The truth is I'm very unhappy when I'm in love. I'm basically a one-man woman. Once the conquest is made, I don't look right or left. I am interested only in that individual. Nobody else matters, because I become very dedicated to that person. But if the guy I love doesn't call, I go right up the wall. I try to call him. I wonder what has happened. What is he doing? Where is he? Voom, voom, voom. I torment myself.

Particularly in later years, I've got so I wouldn't trust any man as far as you can throw a piano. Over the years there have been a number of people who have tried to take advantage of me. They wanted to be linked with me just because I'm Ethel Merman. They come on too strong. I've got so I can recognize them right away and fade them fast. So I don't want to fall in love, go steady and get married. I'm never going to be hurt again. Never.

I don't think I'll ever get married again. Oh, if somebody came along and swept me off my feet, maybe. But there are too many complications in relationships. Who's happy these days? As I told Johnny Carson when he asked me about marriage plans on his show one night, "Who needs to buy the cow when you can get the milk for free!"

I have a comfortable life. I live in a three-and-a-half-room East Side hotel apartment—living room, den, bedroom and kitchenette. The walls are covered with paintings—some by famous artists, some by talented friends and some that I just happen to like. Curios and miniatures and bibelots long ago spilled out of their case into the rooms. And since I've taken up needlepoint, there are pillows of my making everywhere. I don't strive for effect. I just like to be surrounded by things that strike me as beautiful.

Maybe that's the reason that about five years ago I began leaving my Christmas tree on a table in the foyer of my apartment from one year to the next. I tell people that, and they think I'm crazy. But every night I light that little tree and get a lot of enjoyment out of it. It's so peaceful and beautiful and it gives me a wonderful feeling. Wonderful! As if nothing can hurt me.

I love having the Christmas spirit the whole year round. Of course there is some sadness in it—remembering earlier times when the kids trimmed the tree and we were all together. My daughter and my mother and my father and my husband I loved best are gone now. But I can recall times when we were all together and that's comforting. It makes me happy remembering the crowds buying presents and seeing Santa Clauses on every corner. But aside from all that, Christ was born. Christmas reminds me to be grateful and to try to live as He wanted. Because I believe that if you think right you're always taken care of. I'm a great believer in faith.

On a typical day, the first thing I do in the morning is read *The Daily Word*, which I subscribe to from Unity Village. A new edition arrives monthly with a message for each day of the week. And it's surprising how often the thought is appropriate to my life. It sort of guides me.

I clip those particular messages that are meaningful to me. The others I give to a maid whom I love. I have a loose-leaf notebook in which I paste my favorites. For instance, one is:

> The presence of God watches over me
> The light of God surrounds me
> The love of God enfolds me
> The power of God protects me
> Wherever I am God is.

Another of my favorites is "God is in my heart and my whole being is healed." Little quips. When you feel down in the dumps or something, you can repeat that and add "Nothing can hurt me." It's surprising how much better it makes you feel.

I was introduced to *The Daily Word* in 1967, when my beloved daughter, Ethel, died and I thought it was the end of the world. A friend subscribed for me and asked me to read the message every day. She said she knew it would help me as it had her. It has.

Not all my prayers come from *The Daily Word* though. I was for many years a communicant at St. Bartholomew's Church at Park Avenue and Fiftieth Street. Once when I was experiencing a heartache, Dr. Irving Pollard, the assistant rector, gave me this brief prayer to be repeated over and over. "Dear God, give me strength to meet whatsoever comes and wisdom to know what to do at the right time." I've always felt you can't very well go wrong with that. Although I'm not a communicant at St. Barth's anymore, I still go to the chapel when I'm moved to do so. I don't feel I have to go during formal services in order to worship.

But to get back to my typical days, I have plenty of invitations to go places, lots to do. If I'm not working, I go to have my hair taken care of and work at needlepoint. I never go to lunch. Luncheon to me is a word. If I feel in need of sleep, I just open a book or turn on the television. Both are better than any sleeping pill. And, incidentally, you'll find neither those nor tranquilizers in my medicine chest.

In general, I suppose that over the years I've simplified my life. On weekends there is nothing I like more than going to auctions and flea markets. I've found some of the choice Raggedy Anns and Raggedy Andys that I collect in that way. At a flea market I always head for the junk jewelry table first. Before some cat burglars cleaned me out in 1970, I had amassed quite a collection of genuine stuff. After it was gone, I decided not to give them another chance. Now most of what I own comes from bargain tables.

My friend Russell Nype loves to tell how his wife, Diantha, and I discovered an attractively designed paste-diamond brooch that went for three dollars at a flea market in Maine. "I'm going to take that back to New York and have it copied in real diamonds," I told Diantha. But when I got home, I looked it over, got out an old toothbrush and some liquid Ivory and gave it a good going over. By the time I'd finished, it looked so attractive that when I was invited to the White House I wore it.

My taste in drinks is simpler too. I've switched from champagne—which produced an acid condition that made my teeth sensitive to heat and cold—to Almadén Chablis, an inexpensive California wine that I order in the fanciest restaurants. At one time I smoked, but in 1959 I couldn't think of anything else to give up for Lent so I stopped—and I haven't had a cigarette since.

I've never cooked. When I lived at home, Mom did it. By the time we moved to Manhattan, I was making enough money to hire a professional. So I can't do much more in the kitchen than make a cup of tea and some toast. Or on that rare evening when I'm too tired to go out, I open a can of tunafish or boil an egg for myself. I go to bed at seven-thirty to watch television and suddenly I'm out. I wake up and it's morning. That's the way I make up for the late nights.

My taste in food is for the most part confined to simple American fare. Once when Tony Cointreau of the liqueur family took me to La Grenouille, I bypassed the boeuf florentine and other specialties and asked whether they served chopped steak. The captain said it could be arranged. It must have taken some arrangement. When the bill came, my eye happened to spot the price. I said to Tony, "Not that it makes any difference, but what could have been in that chopped steak that made it fourteen dollars?" He called over the captain, who explained that it was sirloin.

"For fourteen dollars?" I asked.

"Oh, yes. We had to chop it," he said—as if that explained everything.

For someone whose life has been associated with Broadway for so long, I attend surprisingly few shows. The type of theater that is popular today just doesn't appeal to me. As far as dramas are concerned, it's considered passé for playwrights to turn out anything the average person can understand.

Star vehicles are out of fashion in both straight plays and musicals. Of course, I enjoy shows such as *Chorus Line* and appreciate the way they are presented, except for the four-letter words. I'm no prude and I may use them myself, but profanity is no substitute for entertainment. Nor do I want to see nudity on stage. That belongs in the confines of your own home. Whatever people want to do in their homes is all right with me, but I don't want to pay my money to see a bunch of naked people. You see one, you've seen them all.

Until his death, on December 22, 1977, before I left on a night when I was dining out, my friends and I generally had a drink with Pop, who was ninety-seven, loved Scotch on the rocks and lived three floors above me.

This is how that came about. After Mom had her first heart seizure and was hospitalized, Dr. Attia told me that she would never again be able to look after my father or herself. This presented something of a problem, since Pop was legally blind, having very little vision in his right eye and none in his left.

While my mother was hospitalized, I moved them from Central Park West into an apartment with the same floor plan as mine, three stories up, in the hotel where I live. But instead of having a den, as I have, in their apartment, that room was furnished as a bedroom for their nurse, Kathryn Shreve.

After the movers finished, I got out the floor plan and the measurements I'd made in their old familiar bedroom, took them upstairs and placed all the furniture in the new one so that it duplicated the layout they were used to. Even though Pop couldn't see much, in a couple of days he could move about as easily as he always had. And with the help of Kathryn, who has become like a sister to me, it worked out wonderfully.

While Mom was at Roosevelt Hospital, Pop and I visited her every day. He and Mom had been married for over fifty years, seldom spending a night apart. Pop was content to sit at her bedside and hold her hand whether or not she was aware of it.

I wanted to be there too. In fact, I was scheduled to go to London to recreate my favorite role, Mamma Rose, in *Gypsy*. I gave up the part to stay near Mom. It wasn't any noble gesture. I did it for my own sake, not Mom's. She didn't know who was there.

That is how I began to contribute each Wednesday that I'm in New York to Roosevelt Hospital. Even though I wanted to be with Mom, I had too much energy just to sit twiddling my thumbs for eight and a half months. In other words, I got tired of hanging around.

After a few weeks I asked whether I could be of some service. At first they put me on escort duty, taking patients in wheelchairs and on stretchers for X rays or cobalt treatments, but as Mom faded I reached the point where I couldn't bear seeing people on stretchers. So I went to the volunteer department again and asked whether they could transfer me. They wanted to know whether I'd be interested in working in the gift shop.

Would I! I'd always liked waiting on store. If I hadn't been a singer or a secretary, I think I'd have loved being a saleslady. I enjoy the intrigue involved in selling and ringing up sales on the cash register. As high school girls, Martha Neubert and I sold hats at Worth's department store on Thirty-fourth Street in Manhattan on Saturdays. Before that I'd known a German family named Staebler who owned a brick building on Third Avenue in Astoria. They ran a saloon on one side and an ice cream parlor on the other. I used to go in and wait on the ice cream crowd. I didn't get paid. I just got a kick out of it. Sometimes I'd hand-pack a quart of ice cream and

Mrs. Staebler would beg, "Please, Ethel! Leave some room at the bottom." The idea was to leave space and let the ice cream melt down.

So I took to the Roosevelt Hospital gift shop immediately. Right from the beginning people would ask whether anyone had ever told me I looked like a *young* Ethel Merman. They still do. Generally I just say they have and that's that.

One woman especially intrigued me. "You're *not?* Are you?"

"Not what?"

"Not Ethel Merman." I admitted I was and she came back with "Well, you certainly don't look it!"

But my favorite Roosevelt Hospital story happened not long ago. I was riding an elevator, wearing my Pink Lady uniform, with this middle-aged couple. The woman looked me over and then asked, "Has anyone ever told you that you look like Ethel Merman?"

Before I could answer, the man piped up. "Ethel Merman just wishes she looked like you."

I grinned and said, "I *am* Ethel Merman," and he wanted to go right down the elevator shaft.

Since my parents passed I have continued working in the gift shop every Wednesday that I am in New York. I do it out of gratitude for the wonderful care they received.

In lieu of flowers at the time of Mom's passing, Pop and I had asked that contributions be made to the hospital in her name. Quite a lot of money accumulated. The hospital used it to develop a beautiful little garden located between Fifty-eighth and Fifty-ninth Streets, near the Ninth Avenue exit.

I didn't know how Pop was going to react to the dedication ceremony on November 3, 1976. At first Kathryn and I weren't going to tell him. We were afraid the emotional strain would be too much. Then we decided there was a greater risk that somebody might mention it to him and he would be terribly hurt.

So Pop attended. It was a wonderful day for him and for me— very cheerful, yet tinged with sadness. Many of our friends were there. A lot of important people who serve on the board at Roosevelt spoke. They had my mother's plaque resting on a bed of crushed velvet with a pin spotlight shining down upon it. The plaque reads: "In memory of Agnes Gardner Zimmermann, mother of Ethel Merman, this ivy garden was contributed by the friends who loved her."

Pop cried a little, but it was also a happy moment for him. He said, "Agnes would have been so happy."

Then I got up to express my thanks. I got about a quarter of the way through my little speech. "Oh, I hope I can get through this," I said, but all I had to do was to look at Pop to pull myself together. That's the way it always was.

By now you've probably gathered that I'm not exactly the kind of dame that people have always thought I was. But if you are interested in hearing about me, my career, my ups, my downs and some of my mistakes, I think you already realize that you'll get it straight from the shoulder, because that's the kind of woman I am.

MOM CLAIMED that I could carry a tune at two and a half or three years of age. Maybe she was a little prejudiced. Then again maybe not. Because at five I made my singing debut at the Astoria, Long Island, Republican Club, of which both my parents were members. Pop accompanied me on the piano, and I must have made a hit, because I appeared there often, billed as "Little Ethel Zimmermann."

Pretty soon I was singing for Pop's brother Masons, for the Long Island Society for the Prevention and Relief of Tuberculosis and in the Parada Community Revue, sponsored by the Knights of Columbus.

When World War I came along, I appeared at Camp Mills and Camp Yaphank. Mrs. Forbes, wife of the doctor who took care of Mom when I was born, was president of the Queens County branch of the Red Cross, and she booked me at the camps. I remember very well one Christmas day when I gladly abandoned my new toys, hopped into an ambulance—since no passenger car was available— and traveled to Camp Mills to entertain the troops.

Those soldiers got a big kick hearing my strong voice coming out of such a tiny body. There was lots of laughter and applause for "Since Maggie Dooley Did the Hooley Hooley," "K-K-K-Katie" and

"Over There," but there were tears too. Pop had bought and taught me Vincent Bryan and Gus Edwards' "He's Me Pal." I changed it to "She's Me Pal" and dedicated it to my mother.

It went something like this:

> She's me pal,
> She's me pal,
> She's the very best friend that I know.
> Her heart's full of love
> As the heavens above,
> She drives away sorrow and woe.
> I'll try to repay all her kindness to me
> And if God be willing I shall.
> I have a friend that's true,
> Dear old mother, that's you,
> You're me pal,
> You're me pal.

You can imagine that when I finished, an awful lot of those big tough fighting men had mysteriously got something in their eyes.

Shortly I became a kind of professional amateur, going from contest to contest. I remember how they held a five-dollar gold piece over each contestant's head and the one who received the most applause got to keep it. I sang loudly and clearly and my voice was distinctive. Invariably I won. Pretty soon I got the idea that I'd like to go into show business. Why not? Everyone was acclaiming the little Zimmermann girl, and I sounded pretty good to myself.

Mom and Pop were proud of my popularity, but from their point of view show business was no way to make a living. They were of Scots and German descent respectively, practical people, and nobody from either side of the house had ever chosen such a precarious field. It's true that they met on one of those hayrides that boys and girls used to organize. And it's also true that Pop was playing piano at the time in a pick-up orchestra. But that was just for fun. He earned his living as a bookkeeper and later as an accountant.

Pop's name, I probably should have said before this, was Edward Zimmermann. Mom's was then Agnes Gardner. My father's mother died when he was eight, so I was never as close to that side of the family as to the Gardners. Grandma Gardner, who was a widow, owned a big three-story house at what used to be 359 Fourth Avenue in Astoria. Since then they have changed the names of the streets in that section and I don't know what it is now called.

We lived on the top story, where I was born in my parents' bedroom on January 16. *The World Almanac* says it was 1909. I say it was 1912. But what difference does it make as long as I feel thirty-three?

Grandma Gardner, my Aunt Mary and my Uncle Harry and my cousin Claude Gilchrist Pickett lived in the middle-floor apartment. Grandma used the street-level floor as rental property.

I spent a lot of time with Grandma and the Picketts. She always had a teakettle simmering on the stove ready to brew tea. That's the reason I always drink it and never developed a taste for coffee. Claude and I were more like brother and sister than cousins until Grandma sold the house. After my family moved to a beautiful fifth-floor walk-up on Thirty-first Avenue, Claude and I sort of drifted apart.

I attended Public School Four and William Cullen Bryant High School, and, strangely, for all my warbling at lodges and amateur contests, I never was active in the glee club or school assemblies. Nor did I appear in class plays. I guess I was too involved in my studies. I'm not even sure whether many of my classmates knew that I could sing.

But there was one boy who did. He was my first big crush, although at this point I can't even recall his name. I do remember I wanted to make an impression. For him to get to the ball park, he had to pass our house. I used to watch for him on Sundays particularly. As soon as I spied him coming down the block, I'd say to Pop, "Feel like playing the piano?" And when my pint-sized Romeo went by I'd be warbling like a bird, so proud of the fact that somebody I liked knew I could sing. My father also taught me to read music and to play the piano—but not well, even though people have said that I'm a natural musician.

I was baptized and confirmed in the Church of the Redeemer on Crescent Street in Astoria. When I was old enough, I attended morning services at nine A.M., Sunday school at eleven A.M., prayer meeting at four-thirty P.M. and Christian Endeavor at seven P.M. Mom didn't go. She was busy at home cooking for the rest of us.

One thing that bothered me was that at the Redeemer they didn't allow girls to sing in the choir. So I shopped around. I tried the Dutch Reformed, St. Patrick's (some of the family on both sides were Catholic), and ended up at the Dutch Reformed Church most of the time. There the choir was mixed.

I'll be honest with you and admit that I resisted attending. But Mom had done it when she was a girl, and I was forced to go too. Today I'm grateful to Mom and Pop for helping me develop a belief in the hereafter. I think everybody should have some sort of faith to see them through. I know it helps me every day.

My parents were loving but strict disciplinarians. I loved them but was scared to death of them. I remember that there was a cat-o'-nine-tails on the wall, but it was for show, not for use. My greatest problem was fear of the dark. When we still lived on Fourth Avenue the whistles of the boats and foghorns spooked me. Mom got communion candles for a night light and sometimes would even lie with me until she thought I was asleep. I wasn't, but I wouldn't let her know it. After she'd gone, I'd silently cry myself to sleep.

I was very close to my mother when I was small—closer than to Pop, who was away at work all day. Mom and I used to spend many afternoons in the orchard beside Grandma's house. In those days there were many open fields in Astoria and people walked a lot. Mom took me almost everywhere she went, but one day she and Aunt Mary were going shopping and left me behind. I can still see them now, walking, walking, walking . . . When they were a certain distance away I couldn't stand it any longer. I just had to be with her, that's all.

She dressed me beautifully. Aunt Jenny, the wife of one of my mother's brothers, used to make all my little pleated skirts and Peter Pan blouses. I guess I was pudgy and my stomach stuck out a little. Anyway she always had to make them longer in the front so they would hang straight. When I dressed up, the skirts would be starched and a big bow would be attached in the back. I always had to be careful when I sat down to pull up the skirt so it and the bow didn't get wrinkled or I'd get whacked.

My Easter treats were Maryjanes that came from Coward Shoes— red kid, black patent leather or brown. If I'd been good, I could put away my long stockings and wear anklets with my Easter shoes.

During the period when I was growing up, I had very few contacts with show business. Like many girls, I suppose, I dreamed of being a movie star. Only I didn't think I was glamorous enough. But I was luckier than most, because the Paramount Astoria Studios were located at Sixth and Pierce, two blocks from my home.

Some of the kids had punched holes in the fence around the studio so that when a company was shooting on the back lot we could vicariously get in on the action. When I knew an Alice Brady or a James Kirkwood Sr. picture was in production, I couldn't wait to get up there and watch. I'd wait around and drool as her big blue limousine passed with the liveried chauffeur sitting out front, and there in the back behind a glass partition was the glamorous Miss Brady in her silver fox furs. To me she was very sophisticated and mysterious and everything I could never hope to be. It never occurred to me that I'd wind up working at that same studio before too many years had passed.

Miss Brady was a famous Broadway star, but that didn't mean anything to me. As far as I was concerned, vaudeville was theater. I never thought of attending a straight play or a musical comedy. But every Friday night Mom and Pop took me to Manhattan to the Palace at Forty-seventh Street and Seventh Avenue. At first we sat in the first row of the second balcony, where the seats cost forty-six cents. Then later we moved down to the back of the first balcony, where seats went for eighty-three cents apiece.

Pop used to get a kick out of me. When I was real little, some famous soprano would be singing and I'd be lost to the world. But let her go a little off key—it didn't have to be much—and I'd dig Pop in the ribs with my elbow. I had a good ear even then.

Blossom Seeley and Benny Fields were favorites. Blossom had great style, great rhythm. If she were alive today, she'd be a headliner. Some of the others I especially liked were Odette Myrtil and her violin, Fanny Brice's singing and comedy, Sophie Tucker and Grace Hayes. When they'd get out on stage, I'd think, Oh, boy, I could do that—and eventually I did.

My only personal connection with the world of vaudeville came through friends of my family, John and Lily Gardner—no relation to my mother, just the same name. Their son, John Jr., was in with the New York theatrical crowd. He knew how crazy I was about performers, so he took me to Grand Central Station to see off a troupe who were going on tour. One fellow was a handsome stilt walker named Archie Leach. As the train pulled out, Archie was on the rear platform waving goodbye. But all I was thinking about was Oh, there they go! Vaudevillians! Nothing about the handsome guy.

That shows how crazy I was about vaudeville, because he, of course, became famous as Cary Grant. Still I'm glad I wasn't a part of that world. When I think of my childhood, I'm grateful to Mom and Pop that through my amateur work I experienced some of the joy of performing without losing the security of an everyday home life. In other words, I was lucky enough to have it both ways.

By THE TIME I entered high school, I wanted to be a singer, but my mother at first urged me to take a general course. She wanted me to follow the example set by one of my favorite cousins, Agnes Shar- key, and become a schoolteacher. But I didn't want to go in that direction. In the back of my mind I had always known I wanted to sing. Finally I compromised. I agreed to take a four-year business course at William Cullen Bryant High in Long Island City.

Now I'm not patting myself on the back when I say I *really* was an excellent shorthand, typing and bookkeeping student. I always got in the 90s on my tests. I can take shorthand—Isaac Pitman method— and type all my own letters even today. My parents felt that by following a commercial course I'd be able to support myself if my singing career didn't materialize.

That early training taught me to be a very systematic person. I do everything in an orderly fashion today. There is really too much perfectionism, I sometimes think. But that is the training. Every en- gagement I have is written in my appointment book. I keep my tele- phone book neatly typed with no handwritten numbers and no crossouts.

My short personal notes are handwritten, but I type long letters. I love typing a letter. It just seems to flow. The only thing is that I'm afraid of breaking my fingernails. So I just use some rubber cushions on my fingers. The alternative would be to wear gloves. But I'd feel like an idiot typing with gloves on.

Still, in order to keep in practice, I sometimes do this exercise that takes in all the keys: *One of the boys quickly threw the large javelin beyond the maximum distance and won the prize.*

It was in high school that I began chumming with Alice Welch. She joined Martha Neubert as a special friend. Alice had lost her parents at an early age and just adored my mother and father. They were fond of Alice too.

I graduated in June and registered with an employment agency down at Long Island City Plaza. Ten days later I was working as a stenographer at the Boyc-Ite Company over on Queens Boulevard. Boyc-Ite was an anti-freeze solution for automobiles. My salary was all of twenty-three dollars a week.

Shortly I got a better offer—twenty-eight a week. We stenographers used to eat in a little lunchroom near the office where we met people connected with other firms. One friendly fellow was Vic Kliesrath from the Bragg-Kliesrath Corporation, which manufactured the B-K Vacuum Booster Brake. He must have heard that I was a good stenographer, because he offered me a job and I jumped at the chance to better myself.

At Bragg-Kliesrath, they had a system that proved a little inconvenient for me. All the stenographers were required to punch in on a time clock. During this period I was going to Manhattan after work several nights a week, visiting music publishing houses. I'd pick up the latest pop songs, which the publishers were happy to give to singers who would use them on club dates. I also was making the rounds of fringe agents who had offices in the Bond Building near the Palace Theater, registering with them. Occasionally one would send me out for an appearance for which I could pick up a fast five bucks—or a bonanza of seven-fifty if the owner was a big spender. I was just seventeen at the time. I remember distinctly because that year my parents gave me my own key to the apartment.

The only problem I had was that I was getting home so late from my occasional extra jobs that it was hard for me to arrive at B-K on time in the morning. So the other girls would punch my card for me and I'd grab an extra hour's sleep. One of those girls, Josephine Schwarz, who worked for the purchasing agent of the company, proved a pal indeed.

Eventually the time clock problem solved itself when I became personal secretary to Caleb Bragg, who was president of Bragg-Kliesrath Corporation. Mr. Bragg—I never called him anything else—wasn't a person you could get close to. I don't think he meant to be snooty, but he was very reserved. It was his nature. He couldn't be any other way.

He was a financier, an inventor, a Florida land promoter, a multimillionaire and ultra-chic. When I worked for him, it was my duty to see that such friends as Gertrude Lawrence, Hope Williams, Frances Williams and Irene Delroy received flowers from him. I'll be honest. It used to drive me crazy. They were singers and big stars, but I thought I was as good as they were.

With all of his interests, it was natural that most of the time Mr. Bragg should come in late and sometimes not at all. So when I'd arrive in the morning, if I felt a little tired, I'd go to the ladies' room, where there was a cot, slip off my dress and sneak a few winks. When Mr. Bragg approached, Josie or one of the other girls would give me the eight-gong signal. I'd hop up, get into my dress and stroll over to my desk by the time that Mr. Bragg was ready to get down to business.

Now I don't want to give the impression that Mr. Bragg didn't work hard. He did. Vic Kliesrath concentrated on mechanical development, but Mr. Bragg defined and refined the ideas and translated them into technical terms to be put in claim forms which had to be sent to his patent attorney, Louis Prevost Whitaker, at 150 Nassau Street. Half the time I didn't know what Mr. Bragg was talking about. I really didn't. How would I know?

A kind of ritual developed. After Mr. Bragg had looked over the letter, he'd say, "Oh, Miss Zimmermann, didn't I say so and so and so and so and so and so?"

"You did?"

"Yes. But it's not here."

"Well, I didn't hear you say it." He'd said it all right, but I didn't get it. So it wasn't down and I hadn't been able to transcribe it. Then he'd have to insert the technical data.

But Mr. Bragg wasn't just a desk man. I can still see him experimenting with the brake on a fire engine. The B-K Vacuum Booster Brake was, as I understand it, an early version of power brakes. Because, like, if you put your foot on the pedal too hard, you'd go right through the windshield. That's how sensitive the brake was. All you had to do was touch it.

There Mr. Bragg would be, wearing a fedora, a beautiful overcoat and highly polished shoes, getting behind the wheel of that fire engine. You'd think maybe a mechanic or somebody would do the test run, but oh no, there was Mr. Bragg with Vic Kliesrath sitting next to him. Up and down Queens Boulevard they'd go.

Unlike Mr. Bragg, Vic Kliesrath was a very regular fellow. At lunchtime he would take two or three of us girls out to eat, and frequently he and his wife would have a few employees to dinner at their home in Port Washington. They had a piano and I'd sing. That's the kind of people they were—down to earth.

I remember one special Saturday they were giving a clambake at a restaurant for certain members of the company. I wore a new Milan hat, a lovely silk dress and new shoes. I was done up in my best.

Now to our great surprise, during the day Mr. Bragg came over to the restaurant. At the time he owned a beautiful houseboat, *The Masquerader*, and three or four speedboats that he sometimes raced in the Gold Cup Regatta. Anyway, he appeared at this shindig and asked if any of us wanted a ride in his speedboat *Casey Jones*. We did and he began taking two or three at a time to the Connecticut shore and back to Port Washington.

Bessie Sullivan, the telephone operator, and I got in, went to the opposite shore and were headed back, cutting in and out among the other boats in the harbor when all of a sudden the *Casey Jones* hit a log and capsized. Over we went—me in my beautiful hat, new dress and shoes. My purse hit the bottom and we were absolutely drenched.

Mr. Bragg's *Masquerader* was standing out there and he insisted that we go aboard. I'd never seen anything like it. It looked like the best New York apartment I could imagine, with servants and all the conveniences.

Bessie and I were each given a pair of Mr. Bragg's pajamas and a robe while our clothes were put in the fireless cooker to dry so that we could wear them home. Of course he reimbursed us for them later.

Now he was having this marvelous party and we were invited to stay. I'd never seen anything like it before either. Two of the guests were Arch Selwyn and his wife, Ruth, both of whom were Broadway producers. She kept talking to me during dinner and asked what I did. I told her I worked for Mr. Bragg, but I also sang. I wanted to get that in. Nobody followed up on it, but she remembered it, because I got to know her later and we talked about it.

It was after that episode that I worked up enough nerve to tell Mr. Bragg that I wanted to be a singer and to ask him for a letter of introduction to George White, who produced George White's *Scandals*, an annual Broadway revue that was very popular. Later some press agent started the story that I wrote my own letter of introduction, but the truth is that Mr. Bragg dictated and signed it.

By this time I had realized that the name Zimmermann would crowd a marquee. So I went to my father and said, "Look, Pop, I can't use the name Zimmermann if I'm ever to become anything in show business. The light bulbs needed to spell it would give everybody heat prostration."

Pop wasn't pleased. I suggested using my mother's maiden name, Gardner. He would have no part of that. Zimmermann had always been good enough for him and it was good enough for me. Then I suggested Ethel Hunter as a pretty name. Hunter had been my maternal grandmother's maiden name. That got Pop's German up. So I finally lopped off the Zim and the final n. The result, Merman—a coined name—made him relatively happy.

After working hours, I went over to the Apollo Theater on Forty-second Street near Broadway and delivered the letter to George White. I was sure I was in. With a hot letter from Caleb Bragg, how could I miss? Well, I did.

Mr. White read it and asked, "What would you like to do? Do you want to be in the line?"

The idea had never entered my mind. "No. I sing," I told him.

He said, "Oh, I'm sorry. Frances Williams is doing the songs this year."

That was the end of my dreams of appearing in George White's *Scandals*—for the time being. Mom and Pop had taught me that if I was going to do anything, I should do something worthwhile or not do it at all. I never could think of myself as a one-liner—let alone a chorus girl. Since I couldn't have a featured role as a singer, I went back to the typewriter and club dates.

Not that the club dates were anything special. I'd finish at the office, go home, pick up my little valise with a couple of taffeta dresses and the standard arrangements of popular songs of the day. I got seven dollars and fifty cents a night. The agents always paid me in cash. Since then I've sometimes wondered how much they actually collected.

I'd sing a verse and two choruses of four or five numbers. If it was a long show, I'd sing a couple of songs, go off while the master of ceremonies introduced another act and then come out in a different dress to do more songs.

The dresses—all of which were taffeta or satin—had little round necks, bodices and full skirts. I thought they were beautiful.

The numbers were current hits, such things as "I've Got a Feelin' I'm Fallin'," "How Deep Is the Ocean" and "Little White Lies." The latter, for some reason I've never been able to figure out, had my picture on the sheet music at a time when I was still a nobody.

One of the first places I worked was on the third floor of Keen's English Chop House at 72 West Thirty-sixth Street. They had a comic, an exotic dancer and me. I worked there several times. To show you how ambitious I was, one New Year's Eve I worked an early show at Keen's, took my little valise and headed for Times Square to take the subway to a show in Brooklyn. Just as I got to the entrance, it turned midnight and I almost got thrown down the stairs by revelers—but I made the second show and that night I collected a total of fifteen dollars.

Up to this time, I ought to explain, life was placid for me. Mr. Bragg's hours more or less coincided with mine—especially in the summertime, when sometimes he didn't come into the office at all. I had no trouble in the clubs. I was never fired. Owners and managers I worked for didn't make serious passes. They could see I was well brought up. I knew what was considered right from wrong in those days. And they knew I was no little fly-by-night gal working clubs and hoping to sleep my way to the top. If I was going to get there, I was going to get there on talent.

My home life was good too. Everything was on an even keel. My father wasn't rich, but he was comfortably well off. Even after I began my secretarial work, I didn't pay room and board. I turned my money over to Mom and she gave me so much for luncheons, carfare and stuff like that. Whatever else I wanted she bought for me—dresses, everything. The rest of my earnings she banked.

At this point there were a few fellows in my life, but nothing serious. I was too dedicated to making a place for myself as a girl singer to bother with romance.

Then in September of 1929 one of the agents with whom I was registered booked me into this place called Little Russia. It was on Fifty-seventh Street, right off Sixth Avenue, downstairs. But instead of being a one-nighter, this engagement was for two weeks at sixty dollars a week, Monday through Saturday. It wasn't any different from the other places I'd worked. I'd do my numbers between ten P.M. and one A.M., pick up my belongings and take the BMT subway to Astoria. Nobody paid much attention. At sixty dollars a week they didn't expect me to be Galli-Curci.

One night shortly after I opened, a man named Lou Irwin was passing by the club with his date. The doorman, whom Irwin had known, suggested that he, as they say, catch my act.

Irwin sent back his card. I wondered whether he was just a guy trying to get a date. But the card said THEATRICAL AGENT and it was engraved, so I decided to take a chance and talk to him.

Irwin told me he represented Helen Morgan, the Ritz Brothers, Brian Aherne and some others. He liked my voice and the fact that he could hear it above all the clatter. He said he had a friend by the name of Archie Mayo, who was a big director at Warner Brothers. Mayo was scheduled to arrive in New York from California next day and Lou Irwin wanted me to sing for him. I told Irwin that I was going to be honest with him. I couldn't make it during the day because I had an office job, but I'd be glad to come over when I got off work. Lou thought that was funny, but he thought it was even funnier when I showed up with Mom because I wasn't of an age to sign a contract.

I remember going to the Mills publishing house on Forty-seventh Street between Sixth and Seventh Avenues for the audition. I brought my music, got one of the staff pianists that Mills employed, went into one of the rooms with a piano and sang. Now I've always claimed that I never suffered stage fright. I never did after I became a professional, but when I sang for Archie Mayo I was scared stiff. Fear arises when you're not exactly sure what you are trying to accomplish.

Later Lou called and said he could negotiate a contract at Warners Studios in Brooklyn at $125 a week making musical shorts. It was for six months, with options for something like seven or nine years. At the time Mr. Bragg was still paying me thirty-five dollars weekly. I was a practical girl with practical parents. So naturally Mom signed me up to become a movie star—or so we thought!

IV

MY CAREER at Warner Brothers consisted of one musical short subject. For some reason, now better forgotten, I was running around in a bear skin. Very chic. Finally Indians chased me up a tree, whereupon I burst into song. It was the craziest thing I've ever been associated with, and if it was ever released I never saw it.

Making that terrible little short gave me a boost though. I *knew* I could do better than that. One thing about the contract that seemed wonderful was that Warners had to pay me whether I worked or not. You might think I would have been in heaven getting money for doing nothing, but first I became restless, then miserable. Finally I went to Lou and told him, "Get me out of the contract before people think I'm a kept woman."

He secured my release. Not long after he arranged for me to join Clayton, Jackson and Durante as the girl singer at their new Broadway nightclub, Les Ambassadeurs. A lot has been written about my audition for Jimmy Durante. It never happened. The boys booked me on Lou Irwin's word. Nor did I work in any numbers with them.

In my first appearance I wore a gown supplied by the club. It was a simple black. Too simple, I thought. I led the chorus line, which included Arlene Judge, who was later married to Dan Topping and five or six other guys. Then on my second appearance I did a solo spot using a few of my regular songs, including "Moanin' Low," which Libby Holman had made famous, "Body and Soul" and "I've Got a Feelin' I'm Fallin'."

I was in heaven now that I was appearing regularly and began getting written about in the columns. Louis Sobol mentioned me in the *Journal*, Jerry Wald in the *Graphic*, Walter Winchell, Mark Hellinger and others. It wasn't anything important, just squibs such as "Watch the little Merman girl, she's going places."

I was. To the hospital. I developed a sore throat and someone gave me a gargle with a lot of iron in it. It didn't help my throat much, but a couple of more doses and all my teeth would have turned black. I went to my doctor, who said my tonsils had to come out.

The operation was difficult because every time the surgeon went in after a tonsil, he found it so diseased it just sort of disintegrated. I had to have stitches on each side of my throat and was sure I would never be able to sing again. I didn't for two weeks. Then my voice returned stronger than ever.

Lou Irwin knew I was heartbroken at having to leave Clayton, Jackson and Durante just when I was beginning to be recognized by the columnists. So he suggested that I get my strength back at a place in Miami called the Roman Pools Casino, located right across from the famed Roney Plaza Hotel. Lou convinced me that it was a wonderful opportunity. He said, "You'll be in the sun while you're not feeling too great. And you'll be pulling down three hundred dollars a week for at least six weeks."

So I agreed. Old programs and reviews say that the headliner was Joe E. Lewis, who was making his comeback after some Chicago gangsters had cut his throat from ear to ear. You couldn't prove it by me. I don't remember ever working with him.

I do recall a girl by the name of Olive McClure. I can still hear her music. She did what was billed as the "Chain Dance." Olive had a gorgeous figure and wore chains on her wrists, ankles and other crucial spots. Later she married Bert Taylor, the society playboy and brother of Countess Dorothy Di Frasso.

My big number was "Moanin' Low." For it I wore—oh please!—a

red beret on the side of my head, a scarf around my neck, a black satin dress, black net stockings and spike heels. If those chains, black net stockings and high heels sound like some sadist's phantasmagoria, most of us innocents then wouldn't have known one if he'd tripped us.

There was a thing that went on down there that may be hard for readers to understand, but I'm not ashamed to mention it. The Roman Pools Casino had gambling. So in the afternoon the girls in the show would get into bathing suits, take a swim, put on lovely robes and go into the casino.

Naturally, being performers, we got to know the guys who hung around there. And it was the custom that if any girl sat around with a guy while he gambled, he would give the girl who had given him her company half of his winnings. Say he won $500, he gave her $250. It was just an innocent custom. No matter what it seems.

At this time I didn't have a checking account of my own. I used to buy postal money orders and send my savings home to Mom to bank. The first week she received $450, the next $600. Well, very shortly Mom was on the telephone. She said, "Hello, Ethel?"

"Yes, Mom."

"Ethel! *Where* is all that money coming from?"

Now just try to explain to your not very worldly mother how it is possible for you to bank $550 when you're earning $300 a week. What made it so funny was that I was really so naive.

Out of my tips I bought myself what I thought were some beautiful new clothes. There was one dress in particular that I remember—an orange and white chiffon. In the afternoon I'd parade around wearing that dress, a felt cloche hat that hugged the spit curls on my cheeks and two red fox furs draped over my shoulders even if I was in Florida. To complete the outfit I had brown and white spectator shoes—something no one before or since has thought of wearing with chiffon. But in those days I didn't know any better. As Dorothy Fields, the songwriter, used to say when she got to know me, "Mermsie, what you didn't wear, you carried!"

When the season ended and I returned to New York, Lou Irwin introduced me to Al Siegel. Siegel had just split up with his wife, a wonderful popular singer, Bea Palmer. He was a very good pianist and arranger, but our professional association turned out to be a mixed blessing. Even though Siegel is now dead, there is still some controversy about what he actually contributed to my career—whether or not he was my Svengali.

Well, this is the way it really was.

We teamed up and broke in our act at the Ritz Theater in Elizabeth, New Jersey. We played several other vaudeville dates, and *Variety* reviewed us at Keith's 86th Street as a "new singing team" (which we weren't) with "interesting arrangements by Siegel." The reviewer added, "And the girl can sing."

If I do say so, we caused quite a bit of excitement and were soon booked into a unit headed by Paul Ash and his orchestra at the Brooklyn Paramount Theater. This was a presentation house. By that I mean the policy was to screen the feature film five or six times a day, with a stage show sandwiched in between movies. In all modesty, I can say Siegel and I broke up the place, staying for seven consecutive weeks.

Even though we were doing four and five shows a day at the Paramount, I nagged Lou Irwin to set us for a guest spot at the Pavillon Royale in Valley Stream, Long Island. Mr. Christo and Mr. Steinberg, who owned the Roman Pools in Florida, had nine Manhattan clubs. The Pavillon Royale, you might say, was their country place. I was dying to participate in one of their All-Star Sunday Evening Impromptus, which Mr. Steinberg arranged. A Sunday Night Impromptu was a fancy name for free entertainment. Stars liked to use it to try out new material; unknowns, to be seen. The reason I wanted to work there was that by this time Al Siegel had made some very, very good arrangements for me, emphasizing a rhythmic approach to songs.

Lou got us a spot and I did "Singin' in the Rain," which always earned a big hand. Steinberg was in the kitchen or the men's room while I was performing. But when he heard the applause, he came running out to see what was happening. His wife told him, "This kid is really good," and he asked whether I knew another song.

I did. A great, great song, "Sing, You Sinners," for which, I must say, Siegel had done an arrangement even better than the one for

"Singin' in the Rain." The upshot was that Steinberg contracted for Siegel and me to appear as *paid* entertainers every Saturday and Sunday night during our Brooklyn Paramount engagement. It meant an extra twenty-five dollars a week. The icing on the cake was that I had my first opportunity to sing with Guy Lombardo, who was already a very big name. At this point, Al Siegel knew his place and I knew mine. Unfortunately, it couldn't remain that way.

Word began to get out that something special was happening at the Paramount. Lou Irwin received an offer for us that some performers wait their entire careers to receive—a spot at $500 a week on the bill at the Palace Theater, the flagship of vaudeville, where I'd spent so many enjoyable afternoons and evenings during the time I was growing up. Of course we grabbed it. But what might have been a high point in my career was overshadowed by what was impending.

Vinton Freedley came to the Brooklyn Paramount. He and Alex Aarons had produced a number of successful musicals, the most acclaimed being those with songs by the brothers Gershwin, George and Ira. Now Freedley and Aarons were preparing another Gershwin show, *Girl Crazy*, this time with a book by Guy Bolton and Jack McGowan.

After catching my act, I guess Vinton thought I was pretty good, even though he never tired of describing the short black dress covered with jet beads, ribbons and bows that I was wearing. Because the next thing I knew he had contacted my agent and arranged for Lou and me to go with him to see George Gershwin. It was my first brush with genius.

George lived at Riverside Drive and Seventy-second Street, overlooking the Hudson River. And as I've often said, not only was I in awe of meeting the great George Gershwin, I was in awe of the apartment building. I was a young gal living with my parents in Astoria, and to me the Gershwin set-up was something beyond my wildest dreams. George occupied the penthouse on one side of the roof. His brother, Ira, lived on the other side. They had the whole thing sewed up—all to themselves.

I was taken into this gorgeous living room to meet this great composer. He was most kind. He sat down at the piano and played three songs which I eventually wound up singing in the show. They were "Sam and Delilah," "I Got Rhythm," and "Boy, What Love Has Done to Me."

Vinton Freedley always said that I then sang "Exactly Like You" and "Little White Lies," in which I always did the second chorus as a slight burlesque of the first. Vinton must have known. You can't prove it by me. It is a total blank. If Vinton had said I sang the "Bell Song" from *Lakmé*, I wouldn't swear that I didn't. I was scared stiff. I should have been. He was the great Gershwin and I was a nobody.

But as *I* remember it, after George finished playing, this humble genius turned to me, a complete unknown, and said something I'll never forget: "Miss Merman, if there's anything about these songs you don't like, I'll be most happy to change it."

I was so awestruck, I managed to get out, "No, Mr. Gershwin, they'll do very nicely." Some people thought that was a put-down. The truth is that I was dumbfounded by his humility. Those were the songs that were to put me on the map.

Bert Lahr had been supposed to do the comedy lead, but he had preferred *Flying High* for George White. Willie Howard had been signed to replace him. Allen Kearns played the juvenile lead and Ginger Rogers was the female star. Ginger, who specialized in vivacious ingenues and Charleston dancing, had committed grand larceny by stealing the musical *Top Speed* from Irene Delroy and the movie *Young Man of Manhattan* from Claudette Colbert the previous season. In the latter she had made "Cigarette me, big boy!" a national catch phrase.

The producers were to pay Ginger $1500 a week; I was to receive $375. Later people implied I was a little jealous. They quoted me as saying of Ginger (and later about Mary Martin), "She's all right—if you like talent." It's a clever line. I wish I *had* said it. The truth is that only a year before I'd been getting sixty dollars a week, so I felt lucky to get $375. Anyway I wasn't worrying about anybody else. I just wanted to make a hit. I thought I had a chance because I was essentially a singer. Willie Howard was a comedian who sang a little. Kearns was a romantic juvenile who could sing. Ginger danced, played comedy well and sang "Embraceable You" and "But Not for Me"—songs that didn't require much power. She did all of her numbers very well, but she didn't feature her singing any more than I did my dancing.

In mid-September Al Siegel and I made our debut in two-a-day at the Palace. The New York *Times* review said that Ted Healy ruled the bill and hailed Harriet Hoctor, Gus Van and me. But again what might have been expected to be a milestone for me as an entertainer was overshadowed by the excitement of *Girl Crazy*. Between shows, Siegel and I hopped cabs and went to the Alvin Theater to rehearse. After the evening show at the Palace we'd go back to the Alvin and beat our brains out rehearsing some more. It seems impossible. But when you're young, you're full of vinegar.

In the beginning I had only a few lines that led into my numbers. Song cues. That was common in Broadway musicals at that time. Some of the biggest stars, such as Ruth Etting and Marion Harris, weren't talking women. They came on and got right into numbers with which they stopped the show. They were great popular singers and it ended there. Acting was not their business.

But when I delivered my lines, I got a response. I wasn't trying to be funny. I never have. I just say the line with the same sincerity the character would—and somehow it comes out funny or sad or whatever it's supposed to be. Anyway, Jack McGowan apparently liked what he heard, because every day or so he'd shove some paper with new dialogue on it into my hand. Pretty soon Kate Fothergill, the part I played, emerged as quite a brash comedy character. This was not as disruptive to the plot as might be imagined, since the story about a girl-crazy Eastern youth and a New York taxi driver who ends up sheriff in Custerville, Arizona, was only an excuse for the comedy and musical numbers anyway.

Howard Lindsay and Russel Crouse used to kid me by saying that as my speaking part grew there was terrific excitement on the part of my parents. Buck and Howard claimed that Mom and Pop ran to the neighbors and excitedly informed them, "Ethel can talk too."

What struck George and Ira Gershwin as riotous was the fact that when Ira wrote additional lyrics for "Sam and Delilah," I took them down in shorthand over the telephone. I didn't see what was so funny. What could be more natural? I'd been a secretary, hadn't I?

News of *Girl Crazy*'s potential reached New York from Philadelphia during the tryout. So on opening night Caleb Bragg, Gertrude Lawrence, George White and all the big shots I'd sent notes and flowers to when I worked for Bragg were out front. I wasn't nervous—just determined to show them that anything they could do Ethel Zimmermann could do better, to paraphrase Irving Berlin.

Girl Crazy was peculiarly constructed in a number of ways. For instance, I figured in the plot in the first act, but they didn't allow me to sing until the ninth number. Up to then the songs had been intimate in style. Things like "Embraceable You" and "Bidin' My Time." So when I came on in my red blouse and black satin skirt slit to the knee and ripped into

> Delilah was a floozy,
> She didn't give a damn.
> Delilah wasn't choosy
> Till she fell for a swell
> Buckaroo whose name was Sam. . . .

the audience yelped with surprise and pleasure. To be truthful, I thought my garter had snapped or I'd lost something. But they were reacting to the first strong singing of the evening.

Almost immediately I followed "Delilah" with "I Got Rhythm," and when I held the C note for sixteen bars, an entire chorus, while the orchestra played the melody, the audience went a little crazy. I don't think they were responding to the beauty of it. I think it was the newness. Nobody had ever done it in a Broadway show before. Thank God I was blessed with a strong diaphragm and lungs. Because I had to sing I don't know how many encores. And that was the song that made me.

During intermission I went up to the third or fourth floor, where I dressed with the DeMarcos and other featured players. Ginger, Willie Howard and Allen Kearns were downstairs, but I was up in the rafters. I was trying to fix my face, put some powder over the eye shadow. One of the cast told me I'd got it on so thick it looked as if it ran into my eyebrows.

There was a knock on the door, and when I opened it there stood George Gershwin. He'd climbed three flights. "Ethel," he asked, "do you know what you're doing?"

"No."

"Well," he advised, "never go near a singing teacher. . . . And never forget your shorthand."

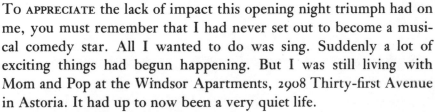

To APPRECIATE the lack of impact this opening night triumph had on me, you must remember that I had never set out to become a musical comedy star. All I wanted to do was sing. Suddenly a lot of exciting things had begun happening. But I was still living with Mom and Pop at the Windsor Apartments, 2908 Thirty-first Avenue in Astoria. It had up to now been a very quiet life.

Occasionally I dated Billy Sussman, who was in the wholesale furniture business, and more frequently Al Goetz, a stockbroker. We went to smart places, such as the Casino in the Park, where old and cafe society intermingled, but even Billy and Al seldom took me to a Broadway musical. The legitimate theater just wasn't of that much interest to me.

So when people ask me how to become a Broadway star, I'm stumped. I just happened to be in the right place at the right time. Or maybe I'm like the shady lady who was asked what a nice girl like her was doing in such a business and answered, "Just lucky, I guess."

I mean I'm human. I enjoyed all the compliments I received at George Gershwin's opening night party. But the greatest thrill of all came later that evening, when Billy Sussmann and I dropped in at the Casino in the Park, were ushered to a very desirable table, and everyone stood up. Only a few nights before we had been relegated to the boondocks.

It was late when I set out for Astoria, and it didn't occur to me to pick up the reviews. Or to buy the papers the next morning either. When I arrived at George Gershwin's the day after the premiere for luncheon and he asked whether I'd read the notices, I admitted I hadn't. It was George who first showed them to me. There was only one word for them: sensational. I didn't know why everyone was so excited about my work. I'd only done what I'd been doing most of my life, but I appreciated the response anyway.

Several years later Grace Moore, the opera and motion picture star, told me she'd spent a fortune learning to sing and every time she heard me she wanted her money back. "Your diction is perfect. Your projection effortless. You break all the rules of nature. Not once tonight did I see you breathe from your chest or abdomen. What do you breathe from?"

"Necessity," I told her.

"But surely you've taken lessons."

I shook my head. "With me, breathing always seemed to come naturally."

These stories bring me around to Al Siegel. Over the years there has been a lot of controversy about what Siegel contributed. As time passed, his claims increased. At first he said he'd been my pianist and arranger. Then he began saying that he was my voice coach for a year. Still later he went so far as to claim he had been my lover. Aside from being my pianist and arranger, all completely untrue.

I teamed up with Siegel in the spring of 1930 and stopped working with him on October 14, the night *Girl Crazy* opened. I'm not rewriting history when I say that he did do terrific arrangements for me. Period.

Let me quote from a February 16, 1931, story by Stanley Chapman that appeared in the *Morning Telegraph*. Mr. Chapman wrote:

> It may be a bit of news to the conservatives, but she never has taken a singing lesson. She is afraid singing teachers make you follow a cut and dried technique. They want you to breathe just so and do this and that according to the

rules. Ethel makes her own rules and willfully goes along singing in her own sweet way. People appear to be satisfied and she refuses to play with fire.

Siegel was like a lot of people who have a small part in someone's career and then begin grabbing credit for things they wish they had had something to do with. They repeat their fabrications so often they finally come to believe them.

Before I teamed up with him, as I said, he had been married to a popular singer, Bea Palmer. Apparently she also found his grandstanding hard to take, because she divorced him and retired. And long after he worked with me he was involved in litigation with Lillian Shade, a singer who objected to his demands for 45 percent of her earnings.

To backtrack, at the time *Girl Crazy* was trying out in Philadelphia, Siegel became ill and had to be admitted to a hospital. His illness was eventually diagnosed as tuberculosis. But on opening night of *Girl Crazy* he insisted upon leaving his sickbed to come to the Alvin to accompany me. At the end of the first act he collapsed and Roger Edens, a young man who was to play an important part in my life, was drafted from Red Nichols' pit orchestra to play my big number in the second act, "Boy, What Love Has Done to Me." That, by the way, was some pit band—with Tommy and Jimmy Dorsey, Benny Goodman, Jack Teagarden, Glenn Miller, Gene Krupa and Joe Venuti among its members.

Siegel eventually was taken to Bethel, Connecticut, to recuperate. For some time I sent him 25 percent of my earnings for the use of the superior arrangements he had made for me. Then, after the opening of the show, I was booked to double at the Casino in the Park, beginning on November 4.

Lou Irwin and I went up to Connecticut to visit Siegel. We proposed a deal for him to write arrangements for some new songs I would be using. He said he'd be glad to do that for 33⅓ percent of everything I earned in perpetuity. Fing! That was the end of Mr. Siegel.

Or, I ought to say, it should have been. But when Walter Winchell ran an item saying Siegel claimed to have taught me all I knew, I finally blew my top and fired off a telegram which Walter printed in his column. I think it makes my point:

DEAR WALTER, I'VE BEEN SINGING SINCE I WAS FIVE YEARS OLD AND I'VE BEEN TELLING THE TRUTH EVEN LONGER. AND I'M TELLING YOU THE ONLY THING THAT AL SIEGEL EVER DID WAS WRITE ARRANGEMENTS. HE NEVER TAUGHT ME ANYTHING.

Winchell printed my rebuttal. I felt pretty good about that. It was as close to a retraction as you could get from him in his prime.

In discussing Siegel's charges, Ed Sullivan wrote in his column that he had never taken much stock in the claims of such as Siegel. "Success is something apart from mechanical tricks," he wrote. "To be successful, a performer must have courage, determination, tact and all the allied virtues. Nobody can infuse these in the heart of another. And once a performer steps out on stage, he is on his own." Amen.

While Siegel was sulking, the critics were calling me a torch singer, a rhythm singer and even a prima jazzerina—whatever that may be. But George Gershwin gave me a photograph of himself inscribed, "A lucky composer is he who has you singing his songs."

Gershwin was a genius and of course I was deeply grateful to him, but truthfully I never felt I learned to know him. It was impossible to reach him. There was an aloofness—not rudeness, but an aloofness—about him. I think basically he was shy more than anything else. He adored me. I know that. But from afar.

If I were asked to select one image of him that I will always carry with me it is of a deliriously happy George sitting at the piano with the pit orchestra pounding out "I Got Rhythm." He loved to do that, and every Wednesday matinee our regular pianist, Roger Edens, would step aside and George would take over. I didn't even have to look. Because he had a certain touch that was his alone. When I would look, I always saw a totally fulfilled man.

I believe that a few of his personal messages evoke him far better than anything I might write about him. On September 29, 1930, for instance, flowers arrived. His card read:

Bobby Jones, Lindbergh, Helen Wills, Queen Mary, Ethel Merman.

Good wishes and love,

George Gershwin

Then on November 17, 1930, with *Girl Crazy* running successfully, he wrote from Beverly Hills:

Dear Ethel,

Well, here we are old Hollywoodites although we've been here about a week. It gets you. We're booked for dinner at a different house every night this week. And always the same routine. First cocktails, then picture talk. Dinner is served starting with soup which is immediately followed by picture talk. Then fried fish or lobster that came on Newburg immediately followed by some more picture talk. Then a delicious steak with picture talk and onions. That continues until after dessert and then demitasse is served in the living room and then the butler leans over a little and says, "I'll tell you what's wrong with those musical talkies." One listens. Perhaps he is right about it after all, who knows? Anyway, here we are in the land of sunshine where it has rained four out of eight days, but we have managed to enjoy it.

We have done no work at all waiting for Bolton to get his story set. The climate, they say, makes one lazy but I'm sure the kind of sweet executives who are always suggesting you go away on a holiday are a greater reason for the laziness. As a matter of fact, this is a fine contrast to the way we wrote *Girl Crazy* that big New York hit with Ethel Merman and lyrics by Gershwin and music by Gershwin. . . .

I am happy you are a big hit at the Casino and you settled amicably the Club Richmond case.*

Thanks for sending the New York *Evening Post* picture. Is the show holding up? I mean the performance. How is Merman behaving? Are there any good records of the

(* I think I was supposed to go in there and reneged because I didn't like the way it was being operated.)

show? Are you going to make "Sam and Delilah"? Write me in detail about everything, won't you please. All the best to you, Ethel, and hope to get back in time to hear and see you at the Richmond Club.

As ever,
George

Not long after, there arrived an undated picture postcard illustrated with a palatial-looking palace in Tijuana:

Dear Ethel,
Down here gambling away all my royalties, but loving it just the same. Thinking of you in your success and wondering how you are.

All the best to you,
George G.

And finally a letter to me from 31 Riverside Drive arrived at a vacation spot, teasing me about wanting to change my name, probably this time to Ethel Hunter:

August 21, 1931
Dear Ethel,
How is my favorite singer of songs getting along in the country?

You couldn't use the name Hunter with about eight million people recognizing your face. You see, Ethel, you're a marked woman. People all over the country will recognize you from now on, so that you better not do anything wrong.

I've been speaking to Lou Irwin quite a lot of late about your new show and I'm sorry to have to tell you that we have not settled definitely on anything yet. I want you to be in a big success next season because I think it is very important to your career. And whatever book they bring me, I will always look for your part very carefully. Something will have to happen in the next few days, because the season is getting on very fast and Aarons and Freedley will have to come through with a book that will be acceptable.

If there is any change in my plans I will let you know because I think we should be together in the next venture.

I hope you have a good rest and your vocal cords are relaxed. And also that your mother is having a good time. All the best.

Sincerely,

George

Unfortunately, I never had the opportunity to work with this great genius again. On August 28, 1931, it was announced that I would join George White's *Scandals*. Since Freedley and Aarons, who had a hold on my services, and White had engaged in a lot of mudslinging and gone into arbitration over the services of Bert Lahr when White had him for *Flying High* and Freedley and Aarons believed he was committed to them for *Girl Crazy*, theatrical people were surprised at the deal. But money is a great tranquilizer, especially to men like Freedley and Aarons, who largely backed their shows personally, sometimes losing heavily. So when White offered to pay them $10,000 to release me and they did, it left everyone smiling.

Over the years, projects with the Gershwins were discussed, but nothing materialized. The producers never found a libretto that appealed to George and contained what he considered a suitable role for me. One project was undertaken but never completed.

With my letters from him, I have another envelope. It contains a pressed flower. I picked it from one of the floral offerings that decorated his grave. The man who had made my subsequent career possible died at the peak of his powers after an operation for a brain tumor on July 19, 1937.

Looking back, I can hardly believe the schedule I met. I was sometimes doubling and tripling during 1930 and '31. On November 4, I opened a limited engagement at the Casino in the Park. Leo Reisman's orchestra, featuring Eddie Duchin at the piano, was playing there.

Roger Edens, or Buster as we called him until he became a high-powered creative executive in Hollywood, had come out of the pit to accompany me and write my arrangements after Siegel became ill. Buster was twenty-one and not long away from Hillsboro, Texas. Both of us were delighted to be working at the Central Park Casino, a spot that many people regarded as the greatest supper club of all time. The clientele included the idle rich, politicians, tycoons, theatrical luminaries and film stars. Naturally, white tie and tails were de rigueur in the main dining room.

Buster and I may have been employed as part of the entertainment, but we got as big a thrill peeking out at the audience as they did listening to us. Before we'd go on, Buster would say, "Eth, look who's sitting there tonight." And we'd be thrilled to see Mayor Jimmy Walker, Marlene Dietrich, A. C. Blumenthal and Peggy Fears, Noel Coward, Otto Kahn, Ethel Barrymore, Leslie Howard, Florenz Ziegfeld or other celebrities of the moment. It was like getting paid for doing something you would gladly pay to do.

Then, on December 4, a full-length feature, *Follow the Leader*, made at Paramount's Astoria Studios, with Ed Wynn and Ginger Rogers, opened. And guess who was also in the cast. That's right. Me.

And who do you think found time to sing "The Star-Spangled Banner" for Franklin Delano Roosevelt, who was revving up his eventual campaign for President? Little old Republican me.

Nor did the Depression of 1931 slow me down. While others were desperately looking for jobs—any kind of jobs—I was one of the lucky ones who could pick and choose. In my first twenty-two months in show business, I earned $100,000, which was something at a time when a nickel bought a loaf of bread.

In March of that year I also signed a contract to make eight musical short subjects, two of which were *Old Man Blues* and *Roaming*.

During the same month, I returned to the Casino in the Park, where Walter Winchell led the cheering for Roger Edens' "lift-you-out-of-your-seats arrangement of 'Just a Gigolo' " and to quote him, "Ethel Merman's enchanting of it."

In June, Rudy Vallee, who was at the peak of his popularity, and I co-headlined at the New York Paramount, and in July, Lou Holtz and I and a gaggle of songwriters were at the Palace. Johnny Green, who had a big success writing "Body and Soul," and Roger Edens accompanied me.

All the while, of course, I was playing eight performances a week in *Girl Crazy* at the Alvin. The energy! Where did it come from? But all of this activity served a good purpose. I had plenty to talk about to interviewers besides my private life. Whenever reporters inquired about romantic attachments, I'd give them my most winning smile and run down my current and future professional commitments. I'd tell them how busy this kept me. Men? I gave the impression I didn't have time for them. I didn't lie. I evaded the issue, and that technique worked beautifully for a surprisingly long time.

VI

IN THOSE PRE-AIR-CONDITIONED DAYS, shows closed in June for the summer. As I've said, I went into the Palace, and when the engagement was completed I looked forward to a nice rest. Mom, Pop and I tootled off to Lake George in a chauffeur-driven Chrysler I had bought. We checked into our hotel and I told the chauffeur to pick us up for a long drive at eight A.M.

That one day of sightseeing turned out to be my entire vacation. Upon returning to the hotel, I found several urgent messages from producer George White waiting for me. I called and he begged me to rush to Atlantic City with Lou Irwin. The eleventh edition of George White's *Scandals*—after ten consecutive years of hits—was laying an ostrich egg.

Lou and I went down to see the production. On paper it had everything. Joseph Urban, the man who had contributed so much to the opulence of the Ziegfeld *Follies*, had designed the scenery. Talented Charles LeMaire had done some knockout costumes. Irving Caesar, George White and Lew Brown, all experienced sketch writers, had handled that department; and the songs were by Lew Brown and Ray Henderson. Henderson had written White's ten previous successes.

As for the cast, Rudy Vallee was hot as a pistol. There were Willie *and* Eugene Howard; Everett Marshall, a glorious baritone who had sung with the Metropolitan Opera; Ray Bolger; the Gale Quadruplets; Ethel Barrymore Colt, of the famous royal family of Broadway; and a little chorus girl named Alice Faye. Yes, *the* Alice Faye. Someone once asked me whether I immediately sensed anything special in Alice and I said no, but obviously Rudy Vallee did. Meow, meow.

I jumped into the production in Newark on September first. George White, who was directing as well as producing, explained that what he wanted was to achieve better balance between the sketches and songs. It seemed a large order.

"Hosanna" might have been wonderful for someone else, but it didn't do anything for me and I wasn't able to do much for it. Then at the close of Act I, I had "Ladies and Gentlemen, That's Love," which was more promising.

In Act II, I worked with Rudy in "My Song," and next to closing I had a spot billed simply "Ethel Merman" in which, as I recall, Mr. White gave me a free hand to sing popular songs of my own choosing.

By the end of the week the improvement was noticeable, but not galvanizing as far as the audience was concerned. Ethel Barrymore Colt did create quite a flap in the newspapers. Reporters described her as "the daughter of Ethel Barrymore, the niece of John and heiress apparent to a rich stage heritage" and quoted her as being "wounded" that White had given me her songs. She announced that she was asking to be let out of her contract because she was too young to be a star and that anyway I was doing a better job with the numbers than she could.

Clearly we weren't ready for Broadway, so White booked us into the Majestic Theater in Brooklyn for another week's shakedown. Miss Colt was persuaded to stay and I was given a new show-stopping number, "Life Is Just a Bowl of Cherries," to replace "Hosanna."

Finally on September 14, 1931, we had our Broadway opening at the Apollo Theater. Gilbert Gabriel of the *American* and other critics cheered White for his eleventh hit review. "Rumors so tear-stained and regretful about the probable fiasco of *Scandals*" were so prevalent, according to Gabriel, "that some of the more gentle-hearted critics had almost made up their minds to go to Mae West instead." Mae was opening in *The Constant Sinner*. Luckily they didn't desert us for Mae, because the majority decided that the flaws had been repaired and both White and I had another hit to our credits.

If I needed further proof of White's confidence in me, I had it in the biography that the producer had the press agent prepare for *Playbill*. It read:

> Ethel Merman is considered by George White one of the outstanding musical comedy stars of the contemporary theater. Born in Astoria, Long Island, where she still resides, she received her education at a local high school and then went into secretarial work as a career. A Broadway casting agent heard her sing at a private party three years ago and was so amazed by her remarkable voice he signed her to a contract. She made her professional debut in a nightclub and then went into vaudeville. Her appearance at the Palace Theater won her new honors and she was signed for an important role in *Girl Crazy* for her first Broadway appearance, last season. Critics and public alike hailed her as one of the real "finds" of the decade. Mr. White plans to present her as the star of a new musical comedy when the current *Scandals* terminates its run.

Ben Washer, then a young reporter for the *World-Telegram* and later a successful Broadway press agent and friend of mine, assessed my feelings pretty shrewdly at the time when he wrote that I gave the impression of being proud and bewildered—proud about the public acceptance I'd received and bewildered by the ease with which we had overcome the problems.

Success was a heady thing. When I'd played Les Ambassadeurs, I had sung two songs made famous by the legendary Helen Morgan. Soon after the *Scandals* opened, I was taken to Les Ambassadeurs to hear Miss Morgan and listened to her announce that she was about to sing two numbers made famous by Ethel Merman in George

White's *Scandals*. It was a gratifying moment for an ex-secretary from Astoria.

I might have been an ex-secretary, but I was still living in Astoria—as if I unconsciously expected all the good things that had happened to me to evaporate, in which case I could easily take up my secretarial work again. But probably the real reason was that I'm a person who puts down roots, and it wasn't easy to dislodge myself and my parents for the move to the city. It wasn't all that difficult to get to Astoria.

Also, by now I was able to admit that I was in love with Al Goetz, who had been pursuing me for some time. It was one of those cases where I should have listened to Mom's advice, but I didn't see it that way then.

Al wasn't tall, but he was dark and reasonably handsome. He was a considerate man, devoted, easy to be with. He was married but legally separated from his wife when I met him. Although he knew his way about town, he wasn't a card-carrying playboy. He had my interests at heart and I'm still grateful to him for advising me on my investments. When I began making what at that time was big money—$1000 a week—I placed my account with his firm, Unger-gleider and Goetz. I had my account with them for years and I'm financially more comfortable today because of Al's expertise in investing.

Even though he was legally separated, we avoided the spotlight, avoided being photographed together and behaved in a dignified way. What the eventual outcome would be, I didn't know. But for the time being, I was as happy as a strictly brought up Episcopalian girl could be under the circumstances.

Meanwhile, at the beginning of 1932, I was again doubling at the Casino in the Park, but I had to cancel out when I developed a sore throat and a 104-degree fever. Which brings me to something I'd like to get off my chest. People are not always sensible about protecting others from exposure to colds. Colds are contagious and it's inconsiderate to spread them under any circumstances. But with singers a cold is a disaster. It means putting us out of business. "Oh, don't worry," people will say. "When she has a cold, she just sings over it." Sings over it? Sings over it! How is anyone going to sing when her throat is closed up? So if you have a cold, do me a favor. Stay away from me.

When George White's *Scandals* closed, I went back to the Palace, opening April 24 on a bill with Jack Haley, Benny Rubin and a tough young Irish comedienne who made my brassy dames seem like debutantes. Her name was—and is—Patsy Kelly and I agreed then with the reviewer for the New York *Times*, who predicted that this was a gal destined to "make quite a name for herself."

I was held over for the next week's bill headed by Mme. Frances Alda, the former Metropolitan Opera soprano who had come out of a three-year retirement to play that week. With Roger Edens and Jack Carroll at twin pianos, I sang "Smile, Darn You, Smile," "There'll Be Some Changes Made" and a couple of now-forgotten numbers. As encores I used "I Got Rhythm" and a hoked-up version of "Life Is Just a Bowl of Cherries," with Jack Haley. Apparently I did all right too. *Variety* was complimentary to Mme. Alda and Haley and really gave me an accolade I treasured, saying that I had "the strength and poise of the Empire State combined with a clear voice, relentless jazz style and a rare ability to charge routines with excitement." What better could a girl ask for?

Offers for a new Broadway show were numerous when *Scandals* closed after 202 performances. Among them: Vincent Youmans' *Sis-Boom-Bah;* Billy Rose and Lew Gensler's *Ballyhoo;* an unspecified Gershwin show to be produced by Freedley and Aarons; an offer to star in the first Ziegfeld *Follies* to be mounted following the great showman's death; and *Humpty Dumpty*.

It's always being said that I've never had a flop. Wrong! *Humpty Dumpty* stunk up the joint. We opened this ambitious satiric survey of American history cast in the form of a Broadway revue in Pittsburgh in September 1932. B. G. DeSylva and Laurence Schwab had produced it and written the "book." I put quotation marks around "book" because no word has been invented to describe what they had come up with. The music and lyrics were by Richard Whiting and Nacio Herb Brown. And the result was a fiasco. The producers found themselves $80,000 in the hole, and all of the experts said the only wise thing to do was to cut losses by closing out of town.

My mood was dark. After a string of triumphs, I didn't relish having a disaster to my discredit. So naturally I took an immediate liking to Buddy DeSylva, who felt that things couldn't get worse and was willing to gamble that they could get better. "Oh hell," he said to his partner in one of those moments that sound like a scene from an old Warner Brothers script, "let's take a chance." And that is what they named the new version of the show.

We closed and returned to New York for seven weeks of rewriting, recasting and restaging. Sid Silvers, who had been a comedian in the original version, contributed different, if not fresh, jokes. Vincent Youmans turned out seven new songs for us—five of which we used. Those songs represented his last work heard on Broadway before he was silenced by tuberculosis. Edgar MacGregor replaced Laurence Schwab as director, and Bobby Connolly was brought in to help choreographer George Hale. A new love interest was added and Jack Haley replaced Lou Holtz as top banana.

For our Wilmington, Delaware, tryout on November 5, the production wasn't in perfect shape, but it was no longer a disaster either. Four days later, after our Philadelphia debut, a couple of the less demanding critics called us a riot. But the management knew better and wisely booked us into Newark for additional polishing of the rough spots.

There is an old cliché that when a show is wrong it is subject to malign influences of every kind. And there seemed to be some truth in that as bad breaks piled up. First I became ill for a couple of days, and then fire destroyed many of the costumes.

Nevertheless on November 26 we opened at the Apollo Theater on Forty-second Street with an offering that didn't make too much literal sense but was a lot of fun. *The New Yorker*'s reviewer expressed my sentiments exactly when he noted, "The plot is eminently suitable for dropping." As for myself, I had four numbers: "You're an Old Smoothie," with Jack Haley; "I Got Religion," a kind of musical revival type number I'd done before; the rousing "Rise and Shine"; and, for me, the unforgettable "Eadie Was a Lady."

Eadie had a strange history. Originally, DeSylva had had the idea for Walter O'Keefe—for some now-forgotten show. Anyway, before going to Pittsburgh with *Humpty Dumpty*, I began making noises about the fact that great and gifted songwriters though they might be, what I had to work with this time out wasn't the stuff to stop shows with.

Whenever I complained, Roger Edens always reminded DeSylva of the song that had been suggested and then discarded because Larry Schwab didn't think it had the cachet needed to grace this satiric historical revue. Finally, more to shut up Roger than anything else, the songwriters told him to make an arrangement for me. He not only arranged their song, he wrote a brilliant new middle section, for which, incidentally, he never received rightful credit.

He played the result for me. I wanted to sing it. DeSylva, Whiting and Brown loved it. Larry Schwab didn't, but he caved in and allowed "Eadie" to be included. Opening night in Pittsburgh only "Eadie" and, to a lesser extent, "You're an Old Smoothie" got over. But "Eadie's" impact was such that one reviewer began his notice: "Eadie Was a Lady opened last night . . ."

The way Roger had set it up, I was what my grandmother used to call "a soiled dove" who'd just returned from the funeral of another dirty bird.

The audience was with me from the moment I came down the stairs swinging my hips in my American Beauty red satin dress and a black boa around my shoulders. As I launched into this seriocomic paean to my dead sister in sin, I felt the current that runs back and forth when something extraordinary is happening on stage. Hearing about this shady lady, who was so refined she drank her brandy with her pinkie sticking out, the audience was convulsed by her "savoir-fairy" and, as the song said, her "class with a capital K."

Roger accomplished a great deal during his too short life, writing for and later even producing some excellent films, but I doubt he ever felt more pride than he did during opening week of *Take a Chance* when the New York *Times* printed the lyrics of "Eadie Was a

Lady"—a song originally thought to lack the cachet to be included in Larry Schwab's flop revue.

At the time *Humpty Dumpty* opened in Pittsburgh, I'd been concerned about being associated with a flop, but after it had been transformed into *Take a Chance* I began wondering where I would ever again find so many audience-pleasing numbers in one show. Luckily I didn't have to worry for 243 performances.

Even after that I bought some time. I decided to go to Chicago with the show. Ole Olsen and Chic Johnson, two vaudevillians who had a following in the Middle West, had taken over the Haley and Silvers roles, and I thought I'd win some new fans on the road. I've always liked Chicago. It's a good town. Besides, it was 1933 and the World's Fair with its theme—A Century of Progress—was running. I decided to take an apartment and give Mom and Pop a chance to see the fair in a leisurely fashion. As it turned out, I lasted only two weeks. At that point I had to withdraw from the show because the chlorine in the water gave me a bad throat. Apparently, despite all the progress, those were the days before your friendly Sparklets man had appeared on the scene. Anyway, no one recommended him to me.

VII

BEFORE APPEARING IN *Take a Chance*, I'd also been churning, and I do mean *churning*, out musical short subjects for Paramount. *Roaming*, *Old Man Blues* (I sang "Hello, My Lover, Goodbye"), *Irene* ("Wipe That Frown Right Off Your Face" had fleeting popularity) and *Be Like Me*. Primitively developed stories received little help from slap-dash production. But I got the idea that making movies could be fun. So during the last week of September 1933 Mom and I arrived in Hollywood.

We rented an apartment at the Ravenswood, located conveniently near Paramount. Mae West, who owned the building then, lived on the seventh floor, while Mom and I were on the fifth—or the other way around.

At that time in Hollywood there was an exclusive clique, and no matter how big a name you were on Broadway, until you had made it in the movies you didn't exist. Mae was box-office dynamite, but she still didn't mingle. I was just another Broadway star and didn't rate.

To put it mildly, this was not a happy time. For the first time since Mom and Pop had been married, they had to spend their nights under separate roofs; because Pop had insisted Mom go to

California with me while he stayed on at his job in New York. We were all lonesome. Pop missed us and we felt lost without him and my dog, Scrapsie, that I'd left back East to keep him company. Since I thought I was in love, my dates consisted of a long nightly telephone call from New York.

There was another custom I didn't take to. The studios all had huge press departments whose job it was to get the actors' names in print one way or another. If a player happened to be having a romance that enhanced his or her appeal, the studio publicized it. If, on the other hand, he or she was dating someone "unsuitable," the publicity people sometimes cooked up a phony romance. Or they planted items that this or that star was on a flower salad diet or washed her hair in champagne.

Since I refused to go along with such nonsense or to discuss the man in my life, columnists made do with non-items. "Ethel Merman claims she will never divulge the identity of her fiancé UNTIL they MARCH UP THE AISLE" was one lulu. Slightly less embarrassing was such a variation as "Ethel Merman says romance is out until she is through with show business."

Billy Rose wrote a song that became popular around that time called "It's Only a Paper Moon." It went something like "It's only a paper moon / Hanging over a cardboard sea . . ." and the more I saw of the movie colony, the more convinced I became that he'd got his idea from a visit there. Everything seemed fake. Worse still, there seemed to be no reason for the way things were done.

I was signed for *We're Not Dressing*, loosely based on J. M. Barrie's *The Admirable Crichton*, with Bing Crosby, Carole Lombard, George Burns, Gracie Allen and Leon Errol. Because Carole played the leading lady, she had to be dressed in pale colors. That left the dark colors for me, even though they did no more for my dark complexion than the pastels did for Carole's blond beauty.

After looking at my wardrobe and makeup tests, someone decided that what I needed was a new hairdo. So over my protests they whacked off my shoulder-length hair, only to have Norman Taurog, the director, take one look at me and announce, "You'll look more sophisticated with longer hair." So I played the part in a wig—while my own locks ended up on the cutting-room floor.

According to the script, Carole owned a pet bear. Bears aren't noted for their cuddly qualities, but this one was about as tame as they get. Before we began working though, the trainer told each of us girls that when that certain time of the month rolled around, she must warn the director so he could shoot scenes she wasn't in. It seems that somehow the bear sensed what was going on and it drove him berserk.

After we began filming, I would gather up some of the eight-by-ten publicity glossies and send them to Pop to raise his spirits. On the back I'd write, "This is Leon Errol," or "George Burns and Gracie Allen." One of the pictures showed Carole, Bing and a bit player. I sent it to Pop. "That's Lombard and Crosby. I don't know who the other guy is." Afterward we all got to know his name pretty well—Ray Milland.

I had another handicap in addition to my inexperience in making movies. Bing, Carole, George and Gracie were under contract to the studio. I was there on a one-picture deal. That's like being in on a pass. Guess who received the breaks. You can bet theirs weren't the faces that ended on the cutting-room floor. As it turned out, audiences caught an occasional glimpse of me and I sang Mack Gordon and Harry Revel's "It's a New Spanish Custom" with Leon Errol and the chorus. That was my total contribution.

What had been planned as my big number, "The Animal in Me," was deleted. After taking two weeks to shoot this elaborate spectacle, the producer explained that it came too near the end of the film. He said it distracted the audience from the story. Wouldn't you think that that would have occurred to the producer and director before they ordered a jungle set with a treadmill? Rented monkeys, camels and kangaroos? And hired a man who spent four days coaxing a herd of forty elephants to stand in a circle and lift their front legs and trunks in time to the music?

I was disappointed because it was my only chance to shine in the picture, which gives you an idea how desperate things must have been for me. Later the sequence was featured in an all-star clambake Paramount called *The Big Broadcast of 1936*. The only good thing about having it shown turned out to be that I was paid a second time, since it wasn't used in the film for which it had been shot.

In *We're Not Dressing* I especially enjoyed working with Gracie Allen, who turned out to be no more like the nitwits she played than I was like my brassy dames. She had a petite figure and a daintiness rarely found in a comedienne. Of course, she and George were huge successes in radio, but they carried the aura of big-time vaudeville with them, which served as a reminder of all those happy evenings Mom and Pop and I had spent at the Palace.

Carole was nice too, and I especially liked Bing. Carole was noted for her sense of humor, but it was Bing who sent me a bottle of seasick pills when he heard I was leaving to vacation in Havana. They were in memory of our location shooting around Catalina, where I'd proved a damn poor sailor.

While I was making *We're Not Dressing*, Roger Edens arrived in Hollywood. By this time Roger and I were like brother and sister. It was a chemical thing. Nobody else has ever understood how to bring out a song's full potential for me in the way Roger did. There was one problem. He was a giver, not a taker. I often felt I hadn't adequately paid him for his efforts.

Now a chance presented itself to rectify that. Even though Roger made a good salary on Broadway, he tossed his money around. So when he had an opportunity to work on films, he didn't have a nest egg to fall back on. And the musician's union had a ruling that an applicant, whatever his background, had to reside in California for several months before he was eligible to join.

While Roger was waiting, he came up short. And I was happy to be able to come up with the cash for him. Then, by the time I signed for my next film, Roger had served his waiting period and the union allowed him to work with me. Although I didn't want him to, he insisted on repaying the loan as soon as he went on salary.

I'm glad that opportunity arose because after Roger became *the* Roger Edens, he was so highly paid by Metro-Goldwyn-Mayer that it was embarrassing to offer him a fee for doing a special arrangement. I learned to keep my eyes open and note when he admired something. Then I'd buy it and send it along as a token of my appreciation.

For instance, he collected paintings, photographs and sculptures of hands. I found some unusual ones. Who knows how much he wanted those gifts? He was in a position to buy anything he really wanted. That's why I'm thankful that I was able to offer him the use of my money before he reached the point where even that wouldn't have meant anything to him.

During my trip to New York and vacation in Cuba, I arranged for Mom, Pop, Scrapsie and me to move from Astoria to 25 Central Park West in Manhattan. I was just getting my collection of rag dolls and the scrapbooks Pop had been keeping for me arranged and was thinking about a Broadway show when Sam Goldwyn called my agent.

He sent over a funny low-comedy script written by Nunnally Johnson, Nat Perrin and Arthur Sheekman. It was called *Kid Millions* and Eddie Cantor was to star. It had songs by Irving Berlin, Burton Lane and Harold Adamson, and Walter Donaldson and Gus Kahn.

I decided to do it. George Murphy, who with his wife, Julie, had worked as a ballroom team during one of my engagements at the Casino in the Park, Ann Sothern, Eve Sully, Jesse Block, Warren Hymer and Burton Churchill were in the cast. Hymer, Churchill and I were to play three flimflam artists trying to con little orphan Eddie out of his million-dollar inheritance. My part in the desperate scheme was to convince Eddie that I was his long-lost mother. The story didn't make too much literal sense, but there were lots of gags and funny scenes, including one where I was wearing a chic hat with a black veil, sitting on Eddie's lap, insisting that I was his dear old mom. Musically, I drew "With an Earful of Music and an Armful of You"—which didn't set the nation singing. Or even tapping their toes.

I know that Eddie Cantor's brand of comedy has gone out of style today, but at the time we thought he was a great artist. He was generous in telling me how to register on camera and was as funny off- as onscreen, which is not always the case with comedians.

Nor did I find Samuel Goldwyn as tyrannical as his reputation led me to expect. I remember in *Kid Millions* Eddie was bugging Sam to let him have a serious love interest. Goldwyn tried to kid Eddie out of the idea. When Eddie insisted, Sam told him the audience just wouldn't stand for it. "Eddie," he said, "you got no sex appeal."

"Sam!" Eddie howled. "What do you mean no sex appeal? How do you think I got my five daughters?"

That stumped Sam. He had the writers work up a comedy romance between Eddie and the sultan's daughter. As played by Eve Sully, this gal was a very funny man-hungry nitwit in the Gracie Allen vein. So, in a sense, Eddie and Sam each got his way.

Sam didn't have as much luck in handling the censors. In one scene Eddie treated a group of eight-year-olds to all the ice cream they could stuff into themselves. When the kids got up from the tables, their little stomachs were bulging. That was okay for the boys, the censor said, but he snipped out scenes with the girls. The public couldn't be dirtied by the implication that these eight-year-olds were pregnant! Now I ask you, Which was obscene? The scene or the censors? Please! They must have been drinking perfume.

After finishing *Kid Millions*, I spent a little time taking stock. While Hollywood seemed a great milieu for Roger to accomplish his ends, it didn't work well for me. On Broadway I'd started playing in dives, progressed to name clubs, movie presentation houses and the Palace. Then I'd gone into musical comedy, where the importance of my role increased with each succeeding production. Without conscious preplanning, I had been at the right place at the opportune time. Looking back, I could see a pattern developing. In Hollywood I just wasn't making it. My contention that talent will out wasn't proving true.

I decided to return to New York. A reporter asked why I was leaving. "Hollywood is all right for a while, but it's not my idea of a good time," I told him. That was an evasion. The truth is that I was certain I had things to offer that Hollywood was incapable of using. The qualities that helped me on Broadway limited me in pictures.

Talent aside, the problem boiled down to something simple. I wasn't under contract. Nobody was planning to build a career for me. Audiences at the time cared about the girl who got the guy. I always played the wisecracking dame who was a friend of the girl who got the guy. On Broadway audiences pulled for the maverick heroine who eventually revealed a marshmallow heart and got the guy.

That's where I belonged.

VIII

THERE HAVE BEEN so many changes in the American musical theater since I broke into the business that the slapdash way producers used to assemble a show seems a little unbelievable when we talk about them now. Take *Anything Goes*. Vinton Freedley, who had recently dissolved his producing partnership with Alex Aarons and was still in a wheelchair from either sunstroke or a mild heart attack (they never decided which), didn't even have a clear idea when he approached me. But that wasn't unique. Producers would sign talent and let the performers' strong points suggest a plot for the show. Vinton said William Gaxton and Victor Moore, the hottest comedy team around, had pretty well committed themselves. I'd lay odds he told them the same thing about me. He hinted Cole Porter was ready to begin writing the score.

When Billy, Victor and I expressed some interest, he sailed for Europe to sign Wodehouse, Bolton and Cole. Cole was faltboating down the Rhine and couldn't be reached immediately. Vinton's task was complicated because Bolton, who was living in England, had a tax problem that made it difficult for him to leave the country, and Wodehouse refused to set foot in the British Isles. Unfazed, Vinton arranged for them to collaborate by telephone.

The outline they turned out sparked Cole's interest. He either pulled some songs out of a trunk or whipped out a score in a hurry. Vinton was so high on its possibilities that he coughed up $5000 to buy back several bars of background music Cole had written for C. B. Cochrane's *Nymph Errant*. It may have been the best five grand any producer ever spent—because Cole developed that fragment into "I Get a Kick Out of You."

The next thing I heard was that Bolton and Wodehouse's book had arrived. The story took place on a Europe-bound luxury liner. The climax was a shipwreck. As Vinton put it, my role "needed expansion." Actually it hardly existed. Vinton's problem was complicated by the fact that while my character was of minor importance in the libretto, Cole had written most of his best songs for me. And since I'd already demonstrated I could play comedy—at least as far as I was concerned—Vinton knew I wouldn't come on, let somebody feed me a song cue and burst into song.

Events took a turn for the worse when a cruise ship, the *Morro Castle*, burned off the shore of New Jersey with a loss of 134 lives. Obviously a new plot was needed. Luckily for me, Wodehouse and Bolton were unavailable for rewrites. So Howard Lindsay, who had been set to direct, was persuaded to undertake the task. But he needed a collaborator.

Cole always insisted that they located Russel Crouse through a dream of Neysa McMein's. Neysa was a famous magazine illustrator who was a great pal of Cole's. Personally, I think that was just one of Cole's fantasies. Buck Crouse had been a newspaper humorist, press agent and an aspiring, if not accomplished, playwright for a decade before *Anything Goes*. But Buck went along with the story, commenting, "That makes me the original dreamboat, I guess, although I feel more like Cleopatra's barge."

Buck had a fey sense of humor and always reminded me of an animated line drawing. Howard had an equally good sense of comedy and was all too solid flesh. He looked like someone's stuffy uncle. Together they made a terrific team, faced with two terrible problems: (a) a fresh plot and (b) a part for me.

They always said that they quickly hit upon the idea of making Victor Moore Public Enemy Number Thirteen, posing as the Reverend Dr. Moon. Billy Gaxton was obviously the handsome light-comedy leading man, who was in love with ingenue Bettina Hall, an heiress. For plot purposes he followed her aboard ship and failed to debark before sailing. This forced him to share a cabin with Reverend Dr. Moon, whose violin case contained a machine gun.

But what kind of character could they create for me? Desperation time arrived. They were lunching at the Algonquin, prior to describing my part to me in order to get my signature on the contract. At luncheon they spied a broad whom they mistook for a notorious evangelist. Inquiry proved she was a famous nightclub hostess. Presto! Reno Sweeney sprang forth full-blown, a tough nightclub singer who had been an evangelist and was in love with Billy Gaxton.

If I'd been wise, I'd have used my shorthand to record the action that they feverishly improvised in selling me on the character. Because none of us could recall the details later and they never quite recovered the fine rapture of their initial comic inspiration. Still, I had no complaints.

My shorthand did come in handy during rehearsals of *Anything Goes* because the book was an on-the-spot project if there ever was one. When there were changes, I'd have them down one-two-three and would read them right back.

Even today if anybody gives me changes during rehearsal for a television show, I take them down. Shorthand is like bicycle riding, once you learn how, you never forget. That's why I've never employed a secretary and never would. I can do it better and faster.

Howard was directing. Whatever worked, he and Buck incorporated into the libretto. But the day before the Boston opening they still had no satisfying climax for the show. Then that afternoon the two of them came rushing out of the men's room clutching wads of toilet tissue and announcing that they had just written the last sheet of the show.

Dress rehearsal was more of a shambles than usual and so was opening night. Billy Gaxton, in top hat and white tie, had a romantic interlude on the moonlit deck during which he sang "All Through the Night" to the elusive Bettina Hall. When Billy finished, he forgot he had to do a short scene in the stateroom with Victor Moore. He ran to his dressing room and had already removed his trousers when he heard his cue. Without hesitating, he rushed out onto the stage. His pants folded over his arm, he uttered his first line to Moore: "What a night, what a dawn, what a sunrise!"

Of course Billy and Moore, who were the number-one comedy team in musicals at that time, got rave reviews. I hadn't ever appeared in Boston, so I was a novelty and they obviously took to me. I mean I stopped the show within the first ten minutes, singing "I Get a Kick Out of You." Next morning one of the critics said that I could have wired home, "Boston surrenders."

My good luck was holding out. Cole and I liked each other immediately. He said a lot of nice things about me, such as "She sounds like a band going by." People tell me he referred to me as La Merman and the Great Ethel. But the nicest thing he said was that he'd rather have me sing his songs than anybody else in the world. I later announced that I would return the compliment. The truth is that I honestly don't have either a favorite song or songwriter. When George and Ira Gershwin, Cole Porter, Irving Berlin, Jule Styne, Steve Sondheim and Jerry Herman have written especially for you, how are you going to pick a favorite?

The Gershwins made it possible for me to flash across the sky like a meteor. But I was typed as a rhythm singer and a belter. Then Cole gave me variety and the opportunity to demonstrate the different kinds of songs I could handle. "You're the Top," in which Billy Gaxton and I rhymed superlatives, wasn't a typical Ethel Merman number. Nor was "Anything Goes." Nor "Buddy, Beware." "Blow, Gabriel, Blow" was a loud pseudo spiritual that allowed me to pull out all the stops.

What Cole had done was to analyze my voice and turn out songs which showed off its variety. "You're the Top" brought audiences to their feet because it was a new kind of love song. There had never been a song like it before. A complete original. So I wasn't surprised that at the peak of its popularity, Cole received three hundred parodies of it a month.

I was caught off guard by the fact that "I Get a Kick Out of You" turned out to rival it as the biggest hit of the show. When I broke the word "terrifically" into syllables and held the second, that "rriffff" killed people. But when Cole first handed me the song, the famous five-rhyme sequence—

> Flying too high
> With some guy
> In the sky
> Is my *i*-dea of nothing to do
> Yet I get a kick out of you!—

was not in it. Cole substituted that for some lines about the fair Mrs. Lindbergh spending nights in the air, for reasons of taste. But even if the final version had been intact, I'm not sure I'd have been bowled over. The song felt like a straight simple tune with no great beat. There didn't seem to be any particularly distinctive rhythm or sock to it. I felt Cole had just written another of his beguines. Which only goes to prove something Cole always said about any song's potential: "Nobody knows." And he included himself.

We opened in New York on November 21, 1934, at the Alvin Theater. Expensive musicals were scarce because of the state of the economy. Well, it might have been the depths of the Depression, but the audience didn't reflect it. Tickets had been scalped at fifty dollars apiece. The orchestra was a sea of sables, with the minks relegated to the mezzanine. Emeralds, rubies and diamonds lit up the place, and all those orchids contributed a tropical effect.

Now I had an inkling the show was a success. But what a hit! Brooks Atkinson wrote in the New York *Times* that though the emotions of "I Get a Kick Out of You" were less exalted than the ones in Shelley's "To a Skylark," the style was as perfect.

What about me? Well, Mr. Atkinson said, "If Ethel Merman did not write 'I Get a Kick Out of You' and also the title song of the show, she has made them hers now by the swinging gusto of her platform style."

The morning after the opening I summed up my feelings when I told Douglas Gilbert of the *World Telegram*, "Me? I'm lucky. Why,

I'm the gal that makes Cinderella a sob story." And that's how I actually felt.

The show ran 420 performances. During that time I returned to the Casino in the Park again; recorded "You're the Top" and "I Get a Kick Out of You" for Brunswick; and told interviewers I disliked coffee, candy, desserts and dressing up. I also starred for twelve weeks in an unsuccessful radio series, *Rhythm at 8*, with the Al Goodman Orchestra on the CBS network until Major Bowes's *Amateur Hour* gave me the gong.

From *Anything Goes*, I made two lasting friends. Not that the entire company wasn't congenial. I liked Howard, Buck, Bettina Hall and my understudy, Vivian Vance, who also played a small role. I never made it a practice to get close to people I worked with. I mean it was like going to an office. You don't necessarily see your co-workers after working hours. But I became lasting friends with Billy Gaxton and Cole.

Cole had a worldwide reputation as a sophisticate and hedonist. I suspect he capitalized on those traits. No other Broadway tunesmith enjoyed a similar image. What's more, it was flattering to receive the attention from him. Who wouldn't enjoy having a Porter song composed for her birthday instead of receiving a Hallmark card or a singing telegram? It's true he sometimes sent flowers, but at least once he surprised me with a full-grown mimosa tree for my terrace. And I wouldn't even try to describe the problems we had with the complicated set of ropes and pulleys needed to get the tree in place.

The wonderful thing is that the longer we worked together, the better Cole and I liked each other. Cole and Linda Porter may have been as sophisticated as their reputations paint them, but it seemed to me they always responded most enthusiastically to people who had the courage to be themselves.

Now ordinarily my closest friends are not entertainers. There's nothing wrong with show people. That just happens to be a fact. But Billy Gaxton and I clicked immediately. He always called me "Toots" and I called him "Babe." He was a great big star, but in "I Get a Kick Out of You" he was called upon to stand with his back to the audience, holding a champagne glass in his hand while I stopped

the show. He never moved a muscle. I admired that kind of professional courtesy and discipline, because Billy had an actor's ego. But
at a moment when it mattered a great deal to me and to the show,
Billy behaved impeccably.

Later we got to be such good friends that we did things I ordinarily wouldn't stand for, let alone participate in. When we'd be doing
our duet of "You're the Top," I'd try to break him up by looking
down and saying sotto voce, "Look at that dame with the big boobs
in the first row." And while I was doing a reprise of "I Get a Kick
Out of You," he'd be in the wings making all kinds of obscene gestures to me about a dwarf in the show. It was awful, but it was
funny.

Billy's dressing room was next to mine and he was always pulling
jokes on me. One night after the show he called, "Hey, Toots, will
you come in here a minute? I want you to meet Princess
Reventlow."

I said, "Oh, horseshit, Babe."

"*Ethel*, I mean it," he insisted. So I went over and there to my
great embarrassment stood Barbara Hutton, then Princess Reventlow. She had come back to see him and his wife, Madeline.
They thought my response was the funniest thing ever.

Before her marriage, Madeline had been on the stage with another
girl as a dancing duo. They weren't related, but they billed themselves as the Cameron Sisters. Madeline played in *Hit the Deck* and
Follow Through. Then when Genevieve Tobin left *Fifty Million
Frenchmen*, she went into the show, married Billy and concentrated
on playing Mrs. Gaxton.

Billy and Madeline were pals of Winthrop Rockefeller. They
knew that things were a little uneasy between Al Goetz and me, so
when Win suggested taking them and me to El Morocco, they were
all for it. A little romance developed between Win and me. Madeline
said it was because Win had never met a girl like me before. To tell
you the truth, I had never met a guy like him either.

We'd go dancing, then hire a hansom cab and go riding in Central
Park. Sometimes we'd be out dancing so late that Madeline would
urge me to phone my mother, who, she said, would be sitting up

worrying. Once I came back from calling Mom and reassured everyone: "It's okay. She's lying down worrying."

Billy and Madeline not only became friends of mine, they also used to take Mom and Pop to dinner at a German beer garden up on Eighty-sixth Street. They'd go in the baby Rolls—a six-cylinder job with a chauffeur sitting on a box in the open air. It had originally cost $38,000, but during the Depression the Gaxtons got it at a bargain—$2000. Then during the winter Madeline got to worrying that the chauffeur needed something to keep him warm. So she called a friend at a thrift shop and picked up a muskrat coat for him. The only problem was that it was a little worn in the behind. Billy solved that by instructing the chauffeur always to stand with his back to the car so that no one would notice the bare spot.

On Sundays during the run of *Anything Goes* I'd often go with the Gaxtons to the professional football games at Yankee Stadium. Billy would drive. Madeline would sit in the back like a White Russian princess. I'd sit up beside Billy and we'd be singing our lungs out all the way to the stadium.

When my daughter was confirmed, I couldn't think of a better godfather for her than Billy. He has passed on now, but Madeline is still one of my closest friends. Aside from all those wonderful songs I got to sing, Cole, Billy and Madeline were the nicest things that happened to me in connection with *Anything Goes*.

I WITHDREW FROM *Anything Goes* to return to Hollywood for *Strike Me Pink*, another Goldwyn-Cantor picture. Benay Venuta replaced me. But the film was delayed and I unexpectedly found myself repeating my Reno Sweeney role in the film version of *Anything Goes*.

When Paramount bought the property, it was intended for W. C. Fields, Queenie Smith and Bing Crosby. By the time they were ready to go into production, Crosby had become a hot box-office property and the moguls decided to hire me for my original role and replace Fields with the less charismatic Charlie Ruggles in Victor Moore's role. Ida Lupino, by the way, played the ingenue lead.

Of Cole's original score only three numbers remained: "Anything Goes"*; "You're the Top," which I did with Bing; and "I Get a Kick Out of You." I sang "Kick" sitting in a crescent moon with an entire bird of paradise nestling in my hair. Below me a couple of hundred extras swarmed over the stage for no particular artistic effect.

I also sang a Chinese ditty, "Shanghai-de-Ho," in front of a chorus of Chinese dancers. The new numbers were contributed by a clutch of songwriters, including Cole's fellow Indianian Hoagy Carmichael,

---

* Additional lyrics certified 100 percent pure by the censor were contributed by Cole's talented cousin Ted Fetter, now curator of the theater and music collection of the Museum of the City of New York.

Edward Heyman, Frederick Hollander, Richard A. Whiting and Leo Robin.

The picture opened at the Paramount in New York and received passable reviews, but for me it lacked zing. If you're curious, a chopped-up version still turns up occasionally on TV under the catchy title *Tops Is the Limit*.

Strike Me Pink wasn't one of the better Goldwyn-Cantor collaborations either. I had three numbers—"Shake It Off with Rhythm," "Calabash Pipe" and "First You Have Me High, Then You Have Me Low," which Sam Goldwyn insisted upon calling "First You Got Me Up, Then You Got Me Down."

I wasn't exactly a failure in those pictures. After *Strike Me Pink* was released, *Photoplay* cited mine as one of the best performances of the month, and *Time* said I had the three best numbers in *Anything Goes*. But somehow the response seemed pretty tepid compared to what I received on Broadway.

While I was in Hollywood, Al Goetz came to visit and all the columnists from Walter Winchell to Dorothy Dey took me to task for withholding word of our marriage—ignoring the fact that Al was only legally separated, not yet divorced. One writer must have still had the needle in his arm because he reported that this very successful stockbroker, this rich man, was giving up his investment business to turn Hollywood agent in order to guide my career.

What they ignored was that there was still enough of Episcopalian-reared Ethel Zimmermann in me to be disturbed by this publicity. As a matter of fact, our romance had begun deteriorating, and by the time Al was free to remarry, the thrill was gone, as the song says.

It was no secret that Cole and I formed a mutual admiration society or that he wanted to write another show for Gaxton, Moore and me. Vinton Freedley saw no reason to break up a winning combination, so he secured Howard Lindsay and Buck Crouse to do the book.

Howard and Buck tried the same gambit Vinton had used in promoting *Anything Goes*. When they wooed Billy, he dominated their story line of *Red, Hot and Blue* while I was only a shadowy figure. Then they visited me at the Paramount Theater, where I was appearing in the stage presentation, and they began spinning in reverse. They were in the midst of telling me *my* version of the story in which I *was* the show, when Billy unexpectedly dropped into my dressing room for a visit. He listened quietly for a few minutes. Then without a word, he walked—right out of the show. Moore followed him.

After toying with several possible substitutes, Vinton signed Jimmy Durante and a nervous young vaudevillian named Bob Hope. Maybe it was this switch in casting that caused Howard and Buck to develop writers' blocks. After weeks of frustration, they finally started gulping Benzedrine and flew right through the first draft. But after they came down from their high they reread their effort, tore it up and started over.

Cole had two songs that had been thrown out of the score of his first movie musical, *Born to Dance*. They were "Goodbye, Little Dream, Goodbye" and "It's De-Lovely." But since he wrote a song a day just to keep in practice, I wasn't worried about songs. In those days, a Broadway musical number was self-contained. Nobody worried whether it fit logically into the score, and the successful songwriters thought more about reaching the top of the hit parade than integrating the song into the story.

Since our rehearsals were delayed while we waited for Howard and Buck to produce a book, I decided to take Mom and Pop to Europe on some passes the French government had given me for singing at the dedication of the *Normandie*. The trip didn't turn out to be the ideal vacation. We sailed on August seventh, and on the seventeenth Pop was taken directly from the ship to a hospital operating table. The King of England's own doctor, Sir James Walton, was in charge of Pop's case, but I was still anxious. Seeking reassurance, I said, "He's the King's doctor. He ought to be pretty good in his line, holding down a job like that, hadn't he?" Some people thought that was hilarious. I didn't see anything funny about it at all. How was I going to make sure Pop got first-rate care if I didn't check out the doctor?

I left Mom and Pop in London and sailed for New York. I returned to find the production ready to disintegrate. My agent and Jimmy Durante's agent had both goofed. Before signing the contracts, each had overlooked inserting a clause specifying his client was to get top billing. Naturally, now that Jimmy and I were committed, neither agent could capitulate without losing face. Jimmy and I stayed completely out of it, but our representatives were issuing frequent ultimatums. Then Cole Porter got a wonderful idea from his wife, Linda, who was a crossword puzzle addict. She suggested having the names intersect.

Everybody congratulated everyone else until the agents began worrying whether people would read down to up or vice versa. Finally some diplomatic genius suggested that every two weeks, our billing be alternated. Once this earth-shaking idea had been hit upon, rehearsals were ready to begin.

Apparently, the friction left everyone irritated. Lew Kesler, who was to be my accompanist for many years, was working with me for the first time. After we got to be friends, Lew often reminded me of the first number we tried. "I'd heard you were a whip with a quip and you might leave me bruised, but I was prepared," he claimed. He also said that he'd been told to find my key—which turned out to be B—and maintained that B is hard to transpose to since it includes five sharps. So he fumbled a bit with the songs, which he hadn't seen before. He played the melody, but not the right harmony. After we had finished, according to him, I turned and said, "Look, pal, do me a favor. Take the Vienna rolls off your fingers!"

I probably did. My second husband, Bob Levitt, sometimes called me "Tactless Tillie."

We opened at the Colonial Theater in Boston on October 7. The plot seems simple enough. A Washington matron (me) was conducting a lottery which was to be run by an ex-convict (Jimmy Durante) and won by a lawyer (Bob Hope) whom I loved, but who was hung up on the memory of a broad (Polly Walters) who as a baby had branded her behind by sitting on a waffle iron. Would you believe that with a plot like that the first act could run for two hours and ten minutes? It did. Critic Elinor Hughes facetiously suggested presenting the first and second acts on successive nights like Eugene O'Neill's *Mourning Becomes Electra* trilogy.

The notices were bad, but audiences who had expected another *Anything Goes* had bought every ticket before we opened. The theater was jammed, but response was tepid. Fuses were short. Vinton and Cole, who usually rose above pre-opening jitters, began feuding over "Goodbye, Little Dream, Goodbye." Vinton said it was too melancholy and was killing the show. They didn't agree on the orchestration of "Ridin' High" either. Cole returned to New York, after which he and Vinton exchanged telegraphic insults.

Changes were made. We moved to New Haven for a week to allow for further improvements. Cole came through with a substitute number for "Goodbye." The new one, "Down in the Depths on the 90th Floor," never attained the popularity of some of his other hits, but it is still regarded by many as one of the finest examples extant of the torchy genre.

It contained a line "In my pet pailletted gown," which caused an explosion between Vinton and me. He didn't want to spring for a pailletted gown. I refused to sing the song without one. So finally he ordered a $1000 gold job which suited me perfectly—except for one detail. He'd had a hen-on-her-nest bustle attached to the back for a sight laugh. When I turned sideways, the audience saw the hen and I'd get a big yock.

To me this gag ruined the musical mood. I told Vinton that the hen had to go. "Any audience that gets a laugh out of me gets it while I'm facing them," I informed him. Then I went to my dressing room, took a pair of scissors and detached the sitting hen.

In spite of all the fuss, I was a happy girl. My numbers included "Down in the Depths," "Ridin' High," "You're a Bad Influence on Me," "Red, Hot and Blue" and a duet with Bob Hope, "It's De-Lovely."

"De-Lovely" caused a bit of friction between Bob and me on occasion. He, whether out of insecurity or because he liked to fool around, began playing to the boxes and otherwise distracting the audiences. At one point a titter arose at the wrong moment and I looked down to discover him lounging at my feet. I didn't mince words when we exited. I informed Vinton that if his so-called comedian ever behaved like that again I'd use my shoe to remodel that ski nose of his. Vinton must have delivered my message to Bob, because we had no more problems.

Among the first-nighters at the Alvin Theater on October 29 were my pals J. Edgar Hoover and Clyde Tolson. I'd got friendly with them because I was spending a lot of time at Sherman Billingsley's Stork Club, and John, as I always called him, and Clyde were there whenever they came to Manhattan.

Now John wasn't the talkative type; Clyde was the one with the quips. And John was careful never to lend the Federal Bureau of Investigation's name to any commercial endorsements, especially anything a little risqué. But one way or another he came through for *Red, Hot and Blue*, telling the *Post*'s Michael Mok, "It's a bright entertainment, put over with lots of style and there's quite a lot of truth in the cracks."

Critics thought that as a judge of shows, John was a great FBI director. To them the book was rowdy, uninspired burlesque. And Richard Watts stated an opinion that a lot of his colleagues were to copy when he wrote that I made Cole's songs sound a lot better than they were. Three or four columnists took up the refrain. Robert Benchley, who did the weekly reviews in *The New Yorker*, eventually worked that idea into his assessment of the show as a compliment to my dynamic approach and then proceeded to contradict himself by adding, "although on a second visit to the show, I was convinced that Mr. Porter's score is much better than I thought the first time."

Apparently unsettled by the complaints, Cole turned out a pseudo-nostalgic number, "The Ozarks Are Calling Me Home," which was added with much fanfare on November 23, 1936. It was, Cole said, for the "common people," not sophisticates for whom he had previously written. In any case the song was quietly dropped after all possible publicity value had been milked.

That Christmas, Cole gave me a painting. It had a red barn, chickens and so on. I looked at it and thought, Boy, this may be great but it doesn't go with my decor. So I gave it away. The sad part is I could never remember to whom I gave it. And it turned out to be an early Grandma Moses.

To get back to *Red, Hot and Blue*, after a few weeks of standing room only, business tapered off. Still we were playing to good houses and could have continued indefinitely, I think, when Vinton allowed Paramount Pictures, which had put up half the investment, to persuade him to close the show and send it to Chicago at the beginning of April 1937.

Vinton sent ahead an order for seventy tons of bagged sand to counterbalance the heavy scenery, allowing it to be raised and lowered from the flies. The head stage carpenter had never heard of a show that required seventy tons of sand. He decided the seventy was a typo and ordered seven tons. When the crew tried to raise the scenery the first time, the seven tons lifted the scenery three or four feet off the floor and left it dangling. Nothing would budge it. Opening night had to be postponed, and from there it was all downhill. Even though reviewers praised the book and tossed their critical hats in the air over the same songs that had only mildly amused their New York counterparts, the public acted as if we were under quarantine. We closed after two weeks.

If I haven't mentioned Jimmy Durante, it's because with temperament exploding all around him Jimmy was the unflappable one who delivered his show-stopping "A Little Skipper from Heaven Above" nightly and never caused problems for anyone. I'd go so far as to say that Durante was a dream. Sweet, good-natured Jimmy befriended anybody who asked. He was a pushover.

But funny. I'll never forget during the Boston tryout, Jimmy contracted a sore throat. Pop went down to Jimmy's dressing room to visit him. He knocked and Jimmy told him to come in. When Pop opened the door, Jimmy was lying down, his throat all wrapped up, with a big cigar in his mouth.

The other thing I remember vividly was the private telephone he had installed in his dressing room. On days when the nags were running, someone had to be assigned to remind him not to miss his cues. "Come on, Jimmy. Get off the phone," you'd hear someone say. "You're on." But Jimmy was just great.

Red, Hot and Blue was in no way innovative. It wasn't even a slick old-fashioned show. But in a day when audiences were content to settle for star turns, it did very nicely for Jimmy, Bob and me.

I WAS CONSIDERED some kind of an oddity because I kept insisting that my private life belonged to me, not to the public. Just as frequently reporters reminded me that there was only one Garbo. Well, I didn't want to be Garbo. I just refused to live my love life on the front pages of the tabloids.

Why doesn't an actress have as much right to privacy as other women? I kept asking. I was telling the truth when I said I hadn't found any man I could marry.

Yet the longer I was in the public eye, the more determined the reporters and columnists were to link me with someone. After Al Goetz faded from the scene, one newspaperman even tried to make a big thing of Billy Sussman, whom I had been dating when I went into *Girl Crazy* in 1930.

So you can imagine their delight when I began going with a rich young high-spirited and very eligible bachelor. Leafing through the scrapbooks that my dad kept so faithfully, the column items leap out of the pages:

> *April 12, 1937:* Ethel Merman and that publisher's lad are getting closer to the edition all the time.
> *May 5:* Ethel Merman and her Wally at the Raleigh Room . . .

May 17: Songbird Ethel Merman floats in the arms of publishing heir Walter Annenberg . . .

Walter lived in Philadelphia then. The Annenbergs were a publishing family who owned the Philadelphia *Inquirer*, the *Racing Form*, the *Morning Telegraph* and later *Seventeen* and *TV Guide*, among other holdings. Walter was running the *Inquirer*.

But he came to New York often to visit his mother and five or six sisters. He was the only boy in the family—very handsome and a family favorite.

I met him through some Main Line people in Philadelphia. Right away for some unknown reason he nicknamed me "East Cupcake." His was a new world to me. When we had dinner at his mother's home, it was the first time I ever visited a family who had gold service.

It was a fine romance, a romance out of a screwball comedy so popular in films then. Walter and I both liked to dance and were footloose and fancy free. But what I liked best about Walter was his sense of humor. You never knew what to expect from him. Once I opened a package and it contained a cage of white mice. The next time I opened a present it was a diamond and gold bracelet.

The day I began an engagement at the Paramount Theater, doing five and six shows a day, Walter sent over a chaise lounge and chairs from Bloomingdale's to make my dressing room more comfortable.

One night when we were on the town, I got a craving for potato pancakes. We went from one restaurant to another until we found them. Watching me put them away struck Walter as funny. Next day a huge sack of potatoes arrived from Walter at the door of our seventeenth-floor apartment at 25 Central Park West.

My romance with Walter was broken up when I decided to go to Hollywood again. Occasionally over the years I'd see him or hear from or about him.

After Richard Nixon appointed him ambassador to Great Britain, Walter had an original presidential star designed and sculpted by Steuben. Along with many other people, I received a duplicate of it from the President.

Then while he was serving as our ambassador, he heard that Benay Venuta, with whom I became friendly after she replaced me in *Anything Goes*, and I were in London, and he invited us to the embassy. It was peculiar, because we'd always had such fun together, but now that he was an ambassador I began to feel a little strange about going. I said to Benay, "Gee, he's a big man now. What are we going to talk about? What's he going to say when we walk in?"

I needn't have worried. The butlers were all standing around. His beautiful wife, Lee, was there—everything was very proper. But Walter was Walter. The minute I came through the door, he boomed, "Hi, East Cupcake! How are you?"

I decided after the closing of *Red, Hot and Blue* not to do another Broadway musical that fall. Lou Irwin was transferring his base to California and had several prospects for me on the West Coast.

Louella Parsons, who always was a great booster of mine, was delighted. On September 23, 1937, she ran a long item about my previous attempts to break into the movie business:

> Pleasing news that Ethel Merman, who was so disappointed with her movie career a year or so ago that she flew back to Broadway stage musicals, is going to take another fling at Hollywood. Trouble was that Ethel never liked the way she was photographed in the pictures she made with Eddie Cantor. But now the popular torch warbler is making a fresh start at 20th Century-Fox, where she is expected in two weeks for *Bread, Butter and Rhythm* with Sonja Henie and Don Ameche. Another good break for Ethel's blues warbling is that Roy Del Ruth will megaphone. Picture should get under way about the middle of October, since Sonja is now enroute to Hollywood from her European vacation and Don Ameche has returned from a brief holiday.

By signing with 20th, I passed up my only opportunity to work with Rodgers and Hart. Prior to this deal, Mervyn LeRoy had been talking to me about appearing in *Food for Scandal*, which had a score by Dick and Larry. Then 20th came along with a better offer. This was publicized as a term contract but actually was a one-picture deal with options.

Truthfully, I wasn't straining at the bit to become a movie star any more than I had plotted to get out of vaudeville and into Broadway musicals. I just enjoyed singing and, once I'd discovered I could punch up a funny line, playing comedy. It wasn't important whether I did it on the stage, over the radio or in movies.

There were drawbacks in making pictures, but nothing serious. Hitting your marks (tape or chalk lines on the floor that kept you in focus for the camera) was difficult at first, but it was only a technical annoyance. The major problem for me was the Hays office's strictures. Those censors were determined to dull down the brass which I'd been accustomed to polishing up for laughs. In "Heat Wave," for instance, Ethel Waters, who introduced the song in a Broadway revue, got a laugh with "She started a heat wave by letting her seat wave." When I sang the lyric in *Alexander's Ragtime Band*, the line had to be changed to "She started the heat wave by letting her feet wave." Please! Where's the wit in that?

Even so, I was serious enough about becoming a movie star to try to persuade Pop to retire and move to Beverly Hills. When he sensibly refused, Mom and I took a suite at the Beverly-Wilshire Hotel, which was convenient to 20th and had good room service.

During this period I made three movies. The not-so-trippingly titled *Bread, Butter and Rhythm* with Sonja Henie, Don Ameche and Cesar Romero came first. I figured I was the rhythm. It wasn't so clear who was bread and who was butter. But it turned out to be immaterial. Before release, somebody sensibly retitled the film *Happy Landing*.

Then there was *Alexander's Ragtime Band* with Alice Faye, Tyrone Power and Don Ameche.

The last was *Straight, Place and Show*. There was great fanfare about Darryl Zanuck, the head of the studio, having it rewritten for me. But it turned out to be typical Ritz Brothers roughhouse—and that's about as much as you'll hear about it from me.

This visit I felt a little less out of place in Hollywood than previously. I never became a part of the clique of contract stars who got big build-ups, but I really didn't want to. I thought their contracts should have been with "Penitentiary-Fox."

The studio took over complete control of their lives. Contract stars were told where to live, how to dress, what to do, and, for all I know, when to go. I got a little taste of it myself.

When I arrived to begin filming *Happy Landing*, some press agent had spread the word that Cesar Romero and I were a hot item. Butch—who's going around calling anyone Cesar?—probably didn't want to cooperate any more than I did, but he was housebroken. As I stepped off the Super Chief in Pasadena, he was waiting to "welcome me back" with what Louella Parsons described as "the biggest bouquet of flowers in town."

I took one look at him and wisecracked, "Been robbing cemeteries again?" Then I pretended to mistake him for an autograph hunter. When he continued to play 20th's game, I loaded him down with my luggage and he ended up riding in the baggage car instead of with me.

Now Butch Romero wasn't a bad guy, but he was so brainwashed by this publicity hooey that he didn't give up even after Ed Sullivan printed an item exposing our "romance" as strictly press agent stuff.

I guess I felt embarrassed and exploited. Anyway I began playing practical jokes on Butch that nearly drove him crazy.

He wasn't free with a buck, to put it mildly. So every time an item about us appeared, I'd order a beautiful floral arrangement for myself, have his card attached and charge it to his account. Upon its arrival, I'd thank him profusely and he'd sputter, "I never ordered that." I'd act amazed. "You didn't? Well, *who* did? I'm allergic to roses."

Sonja finally got in on the fun too. Butch lived at the Garden of Allah, where he employed a Chinese man-servant. Once Sonja and I called this man of all work, pretending to represent the Los Angeles water company. We told him that water in the area was being cut off indefinitely. He was to fill every vessel in the house. Hours later Butch arrived home to find sinks and bathtubs full of water after he managed to pick his way among the brimming pots and kettles that covered the floor.

Another time various Chinese laundries arrived hour after hour, insisting someone had asked them to pick up the wash.

On one occasion a hearse drew up to collect the body. Guess who was behind all of this.

Something that I didn't think was funny happened in the big ice-skating finale filmed the first week in November. In this scene we made a big circle of the rink, holding on to each other's hips. I was at the tail of the line when Sonja made the circle that gave my end terrific momentum.

All skates had a point at the back and suddenly I felt something hit the tip of my beautiful white kid boots. I didn't think anything of it. But when we got through the take, they found the skater in front of me had accidentally put the point of his skate right through my shoe and sock into the top of my big toe. Filming was called off for the day. I was bleeding like a stuck pig.

Aside from that, making *Happy Landing* was a nice experience. Don Ameche was fun, had a great laugh and beautiful teeth. Sonja was good company and gave beautiful parties with big tents over the garden. She always wore her fabulous jewels. There was one party in particular—very elaborate. I remember it as if it were yesterday. Sonja had on her best jewels and Joan Crawford arrived in a sleek black dress with shoulder straps. That's all. Not even a brooch. That's being smart. Joan was the center of attention—and not a sparkler on her.

Happy Landing turned out to be a popular picture. Sonja skated a lot, the plot was some nonsense about an orchestra leader (Romero) and his manager (Ameche) being forced to land their private plane near a village where custom had it that if you danced twice with a girl, it was a proposal of marriage. Romero and Ameche danced and then fled to New York. Sonja followed. I was the opposition and sang some fairly singable songs by Sam Parkass and Jack Yellen, Walter Bullock and Harold Spina. They weren't up to Rodgers and Hart—but then who is?

Irving Berlin. That's who. I'd met Irving briefly in New York years before, but I didn't get to know him until he came to 20th to play the songs I was going to sing in *Alexander's Ragtime Band*, whose plot was an excuse to include twenty-six of Irving's numbers. I drew the title tune plus "Heat Wave," "Walking Back," "Blue Skies," "A Pretty Girl Is Like a Melody," "Everybody Step," "Pack Up Your Sins" and "Let's Go Slumming." I knew right away when I sang those numbers that ranged from pseudo ragtime to swing that Irving and I were going to work together in the future under more propitious circumstances.

Cute, cuddly Alice Faye and Tyrone Power were the stars. I didn't appear until the second half, even though I'd followed the studio dietitian's plan and managed to transform myself from zaftig to willowy. And, for the first time, my naturally dark hair had been lightened to a more flattering auburn. Incidentally, I've kept it that way ever since. So with that and the beginning of a friendship with Irving, the picture was definitely worth making.

My high spirits got out of hand only once during the filming. Ty Power was terrific looking. Now, recently, a lot has been made of Clark Gable's poor teeth. Ty's weren't bad, but they weren't as perfectly formed as Don Ameche's either. So Ty had temporary upper caps that he slipped on for close-ups. One day I was bored and feeling devilish, so I hid his caps. The company was frantic. It held up production until the caps could be found. I don't know why I did it. I had nothing against Ty. Maybe I just resented being relegated to secondary stature by 20th.

Some reporter shortly after questioned me about Ty. Sonja and half of the women in America were insane about him, but I just shrugged and said that he wasn't my type. That quote received wide play in the press. But I didn't mean it the way they interpreted it. Ty and Clark Gable—they just don't make them like that anymore. I admired Ty, but when I said he wasn't my type, I should have gone on and said I probably wasn't his type either. Once after work I had a drink with him, and that's the closest I ever got to Tyrone Power. He was glamour personified and so was the girl he married, Linda Christian. In fact, he was so glamorous he might not have become a star today. Maybe today's audiences would consider him plastic. It's the same as with music in the past few years. Anything singable or understandable is square.

Anyway, after *Alexander's Ragtime Band* I made that third picture for 20th—the one I promised not to mention. I won't, but I can't resist quoting Frank S. Nugent, who wrote in reviewing it for the New York *Times* that it "seems to have been one of those pictures produced by the trial and error method—a trial to its audience and an error on the part of the producer." The end of my work in Hollywood also wrote finis to Lou Irwin as my agent. He was going to stay in Hollywood, and I didn't want to be handled by some associate in New York. Our professional relationship had been mutually beneficial, but now it was over.

Reporters often used to ask me how I felt about movies in comparison to the stage. I now knew I preferred delivering my performance in person. I liked to be in control. You couldn't be in films. And I'd already learned that it was cold down there as the face on the cutting-room floor.

IN SEPTEMBER 1938 I went into the Strand Theater on Broadway. *Variety*'s Abel Green, who could inject excitement into a turtle race, covered my work under "New Acts." That was fair enough. The last time I'd been reviewed there was in July 1930. After the buffeting my ego had taken playing supporting roles in films, his notice perked me up. In part he wrote:

> Back on Broadway, Miss Merman, in varieties, is now an expensive name entry. She brings with her an air and an aura of polish, and the ultimate in big league vocalizing. She made her Friday preem at the Broadway Strand something of a gala occasion, with the entire loge section roped off for her friends who had feted her earlier in the evening at the Stork Club.
>
> In a nifty hoop skirt creation that looks like a fugitive from a Champs Elysées couturier, Miss Merman doesn't let the class clothes keep her from singing about "Eadie" who spelled class with a capital K. She opens with "Pocket Full of Dreams," does "So Help Me" in a manner that sounds almost new, reprises "Heat Wave," another Berliniana out of *Alexander's Ragtime Band*—wherein she's featured—and whams them with a medley of musical comedy

hits and songs she's introduced. Latter pot-pourri unreels like a double-A rating in ASCAP and impresses anew in the association of hit singers with songs.

The Stork Club, its owner Sherman Billingsley and the people who frequented it were central to my life during this period. Paley Park now occupies the site where the Stork once stood, and I hope the people who use it have half as good a time as we did at the Stork Club. For the information of Johnny-come-latelies, the Stork was about as "in" as you could get during the 1930s and '40s. It and El Morocco were to that era what the Casino in the Park had been to the late 1920s and early '30s. Cafe society, with its adventurers, stage and movie stars, writers, press agents, new and old rich, play-girls and playboys, intermingled at 3 East Fifty-third Street. Eleanor Holm, Billy Rose, Walter Winchell, "Shipwreck" Kelly, Brenda Frazier, Peter Arno, J. Edgar Hoover, Clyde Tolson, Bea Lillie, Eddie Dowling, Lois Long, Dorothy Kilgallen, Dorothy Fields, John McClain, several Whitneys, several Rockefellers, "Honeychile" Wilder, the Duke and Duchess of Windsor, Charles MacArthur, Helen Hayes, Radie Harris, Lucius Beebe, Ben Hecht, Billy and Madeline Gaxton—these were only a fraction of the regulars.

The era emphasized the right of a man to exclude others from his premises. Prior to World War II people weren't sensitive to equal rights. You could be a rich, famous, amusing WASP and still be barred with no explanation.

Sherman, who had transformed his former speakeasy into one of New York's favorite playgrounds, succeeded by selling the assumption that everyone was not equal. On his own turf he acted the absolute despot. He made rules of dress and conduct. He might welcome or banish someone on the basis of her hairdo. If a favorite misbehaved, woe unto him or her. If the infraction was minor, a warning or temporary banishment might suffice. If major, thereafter whenever the offender appeared at the gold chain that barred the door, the word was that the joint was jammed, even if there were dozens of empty tables in plain view. That meant you were permanently banned—or as they said on Eighth Avenue, eighty-sixed.

I know that the present-day theme is Anything Goes. I'm not sure I agree. I think there is such a thing as good taste and I don't think that's a copout. There are, for instance, details of my life that I would confide to close friends but that I wouldn't consider telling to just anyone who happens to own a library card.

If I am of interest to readers, it is because of what I have accomplished as a musical performer and the way I've coped with lots of success and occasional failure.

I pride myself on being honest, and I'm not going to omit mentioning the affectionate relationship that existed between Sherman and myself. I'm going to tell you what you need to know, but I'm not going into intimate detail. I will say that those "friends" who hint that he was "the love of my life" don't know what they are talking about. When the time comes to discuss the love of my life, I'll tell you about him—the happiness we shared and the heartbreak too. About my relationship with Sherman, I'll only note that it was one of those times when I'd have been better off if I had listened to my mother when she said, "Ethel, are you sure you know what you are doing?"

Sherman liked me from our first meeting. I liked him and the Stork Club. Why wouldn't I? I was treated like royalty. All the regulars received presents. There was perfume, lipsticks, cologne, red suspenders, wallets, cases of champagne or Scotch that seemed to be handed out almost indiscriminately. Sherman would give you his right arm. He was overgenerous. I think that's why he died almost broke—if he did. And that's what I heard.

It's also true that he was spectacularly generous with me. During that period of my life I drank only champagne. Sherman was always having replenishments delivered to my dressing room, so that I could have a bottle after the show. There were some eye-popping opening night jewels too. And people still mention—some of them enviously—how Sherman had a catered after-theater supper for the entire cast of *Stars in Your Eyes* delivered to Boston during the tryout.

It wasn't only with me either. Anyone who was a friend of mine got the treatment. Dorothy Fields got it. And Radie Harris, who was living at the Algonquin, still talks of coming home one Christmas and having to pick her way through the living room, which was piled with gifts from Sherman.

I also met many friends there. That's how I became so friendly with J. Edgar Hoover and Clyde Tolson. When they were in town, the Stork Club was their hangout.

Clyde was younger and very good-looking. On one of my opening nights they sent me a telegram: "Sincere good wishes to you and your new show. We are sorry we can't be in the front row to hiss— no kiss you. Tenderest regards. John Edgar Hoover. Clyde Tolson."

Clyde undoubtedly sent it. He had a wonderful sense of humor and was much easier to talk to than John. John was quiet and not easy to get to know. But since they were always together, Clyde kept things moving and we became good friends.

I remember right after the New York World's Fair opened in 1939 Sherman took all of us to dinner at the Italian Pavilion. Afterward we walked around the grounds. When we came to the shooting gallery, John and Clyde picked up guns and knocked off all the rabbits and ducks—bang, bang, bang—one right after another.

John didn't look especially like his photographs and nobody knew Clyde. So people wondered who we were with that could shoot like that. Some gangsters, maybe?

It was at the Stork that I met the one-of-a-kind Bea Lillie and became a pal of hers. Bea and I used to hold court in the Cub Room. She looked as if she had just come out of a bandbox—always with that little Juliet cap she wore. She had lovely skin and wore only light powder and little rouge. In her own peculiar way, I thought she was stunning.

And funny! Some of the things she would say were to die from. When we'd get to wisecracking, Dorothy Kilgallen was always wishing she had a microphone to broadcast "our show."

While I was drinking champagne, all I ever saw Bea drink was beer, but she'd have quite a few. There was always a big glass in front of her. The waiter would approach with another bottle. Bea would put her two fingers on the edges of the glass and say, "Oh no, no. No more for me, please"—while he would pour the beer between her fingers into the glass.

When it got late and there were very few people in the club, Bea didn't bother to climb the flight of stairs that led to the ladies' room. The men's room was on street level. She'd wait for an all-clear and scoot right in there and out again.

In New York I went to see poor Bea recently and it was enough to break your heart. She didn't even realize that I was there. My heart ached as I remembered all the fun we'd had. I hugged her and kept saying, "Beasie, it's Ethel!" but there was no way I could reach her.

I mentioned Dorothy Kilgallen earlier. I had a wonderful relationship with her, Leonard Lyons, Ed Sullivan, Hedda Hopper and Louella Parsons, as well as Radie Harris, Earl Wilson and Louis Sobol. But I can't say the same for Walter Winchell, who probably did more than anyone else to popularize the Stork Club. Sherman tried to keep us friends, but it was difficult.

I had several run-ins with Walter and I never felt free to talk openly in his presence. If anything was said, there was always the danger that he would misconstrue or even distort the meaning in some embarrassing way. As for a retraction? Please! Winchell never retracted. He was notorious for that. So when he was present, I always felt as if there was a scrim between us. Not that I was afraid of him, but he was a very difficult person to talk to. For a reporter he was not a good listener either. He talked through you.

Once later, when Walter again printed some stuff about Al Siegel coaching me, I blasted him in a letter. That night he came up to my table and I let him have it. "Don't you talk to me," I said coldly. "You're no friend of mine." That's how scared of him I was. Not much maybe, but unusual enough for another columnist to print as an item.

To get back to Sherman. Years after I stopped going there Russell Nype and I were passing the Stork, which had had a lot of trouble because of Sherman's refusal to employ union help. Suddenly we decided to go in and say hello for old times' sake.

There was no one at the door. Three people were sitting at a table—Eleanor Whitney, Freddie Backer, who became Judge Backer, and a gray-haired man who had his back to us. He jumped up. It was Sherman, but I give you my word of honor I didn't recognize him until he spoke. He was so old and stooped and thin.

Except for a couple of waiters, we were the only people in the place. In the course of the conversation, I mentioned that Sherman had closed the Cub Room. He nodded and for a moment there was a flicker of the old Sherman. "Yes, after you stopped coming," he said. "I only opened it so that you'd have a place to go." That was only a part of his courtly charm. Of course, he had closed it because nobody went there anymore.

XII

Stars in Your Eyes looked like a sure winner and came closest to being a flop of any show I ever did. It was designed to cash in on the influx of tourists visiting the 1939 World's Fair.

Back in the 1930s, playwrights often devised plots by asking themselves, "What would happen if . . . ?" One even called his play about Abraham Lincoln *If Booth Had Missed*. Well, composer Arthur Schwartz began wondering what would happen if a conservative Hollywood mogul hired a leftist genius to direct a movie musical.

My friend Dorothy Fields liked the idea enough to write the lyrics. J. P. McEvoy came on from Hollywood to develop the script. And Dwight Deere Wiman, who had just had a big success with ballerina Vera Zorina in *I Married an Angel*, agreed to produce if the script provided a part for another of his dancing discoveries, Tamara Toumanova.

When Josh Logan, the boy-wonder director of *I Married an Angel* and *Knickerbocker Holiday*, read McEvoy's book, he persuaded the others that this satire on left-wing politics and Hollywood hijinks wasn't either funny or valid. What would work, he said, was a combination of sex and Hollywood. So McEvoy and Logan set about making revisions.

Jimmy Durante and I were co-starred with Richard Carlson, Mildred Natwick, Bob Ross and Mary Wickes in important parts. Jimmy played "Bill," a character based on Hoppy Hopkins—the idea man whose fame grew out of approaching film producers and saying such things as "I'll give you a couple of quick ideas: Jeanette MacDonald, Clark Gable and the San Francisco earthquake."

I was cast as a glamour star who had inherited Monotonous Pictures from my late producer husband. I now had eyes for the new left-wing director (Richard Carlson), who was so in love with the Russian waif (Toumanova) that he was trying to throw my starring vehicle to her—over my dead body.

Lindsay and Crouse's book for *Anything Goes* was a perfectly formed pearl compared to the grain of sand we had for *Stars in Your Eyes*. We sometimes had to suspend rehearsals while McEvoy and Josh rewrote scenes. Still I was happy as I saw my character grow as grand as Norma Shearer, as tough as Carole Lombard and as pampered as Joan Crawford, with a coach (Mary Wickes) following me with a Victrola playing atmospheric music to get me in the mood, as Joan had done at one point in her career. It was my best shot at acting yet.

At our premiere in New Haven the show seemed destined to be a hit. Since Toumanova didn't speak English too well but was a terrific dancer, she was given no dialogue on her first entrance, but zipped through a spectacular dance with which she stopped the show. As the bravos echoed through the theater, her agent, "Doc" Bender, made a typical agent-type remark as he nudged Dwight Wiman and gloated, "I said she was sensational, didn't I? Now I *believe* it!"

Jimmy and I had our moments too, but the show was running an hour too long. In a major operation, Josh and McEvoy sliced fifty minutes overnight. Then the material was gradually restored. By the time we opened in Boston, the curtain came down after midnight. Further surgery was required and the production never quite fully recovered.

During all these changes, Dorothy Fields, who had written lyrics for the music of Jerome Kern and Jimmy McHugh, to name only two of her many collaborators, and Arthur Schwartz, her current partner, found that several of their favorite songs had to be discarded. One was "My New Kentucky Home." Josh proved what a master psychologist he was by persuading Dorothy and Art to remove it on the grounds that it was so good that it was ruining the rest of the show by comparison to it.

The numbers that I eventually performed included "This Is It," "A Lady Needs a Change," "Just a Little Bit More" (which after the reworking of the libretto no longer really belonged in this show), "I'll Pay the Check" and "It's All Yours."

"It's All Yours," a duet with Durante, had no real relationship to the plot either, but it was a rousing roll-'em-in-the-aisles show-stopper—and none of the critics demanded relevance. They just enjoyed the song and the interpolation of some corny joke every time we got to "It's all yours, everything you see."

At that point, Jimmy tossed hats or telephones or whatever and we threw in a joke: Example:

> Jimmy: Jeanette, does this bus go over the Queensboro Bridge?
> Me: Well, if it don't, we're all going to get a hell of a duckin'.

Then, on with the song.

"A Lady Needs a Change" was a sexy number, but my best ten minutes were a scene in my dressing room in which I attempted to seduce the naive Carlson. After plying him with booze, I thought I had him made when his bleary eyes spotted his favorite book, *Alice in Wonderland*. Nothing would do but that I read to him.

What followed, according to the critics, were some of the biggest laughs I had ever collected, beginning when I read, "Chapter One: Down the Rabbit Hole."

By the time I delivered the line "Alice was getting very tired sitting by her sister with nothing to do" to the inert form on my couch, the audience was literally screaming, and the scene got funnier and funnier. I was practically laying the audience in the aisles no matter how unsuccessful my attempts with Carlson were.

Then the mood changed, leading into Dorothy Fields and Arthur Schwartz's heartbreaking torch song "I'll Pay the Check." In it, as a rich, worldly-wise woman, I assured the young director that he owed me nothing. In our relationship I might be heading for an enormous wreck, but he was not to worry. It was my party and I'd pay the check.

We opened on February 9, 1939, at the Majestic. As we were leaving the theater after the premiere, Pop got detained. We climbed into the car and waited. Pop, who was always a snappy dresser, finally came out of the stage door wearing his derby hat. Someone in the crowd spotted him and shouted, "Oh, here comes the Governor." The fans crowded around Pop and he graciously signed "Alfred E. Smith" three or four times, with just the flourish they expected. Then he hopped into our limousine and we took off.

The reviews were generally excellent for the cast, favorable for the score and disappointing for the book. Even so, the consensus was that we would settle in for a run. But patrons of the 1939 World's Fair spent their money to see Eleanor Holm and Johnny Weissmuller in Billy Rose's *Aquacade*, attended Mike Todd's all-black *Hot Mikado* or went to the *Frozen Alive* and other Flushing Meadow sideshows. They had no money left for Broadway.

The principals of *Stars in Your Eyes* took a 50 percent cut, hoping that we would catch on. Only we never did. After 127 performances, we had had it. In addition to the stars I've mentioned, we had quite a chorus. Some of the unknowns who were thrown out of work by the closing included Nora Kaye, Jerome Robbins, Dan Dailey and Maria Karnilova. Choreographer Carl Randall must have had some eye for talent.

Stars in Your Eyes was even more disappointing for me than for most of the others. Because many critics agreed with Brooks Atkinson of the *Times*, who gladdened my heart by writing, "La Merman plays the part with enormous relish. She knows comedy as thoroughly as she knows singing, and her screen hussy is enormously hearty and enjoyable."

To this day I have in my curio cabinet the little silver cup decorated with the masks of comedy and tragedy, laughter and tears, that our director presented to me on opening night.

On it, he had inscribed, "To Sarah Bernhardt, Jr., from Josh."

BUDDY DESYLVA HAD ABANDONED Broadway for movies, where he'd written songs, collaborated on screenplays and produced pictures since I'd appeared for him in *Take a Chance*. He'd been responsible for several Hollywood hits, but hadn't achieved the power or acclaim he craved. So when he left Universal, he took along a story that he thought would make a blockbuster movie.

Pandro M. Berman, who was head of production at RKO, agreed. So did Norman Krasna, who wrote it, and Garson Kanin, who was assigned to direct it. Ginger Rogers didn't share their enthusiasm. But Berman forced her to make it anyway.

Buddy had been an astute judge of material in choosing *Bachelor Mother*. The film covered Ginger, Gar Kanin, Norman Krasna and Pan Berman with glory when the reviews appeared. Only Buddy was ignored.

He complained to Louis Shurr, the agent. Louis' client Bert Lahr, who had scored as the Cowardly Lion in *The Wizard of Oz*, was being dropped by Metro-Goldwyn-Mayer. As Bert said, "How many cowardly lion parts are there?" Louis suggested that Buddy find a story for Bert and produce a Broadway show that would score the kind of success Hollywood couldn't ignore.

Buddy and Herbie Fields, brother of my friend Dorothy, knew of a story they'd written for Paramount which had never been produced. They thought they might be able to buy it, but what composer was available to write the score?

Louis was aware that *Stars in Your Eyes* was foundering. He also realized that Cole Porter had become a hot property again with *Leave It to Me*, which had made a star out of Mary Martin. Cole in 1937 had suffered a riding accident that had left him permanently crippled. But with *Leave It to Me* a success, Broadway's confidence in him was restored. Louis felt certain that Cole and I were available and eager to work together again. So Louis told Buddy to write the female role with me in mind and he would deliver Cole.

That's how I happened to open on February 9, 1939, in *Stars in Your Eyes* and on December 6 of the same year in *DuBarry Was a Lady*, which ran 408 performances. Bert played a washroom attendant in a nightclub. He was hopelessly in love with the singing star (me) and tried to do away with his competition (Phil Regan) for the singer's affections by slipping Regan a Mickey Finn. Drinks were switched and Bert got the Mickey. While he was out cold, he dreamed he was Louis XV and I was DuBarry. You take it from there.

It was what we used to call a tired-businessman's entertainment. In fact, the critics felt the situations would have suited a burlesque show if everything hadn't been first class—the writing, songs, cast, direction, scenery, costumes—everything.

Not that there weren't a few problems. I had a beautiful white dress and a gorgeous black one. They were created for me by Raoul Pene DuBois, who also designed the scenery. But apparently the couturier didn't speak to the scene designer, because at dress rehearsals I couldn't maneuver my skirts through the door without doing a fancy sideways dip. So the doorways had to be remade.

Phil Regan, the singing cop, didn't seem to be able to project his songs beyond the proscenium arch, so Ronald Graham was brought in to replace him before the Broadway opening.

And Chuck Walters, later a Hollywood director, succeeded some guy who refused to look into the soubrette's eyes as though he loved her, because he was really in love with a brunette back home.

"Help! I'm not that repulsive!" the soubrette cried.

She certainly wasn't. Her name was Betty Grable. And a couple of years later she became just about the ultimate peaches-and-cream blonde as moviegoers and World War II G.I.'s were willing to swear. She was also wonderful to work with, very congenial. Now Betty was the first to admit she didn't have much of a voice, but her provocative looks and sexy dancing nearly stopped the show. What's more, no one loved her better than the chorus kids, the gypsies.

Bert Lahr was another story. I don't think I've ever worked with a more talented or insecure man than my co-star. I never knew anyone else who took everything so seriously—to the point where he was his own worst enemy. During rehearsals he was convinced I had received all the funny lines. He had nothing. Now Buddy DeSylva and Herbie Fields had made it a point to divide the laugh lines equally, but nobody could convince Bert of that. Or that he was such an inspired comedian that he could get laughs that weren't really there.

At dress rehearsal in New Haven he turned in a brilliant performance. Afterward he appeared to be unhappy. He insisted that I had got more laughs than he had. At that point he couldn't trust his own ears. Something disturbed him so much that he consumed a whole bottle of Scotch. Then *we* were really scared. We doubted that we'd be able to get him in shape for the first performance.

Opening night he was hilarious. Belly laughs! Gee, he could really get them. But he convinced himself that the producers had a claque out there laughing it up for him.

Nothing reassured him. There was one scene where Bert used to chase me around the bed, downstage, upstage, around the bed, over the bed, around and around. He wore a nightcap with a tassel and a long nightgown. He was so slow that one night I passed him on the bed, the way one race horse passes another. The audience screamed and the producers decided to leave it in. Then Bert began to worry whether that was his laugh or mine.

He was such a marvelous performer that he couldn't defeat himself, but he tried. He was a hypochondriac, and in "Friendship," our big duet, we'd be out there singing, and during the time I was doing my couplet, Bert would say under his breath, "Ethel, I'm going to faint."

While he was singing, I'd reassure him: "No, you're not."

And when I'd take my next couplet, he'd insist, "Yes, I am."

Well, he never fainted. He was just a chronic worrier, which may have been part of his talent. Anyway, he never let the negative side of his personality destroy him.

His agent told me of going backstage after the opening in Boston. The audience had loved "Friendship" so much that we ran out of verses. When they wouldn't let us off, Bert called out, "Come to Philadelphia next week, we'll have some new lyrics for you."

Afterward in his dressing room everyone was congratulating him on the hit he had scored and predicting the show would run a year. Bert just sat there twisting a button on his robe.

Louis said, "Bert, you're a smash! You're in!"

Bert looked up at him and said in a pitiful little voice, "Yeah. But what about next year?"

We were a hit in New Haven, Boston and Philadelphia. Then for some inexplicable reason, the show failed to go over on opening night in New York. The comedy scenes didn't play well. Cole's numbers for me included "When Love Beckoned," "Come On In," "Give Him the Oo-La-La" and "Katie Went to Haiti." With Bert I had "Friendship" and the controversial "But in the Morning, No!"

"Friendship" gave first-nighters a few laughs. "But in the Morning, No!" which enumerated things that could be enjoyed at night but not in the morning, aroused outright hostility.

When the reviews came in they were mixed, but Cole was reprimanded for his "slatternly" lyrics. And later when *The New Yorker* review appeared, "But in the Morning, No!" was cited as "dirt without wit."

This time, whether the critics praised or damned us didn't make any difference. The second-night audience was with us from the beginning, disproving the old theatrical bromide that negative notices invariably halve the laughs the next night. By the end of the week we were playing to standees.

After watching performances every night for a couple of weeks, Buddy DeSylva paid me one of the greatest compliments I've ever received. "Watching Merman is like watching a motion picture," he said. "Her performance never varies."

From Buddy's point of view, with *DuBarry* he had at least partly achieved what he had set out to do—produce the kind of smash that Hollywood couldn't ignore. But before the show began to show any signs of slackening, Buddy brought out *Louisiana Hayride* and began plotting a new move. It is no wonder that I was so enthusiastic about him, telling a newspaper interviewer, "It isn't because he's my boss, but he's a great guy. He knows what is best for me before I do. He's out of another world, that man."

What I was getting at was that he'd decided to build his next show around me. Always before, I'd shared honors with Gaxton and Moore, Jimmy Durante or Bert Lahr. Now Buddy was convinced that I was ready to carry the show by myself.

C
H
A
P
T
E
R

WITH THE BROADWAY OPENING OF *Panama Hattie* Buddy DeSylva established himself as the top musical producer of that period. His three simultaneous hits equaled Ziegfeld's record. The movie industry had to take notice. It did. Before long he was running Paramount Studios.

I was feeling pretty happy and successful too. I left *DuBarry*, took a two-week vacation and plunged into rehearsals for my new show. On October 28, 1940, my picture appeared on the cover of *Time*. Two days later I opened with my name only above the title of *Panama Hattie*. When I saw my billing on the 46th Street Theater marquee I felt like stopping strangers on the street and shouting, "That's me, that's me, that's me!" Oh yes, on Friday, November 15, I married William R. Smith.

Let's take things one at a time. I'll admit I was honored to be on the cover of *Time*. Not many Broadway personalities made that position in those days. It didn't hurt my feelings either when the writer called me "the undisputed number one musical comedy songstress of these harassed times."

Then on October 30, *Panama Hattie* opened. Cole Porter had written the songs; DeSylva and Fields the book. Raoul Pene DuBois designed the scenery and costumes. Edgar MacGregor directed. Robert Alton did the choreography.

As they had with *DuBarry*, the critics called the show high-class burlesque. But this time they didn't stint their praise. They knew audiences would love it, and at the end of the season when *Variety* toted up the reviewers' batting averages on calling hits and flops, none of them wanted a wrong call tallied against himself.

Hattie Maloney was an expansion of the Katie who went to Haiti. Only Hattie had the capacity to grow. In fact, she was quite a dame. Hattie was a brassy broad who hung out with sailors and didn't speak correct, but she had a softer side. Especially after meeting U.S. government official Nick Bullett (Jimmy Dunn). She determined to marry him and, after some problems, enlisted the aid of his eight-year-old daughter, Geraldine (Joan Carroll), in helping her win him away from the heartless Philadelphia society gal (Phyllis Brooks).

That production had a line-up of top talent. Among the principals were Arthur Treacher, Betty Hutton, Nadine Gae, Rags Ragland, Frankie Hyers and Pat Harrington. June Allyson (who understudied Betty Hutton), Jane Ball, Betsy Blair, Lucille Bremer, Doris Dowling and Vera-Ellen, all of whom later had some success in Hollywood, danced in the chorus.

Betty Hutton and I enjoyed a nice friendship. In fact, I still have a note from Betty in the scrapbooks Pop kept. In it she thanked me for a topaz ring I gave her when she left the cast to go to Hollywood. There is also a wire she sent on March 15, 1943:

> DARLING, I AM FEELING VERY BLUE AND LONELY TONIGHT. STARTED REMINISCING WITH EDDIE DUKOFF ABOUT THE FUN I HAD WITH YOU IN PANAMA HATTIE. HE TELLS ME YOU'RE THE TOAST OF NEW YORK AND I'M VERY HAPPY YOU ARE. NO ONE DESERVES IT MORE THAN YOU. MY LOVE, BETTY.

She had three numbers when we opened in New Haven and the same three numbers when she withdrew from the cast to go into films. So why twenty-three years later she tells talk-show audiences that I insisted upon her best number being cut I'll never know.

I didn't need to diminish the impact of anyone else's triumph. Not when Cole was writing "Make It Another Old-Fashioned, Please," a torch song to end torch songs, for me. To say nothing of "Visit Panama," "My Mother Would Love You" and "I've Still Got My Health."

That ignores the show-stopping "Let's Be Buddies," with a precocious Joan Carroll. Prior to that song in the show, Joan hadn't considered me enough of a lady to marry her daddy. But as we sang it I won her over. At the beginning of the number my hat had a bird on it and there were bows, bows, bows all over my dress and shoes. During the song Joan, who had converted to my side, appeared to be snipping the trick bows with scissors so that as we finished singing she had turned my outfit into a simple orchid-colored dress. Audience reaction to that moment reminded me of the Christmas I sang "She's Me Pal" at Camp Mills, dedicating the song to Mom. Only this time instead of soldiers it was tired businessmen who seemed to be getting an awful lot of specks in their eyes.

There was another song too, the rambunctious, nonsensical "You Said It," which Pat Harrington, Frankie Hyers, Rags Ragland, Arthur Treacher and I batted out to the audience.

What a group! Were they funnier off- or onstage? One matinee just before Easter, Pat Harrington came to the theater without his toupee. He had to. His kids had been coloring their eggs and decided daddy's toup made a great nest for them.

Harrington and Frankie Hyers worked at a celebrity hangout on Fifty-second Street, Jack White's Club 18. Their sidekick was a young guy named Jackie Gleason.

Club 18 was very informal. If you felt like getting up and singing, they welcomed you. If you didn't, the regulars performed. The management had so many tables jammed into the place, there was hardly any room for the entertainers to work. And if a gal wanted to go to the ladies' room, God forbid, she had to cross the floor with the guys chanting, "We know where you're going! We know where you're going!" When she came back, one of them would shout, "You were in there long enough to read *Gone With the Wind*."

Or one of the guys would ask, "Anyone here from Philadelphia?"

Somebody would admit he was, only to be told, "Well, there's a bus leaving. Get on it!"

The 21 Club was located right down the block. For a while a stooge would walk through Club 18 carrying a big old garbage can on his shoulder, and Hyers would yell, "There goes more garbage for Twenty One."

Or some debutante would come in wearing a fur coat. The fellows would look at it and ask, "What kind of a fur is that?" And the dame would say it was mink. Then they'd come back: "You think it's mink. Wait till the wind changes."

Their routines were a combination of Olsen and Johnson and Don Rickles.

I loved Rags Ragland, who along with Hyers and Harrington was one of the sailors in *Panama Hattie*. Now I have never approved of drinking before or during a show. For myself, I wouldn't even have a glass of sherry. I've been known to complain about other cast members because their tippling interfered with the performance. But a few people cannot perform without drinking. They need liquor for that push, that crutch. Poor Rags, whose finishing school had been burlesque, had to have booze to be funny. He used to drink Old Grand-dad. So against all my principles, I kept a bottle of it underneath the dressing table's skirt. Rags would come off stage and head for that table. He'd take the top off the bottle and he'd go—I mean, he'd take a big swig—and put the bottle back. It was as if he were drinking water. He could drink a whole bottle and never vary his performance.

He had one line I'll never forget. He was peering through binoculars supposedly looking at a broad across the street, making comments about her, and finally he'd say, "That's a hell of a place to wear a Willkie button." I used to wait for his reading of that line every night.

Arthur Treacher, the other member of the "You Said It" group, became a friend offstage. He and his wife, Virginia, always called me "Hattie." Arthur's passed now, but when I see Virginia it's still "Hello, Hattie."

I was at Arthur and Virginia's home when I met Bill Smith. Bill, who was an actors' agent with the Feldman-Blum Agency on the West Coast, accompanied Charles Boyer, a client, to New York, where Boyer was doing a radio show.

Bill was tall, broad-shouldered and handsome. He came from a Brookline, Massachusetts, family and had had a little experience as a manufacturer on Seventh Avenue before becoming a theatrical agent. After rehearsals all of us began going out. Generally Bill and I found ourselves sitting together. But to this day I can't explain how I happened to marry him. I do know I married him for all the wrong reasons.

While I was in Boston during *Hattie* previews, I gave an interview saying that my greatest ambition was to be a wife and mother. I hinted that newspaper readers might be in for a surprise some morning soon. Now there was nothing wrong in that. But then I went on to make what now seems to me like a lot of excuses to myself. "Yes, it's marvelous knowing you are a star and being able to do things for people . . . but when you become successful on stage you no longer belong to yourself. You are at the beck and call of people who made you a star by going to your shows. You have to sign autographs by hundreds and smile no matter how tired and sick you may feel."

I don't think I'm usually given to self-pity, but that's what the quote sounds like. Or else I'd been reading too many fan magazines. The problem with being the kind of person I am, once something is finished I try to put it out of my mind—and I succeed.

So what I can tell you about my first marriage is mostly from having my memory jogged by my scrapbooks. A sob sister from the *Daily News* wrote, "She thinks 'My Bill' is the greatest number she's ever met and 'My Bill' is not a song." From the scrapbooks, I find that after our meeting Bill went back to the Coast but that we talked nightly on the telephone, and when he asked me to marry him I said yes.

Why? I'd had some fairly serious involvements without rushing to the altar. Did I think it was time to get married? I was around thirty years old.

Anyway, Bill came back to New York for the opening of the show and then on November 15 Mom, Pop, Arthur and Virginia Treacher, Bill and I took a train to Elkton, Maryland, at eight A.M. for a surprise wedding. During the ceremony I cried like a baby. Afterward Pop asked me what I was bawling about. I said because I felt so happy. The truth is I realized the marriage was all wrong right then.

That night I was back on stage at the 46th Street Theater, and during curtain calls the chorus gypsies and musicians showered me with rice. One joker in the orchestra pit tossed an old shoe on stage. Three days later Bill flew back to the Coast and his job.

We tried to make the marriage work. We took a year's lease on an apartment at the Pierre Hotel, a move that didn't make much sense, since Bill continued working out of California rather than Manhattan as we had planned. And I told reporters that when *Hattie* closed, I'd be leaving the stage to become Mrs. Bill Smith, wife and mother.

Even so, I couldn't resist making jokes about how tough it was to get married and then have to sign the hotel register "Mr. and Mrs. Bill Smith."

I don't suppose it did Bill's ego any good either when I phoned and attempted to reserve tables at the Gripsholm Restaurant in the name of Mrs. William B. Smith. Somehow or other, the headwaiter couldn't seem to get the name straight. So I told him, "Smith. Spelled M-e-r-m-a-n."

Before long there were rumors of a rift and plenty of reasons for them. Tempers flared. Some ugly things were said. Then we decided that we should get together and talk things out. Relations must have been pretty good long-distance. Bill had an engraved tag which he wore on a chain around his neck: "My name is Bill Smith. If I am lost, please return me to Ethel Merman, *Panama Hattie*, 46th Street Theater."

Since I couldn't go to the Coast and Bill couldn't manage another trip to New York, we agreed to meet in Chicago the weekend of February 24.

Almost a week beforehand, I received a wire from Hollywood:

February 18, 1941

DEAR MERMO, BILL WAS IN TO SEE ME AND SAID YOU WANTED TO FLY TO CHICAGO SATURDAY NIGHT. I REALLY

DON'T THINK YOU SHOULD TAKE SUCH A CHANCE WITH YOUR VALUABLE SELF. IT IS EXTREMELY BAD FLYING WEATHER AT PRESENT. I AM NOT SPEAKING SELFISHLY FOR PANAMA HATTIE, BUT FOR MERMO. WHEN YOU WON'T LET BILL FLY AND YOU WANT TO FLY YOURSELF, I'D LIKE TO ASK YOU WHEN YOU ARE GOING TO GET SMART. MUCH LOVE AND HOPE YOU ARE HAPPY. BUDDY.

Although I don't recall what happened, apparently everything went smoothly, because on February 25 Buddy wired me:

DEAR MERMO, GLAD YOU HAD A GOOD TIME OVER THE WEEK-END. I GOT A BIG LAUGH FROM THE TELEGRAMS. AFTER SUCH A BIG DAY I WOULD EXPECT YOUR PERFORMANCE THIS WEEK TO BE SO GREAT THAT BUSINESS WOULD JUMP. BUT HOW CAN IT JUMP WHEN YOU'RE ALREADY SELLING OUT? LOVE TO YOU AND THOSE THAT REMEMBER ME. BUDDY.

With Bill in Beverly Hills and me in New York, there was no way the marriage could work. I realize now I hardly knew the man. I got into it too soon. It was a mistake. But we all make mistakes. That's why they put erasers on pencils.

By LATE 1941 Bundles for Britain, Lend-Lease, the Atlantic Charter and the success of the fascists against the Allies made it unlikely that the United States could stay out of war. Theatergoers found just the kind of relief they were searching for when Panama Hattie snagged her man and foiled the plotters who were trying to blow up the Canal.

Personally, things were looking up for me. Bill had secured a Mexican divorce charging desertion, so I was free again—but not for long.

I promised earlier that when I met the love of my life I'd tell you about him. Well, to backtrack to 1940, this is where he enters. I was introduced to him by Walter and Ella Young of Hearst's *Journal-American* at Dinty Moore's restaurant, which was located next door to the 46th Street Theater. His name was Robert Daniels Levitt and he also worked for the *Journal-American*.

Bob was broad-shouldered, dark and handsome as the devil. He wasn't a theater bug at all. He knew who I was, but didn't seem all that impressed. In fact, we didn't talk much even after the four of us left the party and went on to a nightclub.

I had an early appointment, and when the Youngs suggested Bob see me home he unenthusiastically agreed. In the cab on the way to my apartment I asked whether he happened to have chewing gum. He didn't, nor did he ask the driver to stop so he could pick up a pack.

As the cabbie pulled up at 25 Central Park West, Bob started to get out. Then he spotted a big snowdrift and changed his mind. No Sir Walter Raleigh, this boy. He muttered something to the effect that there was no point in both of us getting wet feet. So I plowed through a big drift on my own.

I know that all this sounds suspiciously like the beginning of one of those romantic comedies Hollywood turned out in the 1930s and '40s in which the hero and heroine start off hating each other and wind up in each other's arms. But that's what happened.

After that night I didn't expect to hear from him again. I don't think he intended to see me anymore either. But the following day, a whole carton of chewing gum arrived.

A day or so later the Youngs called from Toots Shor's and wanted me to join them and Bob. I refused, but he kept trying. Finally I agreed to go dining and dancing with him at El Morocco after my performance. When he suggested formal attire, I knew this wasn't just a way to pass another evening as far as he was concerned.

To him, that I was a star was incidental. For all the interest he showed in my professional life, I could still have been a secretary in Astoria. Not only that. If anyone else mentioned show business, he switched the conversation to another channel.

By the latter part of September we were together so often that columnists began running items such as this one from the old *World-Telegram*: "*Panama Hattie*'s Ethel Merman and her constant companion these midnights, Bob Levitt, enjoy the easy-goings-on at La Martinique."

Some people who knew of Bob's interest in Middle English thought it was pretty funny that he should have anything in common with a girl who never read books. But Bob was a well-rounded man and he wouldn't have thought of choosing a wife just because she could discuss Middle English.

About that time I accidentally discovered that Bob had not only never seen my current show but also had never seen me perform anywhere. So I told him there would be two tickets in his name at the box office next night, my compliments, and he'd better see the show—or else.

He took along book reviewer Sterling North and quite a few drinks. In fact, Sterling said Bob took along so many drinks he had difficulty trying to stay awake. It wasn't that my voice was so soothing to his ears. Much later Bob told me that he wasn't drunk, but musical comedies bored the hell out of him and always made him sleepy.

He might not have wanted to watch me onstage, but he wanted to see me every night. One thing I didn't have to worry about in his case was that he was interested in Ethel Merman the star. He couldn't have cared less about my celebrity status. It was obvious he loved me for *me*.

Not so strangely, the more I saw of Bob the better I liked him. He wasn't just handsome and broad-shouldered. He was a darling guy with a wonderful sense of humor. His lack of interest in the theater didn't arise from the fact that he was unintelligent. He was brilliant, very brilliant, and a real newspaperman. He was friendly with the Hearsts, especially Bill, and other newspaper people. He just didn't care for actors.

When we first met, he was circulation manager for the *Journal-American* and highly regarded for the job he was doing. So when the *American Weekly* got into big trouble, the Hearst organization named him publisher. Before long he pulled it out of the red and into the black again.

Bob was also a marvelous writer and in the beginning he composed and dedicated poems to me, as well as writing me love letters even though we saw each other every night. I wish I could include a few of them, but I gave them to our daughter several years ago and they were lost when she moved from Colorado to Los Angeles. The only example I can recall was etched on a beautiful gold heart on the charm bracelet that Bob gave to me. It went:

> If you are mine,
> As I am thine,

You are indeed,
My valentine.

When all of my jewelry was stolen a few years ago, even that went. On the wall of my den I do have a painting he had done of me as I appeared on the cover of *Playbill* for *Panama Hattie*. It was a surprise gift and I'll treasure it always.

Spending time together after the show regularly caused a problem. Since Bob was accustomed to being up and going to work early and I liked to have a bite to eat and a chance to unwind in some club after the show, our hours didn't coincide too well. Finally he solved the dilemma by leaving work and going directly home to bed, sleeping a few hours and then meeting me at the stage door to go on the town.

When I meet somebody and fall, I go head over heels—hook, line and sinker. That's the way it was with Bob. So in the late fall we were married in Connecticut. North or Brook—one of those Havens that are bunched together around New Haven.

Bob was earning $200 a week, which was big money for a news-paperman or almost anyone else in 1941. I was making about eighteen or twenty times that amount. But Bob was secure enough so that he didn't look upon our respective salaries as establishing superior and inferior positions. Neither did I. I felt if I wanted things that $200 a week didn't provide, it was up to me to get them.

We discussed the situation and agreed that there was nothing humiliating to either of us in arranging that I spend my earnings to maintain the standard of living that was expected of anyone of my standing in the theater. Bob could handle that just as he could shrug it off when some stranger would refer to him as "Mr. Merman." Being a newsman, he knew that one day an entertainer can be the rage, earning big money; a year or so later that person can be broke and without a job. He recognized fame for what it is, and he knew it had nothing to do with love or happiness.

After our marriage we decided to stay in the building where I'd been living with Mom and Pop. Bob and I took a ten-room duplex with a huge roof-garden terrace on the twenty-first and twenty-second floors at 25 Central Park West.

My mother helped me hire a staff to look after Bob and me, since I had never taken time nor had any special inclination to acquire domestic skills. Mom, on the other hand, was a whiz at those things. After I'd become successful, we had hired a cook and maids briefly. But Mom couldn't stand seeing her pots and pans being ruined. None of her servants lasted long.

I didn't find it easy to keep domestic help either. Most were reluctant to work for actresses. Not that actresses are any different from other people. But our employees were convinced that because of my profession Bob and I would be entertaining often and late. No amount of explaining that one of the penalties of theater work is that a performer usually has to begin to get ready about five-thirty in the afternoon was of any help. Since I'd be dining early, it usually meant that I'd be eating alone. It was necessary for me to do that, get my hair in curlers and then relax and conserve my energy so that I could give my best performance. I explained that when I did entertain it was at home. I felt people weren't real friends if I had to take them to a nightclub or restaurant.

One thing I was good at was keeping track of expenses. I still had my business training, and when the housekeeper marketed and presented me with the bills I entered each expenditure into a ledger on a page for that day. That way I could see the cost of running a home, day by day, week by week. It wasn't that I didn't trust the help. I just wanted to know where my money was going and why expenses suddenly jumped—if they did.

It was right after our marriage that Bob and I decided the warmest contribution to a room is a painting, and we just started collecting. We used to go to galleries on Saturday and we bought what we liked. I mean, if I enjoy looking at a painting I don't care who painted it. Sure, I enjoy the Renoir that Bob gave me, and I have a lovely Edzard. Naturally I treasure those. But before I had the real Edzard, Benay Venuta painted one in his manner and signed it Benayzard. As a matter of fact, I enjoy looking at her painting as much as at the real one. I also have one that looks like a Dali that Benay did for my daughter. Everyone admires it. What I can't stand are abstracts that I don't know what they mean.

Jumping ahead, in 1976 Janet Gaynor had an exhibit on Fifty-seventh Street. By the time I got there, everything was sold. But there was one painting of flowers in baskets in a hothouse that I loved so much I cut it out of the brochure and had it put in a little gold frame. I keep it by my bed and look at it all the time. It doesn't matter to me that it's only a reproduction. It's lovely.

My newfound domesticity wasn't to last long. On December 7, 1941, after the bombing of Pearl Harbor, America declared war and all able-bodied men were being called up. Very shortly my intelligent, able-bodied new husband was out of the apartment and into the U.S. Army.

I was pregnant, and during the third month I really began to balloon, so I decided to withdraw from *Panama Hattie* in order to take good care of myself and spend time with Bob in case he should be shipped overseas upon graduation from officers' school. Happily he was assigned to the Quartermaster Corps at the Port of Embarkation in Brooklyn, where he eventually became an aide to General Homer Groninger.

This meant that he would be around when the baby arrived. It also meant I was expected to attend parties given by his army friends. If there was one role that I was never born to play it was the army wife. Bob did his best to brief me on what was expected of an officer's spouse and how to carry off the situation. But everything in my nature rebelled against this phoniness.

One thing I will say of the military, they would never have trouble arousing my fighting spirit. Nothing was served but warm Manhattans at the first party I attended with Bob at the officers' club. I hated Manhattans—warm or cold—but I put away quite a few in order to get through the evening. Then during dinner a band played. I was in the midst of my entree when General Groninger's wife came up and asked whether I wouldn't like to get up and sing a few numbers.

I said, "Get out of my way, Cuddles, or I'll spit in your eye," and went back to eating. Later Bob told me he hoped the General's wife would understand my humor, because to him I'd sounded serious. I was. But Mrs. Groninger seemed to think I was being funny and we got along fine. She never asked me to sing again though.

The General wasn't so friendly toward me. He liked playing old-fashioned rummy and bragged that he never lost. The evening he suggested a game, Bob turned ashen and did his damnedest to get the message to me. Somehow I turned out to be unusually dense that day. I proceeded to take every trick until the General called off the game. I think if I hadn't been pregnant he might have slugged me. For a while after that Bob claimed I was insurance against his promotion in the Army, but by December he was a major and eventually he rose to the position of lieutenant colonel, so I couldn't have been too great a handicap.

Everything went along fine until July, when I entered Doctors Hospital for what turned out to be a Caesarean section that brought us a seven-pound, one-ounce baby girl on July 20. Bob, who had never been around a newborn baby, thought she was so small that he nicknamed her "Little Bit," which was what we ordinarily called her. When she got to be about three years old, she told a tenant of the building where we lived, "My name's Little Bit, but they call me Ethel Merman Levitt the Second for short."

XVI

DURING MY PREGNANCY I had made up my mind to take off a full year before returning to the theater, but by June producers were bombarding me with offers. Two projects particularly interested me. One was the late George Gershwin's *Birds of a Feather*, which I wanted to do for sentimental reasons; the other was Cole Porter's *The State of Texas*, or *Jenny Get Your Gun*.

Jenny had been a book by Dorothy and Herbie Fields. Since Buddy DeSylva was busy in Hollywood, the idea was to let Vinton Freedley produce. That set-up appealed to me. I decided to do the Porter show after hearing only three songs and without reading the finished script. Of course with such experienced people I wasn't taking too great a risk. Even though *Oklahoma!*, which emphasized a new cohesive approach, was about to open, hit musicals were still pretty freely slapped together. Cole used to say it was a joy to be working with one of the Fieldses when you developed second-act trouble out of town, because both of them could dip into their father's trunk—he was half of the comedy team Weber and Fields—and pull out a great comedy routine that saved the day.

None of us was prepared for Vinton's reaction. He wasn't enthusiastic about what he heard. The three collaborators were offended, and the upshot was that Cole called a hot new producer named Mike

Todd to suggest auditioning material for him. Mike brushed aside the suggestion and offered to sign a contract. Period. He didn't have to hear a note or read a word. It was a shrewd move. Whatever the show turned out to be, Mike would have established contacts with a leading songwriter, a prominent lyricist-librettist, another librettist and me.

Happily, the only major change that had to be made was the title. *Jenny Get Your Gun* became *Something for the Boys*. The production represented a case of perfect timing. Because of wartime shortages, there hadn't been a big splashy musical for almost six months. And Mike Todd, with his carnival background, was the perfect producer. He had all kinds of ways of getting cheap, colorful substitutes for conventional materials. Under the lights, the make-do stuff looked dazzling.

We opened in Boston on Christmas night 1942, and the audience was with us from the start. The plot was the kind that audiences of that era preferred—easy to follow, or to ignore if they just wanted to concentrate on the singing and dancing. In this case, Blossom Hart (me), a defense worker, inherits a 4000-acre Texas ranch located near Kelly Field. Unfortunately, two cousins, a pitchman (Allen Jenkins) and a stripteaser (Paula Laurence), are also heirs. To complicate matters further, a piece of carborundum filling in my tooth serves as a radio receiving set which I use to get messages for the Kelly Field soldiers. This gets me into a lot of hot water with military authorities who think I'm providing another kind of service.

Both Cole and I thought his score was one of the best he had ever written for me. I still think it was good. Lewis Nichols, the wartime drama critic for the New York *Times*, agreed with me. He thought the show had almost everything and wrote of me,

> Ethel Merman in good voice is a raucous overtone to the trumpets of a band, it is a soft trill for a torch song, it is tinny for a parody and fast for one of Mr. Porter's complicated lyrics. Accompanying the voice are all the necessary gestures, the roll of the eye or the wave of the hand to suggest ribaldries or separations forever more. In "Hey,

Good Lookin' " she is loud, in "He's a Right Guy" she is soft; it is one of Mr. Porter's lines that sums it up pretty well: she is "the missing link between Lily Pons and Mae West." And a credit, of course, to the pair of them.

As a score it was excellent, but at the time the object was to turn out numbers that would top the Saturday night *Hit Parade* for fifty-two weeks, plugging the show and selling tickets to people who otherwise didn't attend Broadway musicals.

By the way, Betty Garrett, who played Mary-Francis and was my understudy, was the one I made the crack to about not being nervous onstage. In addition, there was another Betty in the show, tap dancer Betty Bruce, who became a personal friend of mine. I got along fine with almost everyone—Allen Jenkins, Bill Johnson, Anita Alvarez and a sixteen-year-old Bill Callahan, who put himself through college with his tap dancing and became a lawyer.

There was also a deadpan comedienne named Paula Laurence in the cast, with whom I was friendly at first. Cole had discovered her at the Ruban Bleu. She was making her musical comedy debut and evidently didn't know much about stage deportment. We had a duet as a couple of sloppy Indian squaws singing "By the Mis-iss-iss-iss-iss-iss-iss-iss-iss-inewa," repeating the "iss" eight times.

Cole had based it on the name of a creek that ran through his mother's Indiana farm. This plain, quiet old creek that minded its own business had provided us with a raucous show-stopper from its first performance. Part of the impact came from the song, part from the delivery, some from the staging. The outfits Paula and I wore were atrocious—funny, long Indian dresses, moccasins and braids. The visual impact broke up the audiences so completely that half the time their laughter drowned out the lyrics, which may have been just as well. Even though the jokes weren't some of Cole's wittiest, a lot of people still tell me that it was the funniest number they ever saw in the theater up to that time.

After a couple of weeks I began getting annoyed. I had found some business swinging my braids that got a laugh. The first thing I knew, Paula was swinging her braids. Then one night I accidentally lost a moccasin. It fell off and went into the orchestra pit. That got a yak and I kept the business in. Then Paula began losing her moccasins.

Now I just don't believe in that. There's such a thing as theater discipline. One player doesn't appropriate another's inventions. I won't stand for that any more than I'd stand for someone coming up and taking money out of my purse. I went to the stage manager and told him to tell her to stop it. That's one thing about me, if anyone does anything to hurt me in any way, I chop them off like *that*. They never hear from me again. I chopped Paula. It was just as if she never existed.

Later she said that I was the star, and if I had wanted her to paint her nose red she guessed she'd have had to. "And don't think she wouldn't," she told the writer Wolcott Gibbs.

Well, I wouldn't. I've never yet shared the stage with any performer where I used anything except my God-given talent and my own hard work to project myself. That other stuff is for amateurs.

On opening in New York, our notices in addition to the one in the *Times* were the kind you dream about. I received hundreds of telegrams that night. I appreciated them all, but there were two I kept around for quite a while before I let Pop paste them in the scrapbook. The first one read:

> DEAR MOMMY, I AM THINKING OF YOU TONIGHT AND WISH YOU EVERY SUCCESS. GRANDMA AND GRANDPA SEND THEIR LOVE. THEY TELL ME YOU WOULD BE A SENSATION IN YOUR NEW SHOW. LOVE AND LOTS OF KISSES FROM YOUR LOVING DAUGHTER, ETHEL.

She was a little over six months old.
The next one carried the same idea:

> WE ALREADY KNOW YOU'RE WONDERFUL STOP TONIGHT A LOT OF OTHER PEOPLE WILL FIND IT OUT AGAIN STOP LITTLE BIT AND BOB.

There was also a card that came with a huge bouquet. I treasured it. It read, "To Miss Show Business—the best performer, the best trouper. I love ya. Mike Todd."

I loved working for Mike Todd too. He had pitched potato peelers; founded the Todd School of Applied Bricklaying; produced *The Moth and the Flame*, a carnival-type girlie show at the 1933 Chicago World's Fair; *The Hot Mikado*, a black version of Gilbert and Sullivan; and brought *Star and Garter*, a deluxe version of Minsky's bump and grind, to Broadway at a $4.40 top.

He had the nerve of the master showman. To steal a phrase from Cole Porter, Mike could charm the birds out of the trees. He was a fantastic man—in the real sense. He spent money before he had it. He smoked Perfectos—the most expensive cigar available—in good times and bad. Once during a lean period he lived in a Park Avenue penthouse where his only furnishings consisted of a bed and six telephones.

I had no trouble with him. Professionally I never worked for a more considerate guy. He needed every penny he could get during the time I was appearing in *Something for the Boys*. Yet a couple of times I was out of the show with laryngitis. Previously if I missed a performance, the producer docked me one-eighth of my salary. But not Mike, who didn't have the money the other producers had.

Not only that, here is one of the notes he sent:

> Dearest Ethel,
>
> I appreciate your spirit in wanting to go on, but if you don't feel fit and if it in any way is going to harm you, the show is second to your health and a very slow second at that. I love you more than the show. So you decide. Get better.   Mike Todd

Mike did have a cute gimmick. When I was out of the show, he would wait until the last minute to announce that my understudy would play my part for that performance and that those who wanted a refund could get it *before* the show began. The moment he stopped speaking, the orchestra struck up "The Star-Spangled Banner." In those patriotic wartime days audiences stood at respectful attention, and with the anthem's last note the curtain rose. Only the most aggressive received a refund.

During the run of *Something for the Boys* I spent a day along with sixty-nine other guest stars, including Katharine Cornell, Helen Hayes, Tallulah Bankhead, Lynn Fontanne, Judith Anderson, Katharine Hepburn and Gypsy Rose Lee, appearing in the film *Stage Door Canteen*. It was produced by the American Theatre Wing, Sol Lesser and United Artists for the benefit of the Theatre Wing.

On all but matinee days during the run of *Something for the Boys* I made it a point to be at home between four-thirty and five-thirty for my play period with Little Bit. By now she had such dark brown eyes they seemed almost black, chestnut-colored hair and so tiny a nose that her fat little cheeks almost hid it if you looked at her in profile. In fact, she was so much the center of my life that people who had predicted I'd make an indifferent mother now accused me of being too indulgent. I felt that was part of the fun of having a baby.

In October Bob and I had her christened at St. Thomas' Church. As her godfather we chose Billy Gaxton and as her godmother Eleanor Holm.

Eleanor was a beautiful fun-loving swimmer who had been bounced off the U.S. Women's Olympic swimming team for having a cocktail. So she had turned professional, starred in Billy Rose's *Aquacade* and married her producer. While she lived in New York, she was one of my closest chums. Bob got along pretty well with Billy too.

Billy was Mike Todd's rival as successor to Ziegfeld in those days. He and Eleanor and Bob and I used to spend a lot of time together. We had lots of laughs. In those days we'd go to Dinty Moore's a lot. Billy had been a shorthand speed champion before he went into songwriting and producing. I had kept up my shorthand too. Many nights he and I would get into a challenge to see who was faster, using the restaurant's tablecloths as substitute steno pads.

Billy and Eleanor used to come down to our apartment almost every Sunday afternoon too. At the time I really believe Bob was probably the best-dressed officer in the Army. He had his uniforms made at Luxenberg's on Madison Avenue and they looked stunning.

One Sunday Billy arrived all excited about having received some kind of a commission to go overseas for the government. It meant wearing a uniform. Of course Billy was so short the press called him the "Bantam Barnum" and the "Mighty Mite," while Bob was a broad-shouldered, nice-sized guy. Anyway Billy went to Bob's closet and put on one of his officer's coats and an officer's hat. He was so tiny the coat just hung on him, making him look like a sad sack. We got hysterical. Then he came out wearing Bob's overseas cap at what he hoped was a jaunty angle over one eye. Eleanor looked at him and said, "You know, Billy, in that you look a little Jewish," which cracked all of us up again.

Bob had been born of Jewish parents, but he had never been bar mitzvahed or anything, because his father was an atheist. After Little Bit was born, I remember Bob saying to me, "We should all be brought up in the same pot." And at his suggestion he and I went over to Dr. Sargeant, who was then the minister of St. Bartholomew's. We talked the situation over with Dr. Sargeant, and Bob was eventually baptized and confirmed an Episcopalian.

We attended church there regularly. In fact, when they had a heavy Sunday there, Bob used to volunteer as a vestryman. He'd take that big silver platter and pass around collecting. There would be a lot of big money on the plate, and when he passed me he'd pretend to case the money and give me a big wink. But he was serious about church. We took communion regularly. In those days you weren't allowed to have anything to eat beforehand. That's all changed now. But that was a beautiful period of my life. As you can see, for a girl who had often proclaimed that a career and marriage couldn't be mixed, I was doing pretty well.

I left *Something for the Boys* after 422 performances. Joan Blondell took it on a national tour. Cole never did another show for me, but we remained friends. Even after the amputation of his left leg, when he saw only a few people, he still invited me. It was sad seeing him so depressed, knowing in your heart that he no longer wanted to live. But even then the wit still occasionally surfaced. I was up to his apartment not long before he passed and asked him about a mutual friend. Had he seen her? He said, "Yes, as a matter of fact, she was here last night." I asked how she looked. "She looked divine"—he paused—"except her pearls were too long."

XVII

COULD WE JUST FORGET 1944?

In April I had a miscarriage. Then in June Bob and I began having serious spats that ended in a trial separation. Some separation! Before the end of the second week we were dating nightly and within a month had reconciled.

Meanwhile, though, I had made a rash move and barely escaped having my first flop. Mary Martin, Marlene Dietrich, Joan Crawford and Joan Blondell had turned down the role of Sadie Thompson, but I thought it was right up my alley.

Sadie Thompson had been adapted by Rouben Mamoulian and Howard Dietz from a short story by Somerset Maugham and a play by John Colton and Clemence Randolph. Vernon Duke composed the score and Dietz did the lyrics. A. P. Waxman "presented Rouben Mamoulian's production." Well, that's what the program said.

We began rehearsing on September 18, and I quit on September 30. It hardly seems possible that twelve days could contain so much dissension. The main trouble was over the lyrics. In earlier shows I never experienced a problem learning them. I would run through a song a few times with Lew Kesler, and the words stayed in my head for keeps.

With the songs from *Sadie Thompson* I had problems. I tried to discuss them with Howard Dietz. He didn't seem to understand what I was talking about. So I had my husband, who was a beautiful writer, make some improvements. I took them to rehearsal. Naturally I didn't expect Dietz to accept Bob's lyrics, but I did think they might cause him to clarify his own. No way. We started rehearsals. In one number I was supposed to sing, "You put some black pencil on your peepers / And some Mal Maison on your lips."

I didn't know what that meant. I asked Dietz, Vernon Duke and Rouben Mamoulian how the layman could be expected to understand the song when I couldn't. Dietz said Mal Maison was a famous lipstick in Paris.

At the next rehearsal I informed him I'd made a survey of between fifteen and twenty-five girls. None of them had ever heard of Mal Maison. That didn't shake his Olympian confidence. I try not to be unreasonable, but I *am* determined. When he wouldn't budge, I delivered an ultimatum: Either the lyric goes or I go.

I went.

That was the low point of my career. I didn't want to walk out on a show, but I couldn't sing something I didn't understand.

Whenever I've sung a number that the audience didn't respond to, I've asked for a new song. After all, the audience is our editor. Every musical production is a group effort that includes the creative artist, the performers and the audience. Take Cole Porter, an acknowledged genius. To write most effectively for me, he studied my voice and decided A flat, B flat and C natural were my best notes. He saw to it that the key words coincided with one of those notes. It gave me my best shot and it helped put his songs across. But others in the production were important too. In "By the Mississinewa," Billy Livingston's costumes and Hassard Short's staging contributed to the smashing effect. The spirit of professional cooperation was missing from *Sadie Thompson*. Without it, in my opinion, there was no way the show could succeed.

Luckily, several columnists rallied to my side when I quit the show. Ed Sullivan wrote that opinion in Shubert Alley inclined to agree with me instead of the management because "there are two stars on the Broadway stage who have never been accused of temperament by chorus kids or big producers. One is Helen Hayes, the other is Ethel Merman."

June Havoc, a vivacious blonde who had made a hit in *Pal Joey* and *Mexican Hayride*, gave up a chance to play in *Carousel* to replace me. Although she received favorable notices, the show folded after thirty-two performances.

I had no show during 1945. Early in the year I discovered I was pregnant, and, having suffered one miscarriage the previous year, I devoted myself to being a wife and mother. Bob wasn't close to his own family. I saw very little of his mother and he didn't visit her often, but he was a wonderful father.

Once he had to go overseas on a secret mission. On the day he was to leave he came home for a last luncheon. Before kissing us goodbye, he removed his Special Services pin and fastened it to Little Bit's dress. "Now you keep this until I get back," he said. It was very touching.

But it didn't wind up so touching, because Little Bit's governess, Miss Koopmann, put her on the toity seat after lunch. And when Miss Koopmann went to take Little Bit off, she said, "Ethel, where's the pin Big Bob gave you?"

Little Bit, who was only about three, said, "In there." I guess that pin didn't seem so important to her, so she threw it away.

When Bob returned, he had grown a Jerry Colonna–type mustache. I hated it. Little Bit hated it too. She wouldn't kiss her father until he shaved it off. She was the only one who could force him to get rid of it.

Bob was widely quoted as saying, "I like Ethel best of all when she's pregnant." It was a provocative remark. I asked him what that was supposed to mean. He explained that since I couldn't work we weren't required to go out for professional reasons, so we could just stay home and listen to the radio or play gin rummy.

One thing I continued to do while carrying Bobby was to entertain at the staging area of Camp Shanks. Bob's friend Walter Gross, who wrote "Tenderly," worked as my accompanist. Once more by the third month I felt—and looked—pregnant all over. But those army stagehands and electricians lit me beautifully, using a flattering off-pink gelatin. As I swelled and swelled, the spot got smaller and smaller until finally a pin spot lit only my face during the month before the baby came. But obviously the soldiers enjoyed it. Pregnant or not, I was made an honorary top sergeant.

Many of the boys would march right out of the staging area to a boat train heading for their ship and overseas. That staging area was the last sight of the States that they would have.

About this time Frank Loesser threw a party one night. Benay Venuta, who was also very pregnant, and I sang a duet. When the guests demanded an encore, Abe Burrows kidded, "We'll now hear from the quartette again."

"It might be a quintette," I shot back. "How do you know what's been going on?"

Well, on August 11, 1945, Robert Daniels Levitt Jr. was delivered by Caesarean section at Doctors Hospital. Two days later when I was still in stitches—and not from laughing—Dorothy Fields called. Dorothy had an idea that couldn't wait.

Before I explain her idea, I want to tell you about Dorothy, who was one of my oldest and closest friends. She was a woman of great warmth and wide experience. As a lyricist her chief collaborators up to 1946 for stage and film included Jerome Kern, Jimmy McHugh, Arthur Schwartz, Sigmund Romberg, Morton Gould and Burton Lane. With her brother Herbert she had turned out librettos for such Broadway hits as *Up in Central Park*, *Let's Face It*, *Mexican Hayride* and *Something for the Boys*.

Dorothy was a gal who took time for friendship. She was as extravagant of her emotions as of her money. When Mom or Pop had a birthday, Dorothy would send flowers and take them to dinner. Everyone was her friend.

She had apartments first on Fifty-seventh Street across from Carnegie Hall and later on Central Park West. But wherever she lived, she had the best—furniture, linens, everything. She collected many beautiful things, including rare teapots. I have a couple of those as well as other lovely gifts she sent me.

Dorothy's idea that couldn't wait was for me to play sharpshooting Annie Oakley. If I'd agree, Jerome Kern would compose the music, she'd write the lyrics and would collaborate with her brother Herbie on the book. Rodgers and Hammerstein were prepared to organize a producing firm to present the show, but only if I'd play Annie.

I was having postoperative gas pains and felt like anything but a lady sharpshooter. I asked Dorothy to give me time to get out of the hospital. Then I'd decide. She agreed.

By the day of my release I was feeling enthusiastic about working with all those talented people. I felt even better when my deal was set: $4500 a week plus 10 percent of the gross. They even agreed to pay my stand-by, Mary Jane Walsh, a then unheard of $500 a week.

Unexpectedly Jerome Kern died, the victim of a stroke. Who could possibly replace Jerry Kern, the father of the American musical? The name that popped into everyone's head was Irving Berlin. But no one mentioned him, because Dorothy had had the idea for the show and Berlin did his own lyrics. When Berlin was finally suggested, Dorothy insisted on stepping aside if he was available.

Irving didn't jump for joy at the offer. He hadn't written a Broadway show in four years and felt rusty. Finally, after talking the proposition over with his wife, Ellin, Irving signed. Then he did a phenomenal thing. In eight days he turned out ten great songs, ranging in form from sentimental ballads to risqué comedy. Never had his range been broader. My share included "Doin' What Comes Natur'lly," "You Can't Get a Man with a Gun," "There's No Business Like Show Business," "They Say It's Wonderful," "Moonshine Lullaby," and "I'm an Indian Too"—and that was only in the first act. In the second I had "I Got Lost in His Arms," "I Got the Sun in the Morning," and "Anything You Can Do, I Can Do Better."

With all due respect to the Gershwins and Cole, Irving had given me range, allowing me a kind of vulnerability that was missing in girls like "Nails" Duquesne, Blossom Hart and Hattie Maloney. And what a joy to work with! I'd sing a number and Irving would say, "Wonderful! You made it better than I thought it was."

Of course he's human. In Boston he began experimenting with "Doin' What Comes Natur'lly," shortening it, trying to make it better. Now it's damned hard to unlearn a song, but I did it—for Irving. Then after the first performance he came backstage and said, "The audience didn't buy it. We'll go back to the old way." I could have killed him—except that I knew he was correct.

Dorothy and Herbie had come up with the title *Annie Get Your Gun* (remember the original title of *Something for the Boys*) and provided me with the greatest star's entrance I'd ever had by inventing a gimmick of having a bird shot off a woman's hat just before sure-shot Annie appears. They also made this diamond in the rough a fully rounded full-fledged woman. She was a character who demanded I act as well as sing. Under Josh's tutelage I turned in my best performance yet. Josh is a director who knows what he wants and how to get you to give it to him. In his autobiography, *Josh*, he describes Annie's first meeting with Frank Butler (Ray Middleton) in a way I couldn't equal and that illustrates how he widened my range from the invulnerable bimbo I usually played:

> The script read, "She looks at him and in a second falls in love with him forever." I felt that the only way I could show such an abrupt change was to have her collapse inwardly and outwardly as if she were a puppet whose strings had been cut quickly. I told Ethel to keep her eyes fixed on Ray but to let everything else in her body and mind go. She tried it. Her mouth dropped open, her shoulders sank, her legs opened wide at the knees, her diaphragm caved in. It was an unforgettable effect. Later, we dubbed it the "goon look," and it won for me the eternal devotion of everyone, including myself. It seemed to be the catalytic moment—the moment at which the play became a hit.

We opened in New Haven. Only some minor tinkering needed to be done. Boston loved us too. We arrived in New York full of confidence for our April 25 opening at the Imperial. We had a dress rehearsal in the afternoon and left. When the crew began hanging the unusually heavy sets on the overhead stage girders, the weight of the scenery tore one of the girders from its anchoring in the brick wall.

If that girder had fallen during rehearsal, I don't know how many people would have been creamed.

The theater's license was suspended for two weeks. After some fast scrambling, the Shuberts booked us into Philadelphia from April 30 to May 11; and we finally opened in New York on May 16.

At home I was having problems too. I don't know what I would have done without Mom. While I was in Boston, the couple who worked for me left without giving notice. Mom took over and helped Bob. He had been discharged from the Army and had returned to the Hearst organization. There was also a nurse to look after Little Bit and Bobby. To keep the nurse happy I relieved her by conducting interviews while bouncing Bobby on my knee.

He was too young to protest. But Little Bit, who was a precocious three and a half, voiced her complaints. After all, she had been able to say "appropriate" and "mischievous" at two and a half. And she had strong likes and dislikes. For instance, she loved all animals. Bob brought her to Boston to see *Annie Get Your Gun*. The instant she saw the bird being shot off the woman's hat, she refused to see any more. She thought it was a live bird that had been killed. She began screaming as she pulled Bob up the aisle and out of the theater. Nor would she return.

When I told her that I had to go to Philadelphia with the show for a couple of weeks while the theater owners repaired the grids, but that then I'd come home to stay for a long time, she gave me a skeptical look and said, "You mean if the scenery doesn't break again."

In Philadelphia, as in New Haven and Boston, the audiences loved us instantly. But one thing I'd learned in theater is never to take either audiences or critics for granted. Opening night in New York, during the first act, response was cool. At intermission Josh rushed into my dressing room asking how I could play to the dead fish out front. "Easy," I told him. "Inside I'm saying, 'Screw you, you jerks! If you were as good as I am, you'd be up here!'"

During the interval everybody must have reassured everyone else that it was okay to laugh, because when the audience returned it turned out to be a responsive group. Even so, with all those hit songs, such an astute critic as Louis Kronenberger—then of *PM*, later of *Time*—wrote, "Irving Berlin's score is musically not exciting—of the real songs, only one or two are tuneful." And Brooks Atkinson of the New York *Times* called the songs undistinguished with the possible exception of "I Got the Sun in the Morning." It made you feel that Cole Porter could have been speaking of all critics when he said that George Jean Nathan wouldn't recognize "The Star-Spangled Banner" unless he saw everyone else standing up.

THE DAY AFTER THE OPENING a friend called offering her secretary to help with thank-you notes for telegrams and flowers. But I'd got up early and the last one was ready to mail by the time she phoned. What's more, I'd gone over the grocery bills and called to complain about being charged for two cans of grapefruit juice when I'd only received one, as I'd pointed out before. To me a secretary would have been excess baggage.

Once again in a hit, I enjoyed my home life as fully as the demands of my job would allow. Bob had long ago adjusted to being "Mr. Merman" and had enough inner resources to live as comfortably as anyone could under the circumstances. Luckily, at work or out having cocktails with newspapermen, he was regarded a successful and amusing fellow in his own right. I wasn't any crutch.

I don't really know, but there may have been some hidden stress. Maybe that's why he talked of leaving Hearst after the war and teaching journalism at his alma mater, Rollins College, in Florida. When we discussed leaving New York, I asked what about me. He suggested that I teach singing and acting. That floored me. "Me? What the hell do I know about that stuff?" I asked. The question cracked Bob up and he repeated the story so that it went all over town.

But Josh Logan said the same thing in ten-dollar words: "You're able to make transitions without asking for cerebral reasons for those transitions," he said. "In other words, as an actress you are able to go from high into reverse without the annoying business of going through neutral."

To get back to my home life, it was as normal as a public figure's can be. Bob liked some of my friends and naturally didn't care for others.

The same went for me. One couple I warmed up to were Leon and Carola Mandel. He was the owner of Mandel Brothers Department Store in Chicago. Carola, a very beautiful Cuban woman, at one time held the title of world's champion skeet shot. Their home at 45 East Oak in Chicago bulged with cups and trophies that she'd won. It also had a swimming pool adjoining the living room long before anyone ever heard of Hugh Hefner's mansion. Leon was a great connoisseur of food and liquor. Visiting New York, they practically lived at the 21 Club. But he had a greater collection in his wine cellar than the 21 had. I remember once in Palm Beach he brought out a bottle of brandy that was so old it had no label on it whatsoever, no year and no number.

We visited them on their 400-foot yacht in Palm Beach too. When they had first married, they sailed around the world on a yacht—the two of them and a crew of forty-three. Then he sold the first *Carola* and bought another, on which they lived. Through the years I spent a lot of time on that one. And I've never seen a dining room in any home to equal the one they had.

While I was busy with *Annie*, Bob, Leon, and Carola went to Europe together. As I've said, Bob was handsome and I'm inclined to be pretty possessive, so I worried about what he'd be up to. But when they came back to the U.S., Carola told me that he hadn't looked right or left.

Another friend of Bob's I liked was Bill Hearst. I liked his mother, Mrs. William Randolph Hearst, too. While I was in *Annie Get Your Gun*, Bob and I were frequently invited to her big parties. There was one black-tie affair that I remember particularly. Bob and Bill went on ahead. I came after my performance. It was that night that I first met the Duke and Duchess of Windsor.

We hit it off immediately. I think it was then that the Duchess told me, "I wish you could hear the Duke going around the apartment singing 'Doin' What Comes Natur'lly'!" Not long after, a signed photograph arrived from the Windsors. It was "To Mr. and Mrs. Levitt—who raised a family, doing what comes naturally. Wallis Windsor and Edward, Duke of Windsor."

When the Duke wasn't speaking, he had a peculiar habit of going "Mmmmmm." I mentioned this to Bob and asked why he thought the Duke did that. Knowing that they lived at the Waldorf Towers, Bob made a funny crack. He said, "Maybe the Waldorf's wired for DC and the Duke's AC."

Soon we all became so friendly that I started calling the Duke "Boy" and the Duchess "Girl." They got a kick out of that. Most people were afraid to be themselves around the Windsors. But I liked her and I loved the little Duke. He knew all the lyrics to popular tunes, which he loved to sing for hours at a time.

Another longtime friend I met through Bob is Dr. Michael Damato. Bob got to know him in the Army. Dr. Damato was the attending surgeon, which meant he was responsible for officers and their families. Bob invited him to dinner and we all got along so well that he frequently dined with us and was always included on the opening night list. After the *Sadie Thompson* fiasco, I was trying to decide whether to do a new show or start a baby. Dr. Damato, who was a dinner guest, spoke up and said, "As a physician, I'd suggest the baby. You can always do a new show." Shortly I was pregnant.

Anyway, he was soon taking care of Bob, Little Bit, Bob's mother, Mom, Pop and eventually Bobby. Over the years I've always had my own physician, but he's become my confidant and close friend. I still talk to him frequently even though he's retired. If I didn't mention him for a little while, Pop would remind me to call.

The people I've been speaking of were personal friends, but I'd like to include one couple who don't quite fit that category—General Dwight Eisenhower and Mamie. While they meant a lot to me, I was never on close terms with them. Yet of the many famous people who have come backstage over the years, I don't think any other visitors have thrilled me as much. Upon hearing they were out front and planning to come back, I sent out for the brand of Scotch I'd heard Ike preferred. At the time, neither the Republican nor the Democratic party was sure of the great war hero's political preferences, but both saw him as an unbeatable candidate. As a lifelong Republican, I wanted to do my part in creating a good impression for our side.

General and Mrs. Eisenhower were so friendly and unassuming that I was crazy about them. And I was a little awed when the General informed me, "This is the first time in thirty years that I've seen a Broadway show, and it was worth waiting for."

After they left, I wouldn't allow the glass he'd used to be rinsed. I kept it in my dressing room under a sign that I typed: "GENERAL EISENHOWER DRANK HERE, November 18, 1946."

I shouldn't have. Somebody eventually lifted it.

Eisenhower was my war hero and the President I admire and respect most. And luckily when I lived at the Park Lane Hotel, they always stopped there when visiting New York. So I often shared an elevator with them or met them in the lobby, where we'd have a chitchat. I have a photo of him inscribed: "To a great artist—" and a lot of other stuff. In 1952 I had the honor of singing at the Republican National Convention in San Francisco, where they introduced me as one of the world's greatest Republicans. In fact, I have so many souvenirs, letters and mementos that when I had a home with a large library, one section was labeled IKE'S CORNER.

If I've said little about Richard Rodgers and Oscar Hammerstein, it's because I lived up to my part of the contract and they lived up to theirs. There were only a couple of very minor problems.

In 1947 I had two weeks' vacation coming and I spent the time in the hospital having minor surgery. When my two-year contract on *Annie* was about to expire, Rodgers approached me about renewing for another year. I was bone tired, but I finally agreed that if they would give me a six-week vacation I'd sign for another year. First I wanted some time with my husband and children.

They hired Judy Garland to replace me as a warm-up for the film version, in which she was to play my part. Judy backed out at the last minute.

Of necessity, my understudy, Mary Jane Walsh, went in on the week of July Fourth. Weather was hot and business was bad all along Broadway. Mary Jane was a talented girl, but she hadn't established herself as a star. Customers demanded refunds, and business dropped $10,000 that week.

As a special treat to the kids, Bob and I took them by train to Glenwood Springs, Colorado. We'd been invited to stay with George and Loretta Summers, who had a big ranch house on a 375-acre spread, but we felt we'd fill up too many rooms. So we booked into the Colorado Hotel. We had luncheon and dinner with the Summerses each day, but we spent afternoons at the hotel swimming and going horseback riding with Little Bit and Bobby.

We'd originally chosen Colorado because of Little Bit's interest in animals, but we all fell in love with the mountains and open spaces. I even went to my first supermarket opening there. George Summers controlled leases to Safeway Stores throughout the country and he had one opening in Montrose, Colorado, a friendly little town with outgoing people. He asked me to go. And I thought, Why not?

I was just getting completely unwound when I received a frantic phone call from Richard Rodgers asking me to come back at once. I said, No way. We'd planned this vacation for months and Bob would be furious if I even mentioned such a possibility. Rodgers told me the box-office take had dropped disastrously and begged me to think of the people whom I'd throw out of work if I didn't return. I still said no. I figured I had lived up to my obligations to the theater, now my family came first.

Initially the newspapers tended to make me look like a villain. But Earl Wilson contacted Mary Martin and Joan Edwards, both of whom had played Annie, and they backed me up. They said they had temporarily lost their voices because of the strain from singing the songs I'd been performing eight times a week for two years. They could certainly understand how much I needed a rest.

The problem was solved when the *Annie* company held an emergency meeting and voted to take a cut to keep the show running.

The previous winter, I'd suggested the Colorado Hotel as a restful vacation spot for Howard Lindsay and Dorothy Stickney, who didn't want to undertake anything as strenuous as a European trip.

I'd even made reservations for them at our hotel. They loved it as much as we did.

One afternoon Howard yelled out the window to me that he had an idea for my next show.

"What is it?"

"Perle Mesta."

That didn't exactly thrill me. To tell the truth, I had to ask around to find out who Perle Mesta was.

When my six weeks were up and I returned to *Annie*, box-office receipts picked up and Rodgers and Hammerstein reimbursed the cast for the salary cuts they had taken to keep the show running. After Christmas the closing notice was posted, but around New Year's business became so brisk that the producers rescinded the closing temporarily.

They also began to apply pressure on me to tour. There were newspaper stories saying that both the supporting players and the management hoped that I would play limited engagements in Philadelphia and Boston, which "would bring in tremendous receipts, thereby keeping the performers working a bit longer."

Whoever was behind the campaign didn't know their girl. Nothing would persuade me to do it. I certainly wasn't going to take two small children on the road, any more than I'd leave them with a governess.

Luckily I'm the kind of person who always has things in writing. As far as I was concerned, Rodgers and Hammerstein and I had an agreement. We had both read it. I had signed it. They had signed it. Period.

But when stories making me a heavy by throwing the company out of work continued, I called the New York *Times* and, as the reporter said, presented my case. I quote:

> Why all the fuss? I have a letter from Richard Rodgers, co-producer of the show with Oscar Hammerstein II, dated March 8, 1948, saying that I am in no way obligated to play outside New York.
>
> This has been known all along. I've kept the company working for two years and eight months—and I've done my part.

On February 19, *Annie* closed after a run of 1147 performances. *Annie* had had a very congenial company. Ray Middleton, my leading man, was a swell guy. I still get a Christmas card from him every year. So was Harry Bellaver, who played Chief Sitting Bull in the original production and repeated the role in the revival several years later. But even though it had contained my best role so far and brought me greater personal acclaim than ever, I felt as if I had been freed. For two years and nine months, with only two brief vacations and two performances missed because of illness, I had fashioned my life to accommodate the demands of every actor's master—the theater. Now I felt I needed something less demanding. People had been saying I was living the part. Maybe I was, but only onstage. Once my greasepaint came off, I forgot all about *Annie*. I had to, or my family would have killed me.

FIVE DAYS AFTER *Annie*'s closing Bob was to make a short business trip to the West Coast by way of New Orleans. He wanted me to accompany him. Since Bob had been adjusting his hours to mine for a couple of years, I decided he should have my undivided attention. So we left the kids in the care of Mom, Pop and a governess.

In New Orleans we checked into the International Suite of the Roosevelt Hotel and I proceeded to enjoy my new freedom while Bob tended to business. On our final day in town, apparently Podine Shoenberger of the New Orleans *Times-Picayune* called while I was out, and Bob, alert to publicity and promotion, told her, "Ma's out shopping. Tell you what you do. Come up and you can probably talk to her on the fly."

I wasn't aware of this until I read it in the paper. So when this woman tried to stop me at the elevator, I told her I had to pack and had no time for interviews. She must have again called Bob, who invited her up, because in her story she quoted him: "Oh no, I don't mind being married to a celebrity. It's no different from being married to any other woman. They all wait until the last minute to pack." Then she said he called, "Ma, come on out."

And I called back, "I can't. I'm cleaning the bathroom."

I probably did. To this day, I worry about what the maid will think of me if she comes in and the bathroom is a mess.

We left New Orleans for San Francisco, where Bob took care of additional business and I did a guest shot on radio with Bing Crosby at the Marine Memorial. Radio was so relaxing, I decided it interested me.

A couple of weeks later I was booked on Milton Berle's television variety show for the second time. I did a medley—"Smile, Darn You, Smile," "Smiles" and "When You're Smiling." Even though this guest shot caused a lot of favorable comment, I didn't enjoy doing a show with horses and all that goes with horses. I told my agent I enjoyed radio more and asked him to look around for something.

Just about then NBC radio was developing a flock of economy-priced shows to be pitched directly to sponsors to try to block the inroads TV was making into radio's advertising revenue. The agent said he could get a program for me paying $1000 a week sustaining and $1500 if sponsored. That sounded fine. I wanted to relax without retiring. I felt I'd earned the right to take it easy for a while after twenty years in the business.

A couple of gag writers, Will Glickman and Joe Stein, who was later to write *Fiddler on the Roof*, worked out a plot about a girl named Ethel, her arranger-pianist-pal and a mob-king suitor who was willing to back her show. The program's premise was based on the difficulty of putting it together. Our search for songs and sketches to be used in the show gave us an excuse to use lots of self-contained revue numbers.

We cut an audition record in June. The network turned it down flat. So I took off for Colorado with Bob and the kids. Then, the last week in July, some vice president apparently changed his mind and I hurried back to New York. After rehearsing all day, we recorded the show that night.

I had high hopes for the series, but critics complained that I didn't sing enough. They weren't too pleased with the character Glickman and Stein had devised for me either. John Crosby wrote that as a radio comic I fell somewhere between Joan Davis and Mae West, and then added, "Normally Ethel Merman has more personality than seems quite fair, but it is seriously diminished by radio, and I have a feeling that those who have never actually seen her in action may find her incomprehensible."

At least a few people enjoyed the show. On September 18 I received the following letter:

> Dear Ethel,
>
> My Linda has been seriously ill for eight months. But if anything can make her well again, it is your broadcast every Sunday night at 9:30. I always listen too. You are wonderful and I sit beside her and watch her revel in your excellence. You probably know after a few years on stage that no one can equal you. This is a love letter from Linda and me to you.
>
> My best to you all.
>
> From your devoted
Cole
>
> PS. If you have time, write Linda, tell her that you are happy to hear from me that she is better (she is not) and that it gives you a great kick to know she enjoys your program. This will do her great good, which she needs. The address is merely Williamstown, Massachusetts.

I wrote Linda, on the pretense of letting her know that I was on the air. On October 22 I received another letter.

> Dearest Ethel:
>
> Linda is being taken down by ambulance to New York on Monday, October 24th, and I can't tell you how she looks forward to listening to you sing again. You are so sweet to have notified her.
>
> Lots of love,
Cole

On October 25 I received a telegram:

> I WAS A' LISTENIN' AND IT THRILLED ME. LOVE TO YOU AND THE BABIES. LINDA.

The next day I received another letter from Cole:

Dearest Ethel:

You have no idea what a great thing you did for Linda when you dedicated "You're the Top" to her on your last Monday's program. She had just come down by ambulance to New York and, for the first time, I felt that she had lost her morale due to exhaustion—but the moment your program was turned on and she heard those wonderful words you said to her it brought back all of her bravery.

You are a darling to have done this and I shall never forget it.

Lots of love,
Cole

My only other engagement during 1949 was non-professional. I did a benefit concert for St. Bartholomew's Church in connection with the annual bazaar.

Two other Levitts performed at St. Barth's that year too. Little Ethel made her debut as an angel in the Nativity play, although at the time she was so madly in love with Hopalong Cassidy that she would gladly have traded her halo for a cowgirl outfit. Four-year-old Bobby stepped in at the last minute to be a shepherd in a mob scene.

I assume some child had heard that untold riches awaited actresses, because later Little Ethel asked me, "Mom, are we millionaires?"

I assured her we were not. Later I heard her on the phone setting her friend straight. "You're wrong," she announced. "We're not millionaires. Mom says not. I guess we're thousandaires."

When I opened in *Annie*, Bobby had been an adorable little cherub whom Little Bit always referred to as "my fat baby brother." And as he became old enough to crawl, he developed a habit I've never heard of in any other child. If you put him down to sleep, he'd hunch up on his knees and bang his head against the top of his bed. *Boom, boom, boom.* You'd have thought the house was falling in. Then the noise would stop and one of us would go to him. He'd be asleep on his elbows and knees. We'd have to lay him out flat.

During this period Little Bit began to develop a personality that was enough like mine so that we gradually took to calling her Little Ethel. Pop used to say she talked to you with her eyes *and* her mouth at the same time. Her favorite way of opening a conversation was "Do you want to know something?" We usually did. Because Bob and I and Mom and Pop all doted on the kids.

One of Pop's favorite stories occurred when we had a cottage in East Hampton one summer, while I was in a show. Mom and the German governess were out there with Little Ethel and Bobby. I bought some toys for the children and a silk sunsuit for Mom. Pop took them out on a Friday night after he finished his week's work. The kids grabbed their toys and Mom went off to try on her new outfit. When she returned, she said to Pop that it was beautiful but she couldn't wear it because it was cut too low. Little Ethel looked up at her with those expressive brown eyes and asked, "Grandma, do you want to know something?" Grandma did. "There's nothing wrong with the suit," Little Ethel announced. "Your bust is just too big."

Little Ethel enjoyed being out on Long Island with the birds and animals. She was a total nature lover. She loved anything that crawled, flew or moved. She wouldn't even allow us to kill a fly or a mosquito. In East Hampton she and her father used to go out at night with a pail of water and gather frogs. Once Bob found a huge crab. That became Little Ethel's pet. She used to tie a rope around it and walk it along the beach like a dog.

In our duplex she had the most beautiful, dainty little-girl's bedroom with an old four-poster and canopy, frilly curtains—everything. One day I went in and saw jars filled with dirt and holes punched in the lids. I looked closer. Inside were these grubs she'd captured in our roof garden.

She especially adored her parakeet. You can imagine our panic after what happened when Bob and I came home from East Hampton one Sunday night. The apartment was stuffy so Bob opened the window to get some ventilation. Later he took Little Ethel's parakeet out of the cage to play with it. Without warning, the parakeet flew off his finger and straight out the window.

We were panicky. That bird was the apple of Ethel's eye. Finally

I called Dorothy Kilgallen, who had a morning radio show with her husband, Richard Kohlmar. I explained what had happened and asked Dorothy to alert their listeners to our missing pet.

She put out the word that if anyone sighted the bird to call her. Well, it just so happened that a man and his wife were having breakfast at the Mayflower Hotel next door to our building, and as Dorothy was talking about our missing pet it landed on our neighbor's windowsill. So we got the bird back without Little Ethel ever knowing about its day of freedom in Central Park.

Dorothy and I were good friends. Whatever others may have thought of her, I always found her ready to lend a helping hand. Since our children were approximately the same age and both had German governesses who were close friends, we saw a lot of each other. It's sad that both Dorothy and Dick should have passed so young.

It was during the interim between *Annie Get Your Gun* and *Call Me Madam* that the first storm signals began to go up between Bob and me. Nothing serious yet, but I couldn't help feeling something was wrong. I was fairly certain there was no other woman. We just disagreed more frequently. He was a newspaperman, and like most of them he wanted to go to a bar after work and have his beaker of martinis. But in the good days he had almost always arrived home in time for dinner. Now he was absent more frequently, and when we were together it wasn't the same somehow. But neither of us wanted anything to happen to our marriage, for our own sakes and especially for the children's.

At one time I considered retiring. I didn't say it was because of marital problems, but I mentioned to several interviewers that I was thinking of getting out of the business after *Call Me Madam*. Even though I knew in my heart that my career had never interfered with either of my marriages, I thought maybe I should become a homebody.

While I was waiting for *Madam* to be put together, I recorded some single releases for Decca. Ray Bolger and I teamed to sing "Dearie" with "I Said My Pajamas" on the flip side. It was released in February and sold 200,000 copies in four weeks. Later we tried to repeat that success with "It's So Nice to Have a Man Around the House" and "If I'd Known You Were Comin' I'd've Baked a Cake" and again with "Once upon a Nickel" backed by "Oldies," but somehow the magic was gone.

"THE PLAY IS LAID in two mythical countries. One is called Lichten-burg, the other is the United States," Howard Lindsay and Buck Crouse wrote in describing the setting of *Call Me Madam*. They also made sure not to offend Perle Mesta, the U.S.A.'s Ambassador Extraordinary and Plenipotentiary to Luxembourg, by running the disclaimer in the script and later in *Playbill:* "Neither the character of Miss Sally Adams nor Miss Ethel Merman resembles any person alive or dead."

I was playing a brash ambassadress who defied the chargé d'affaires and did things my way, letting protocol be damned, but melted when the Prime Minister of Lichtenburg kissed my hand. As a sub-plot, a bookish Harvard type fell in love with the Princess. And a series of gags that had me phoning President Truman punctuated the script. We weren't too sure how the President or the public would react to our good-natured ribbing, but the public loved it. The President never saw the show, but at least none of us got personal notes calling us s.o.b.'s as the critic of his daughter Margaret's vocal efforts had.

In April columnist Leonard Lyons suggested to Perle Mesta that he introduce us. She enthusiastically agreed. "Who knows? Maybe I can teach Miss Merman a few things," she said. When Lenny reported this to me, I wasn't fazed. I told him I might be able to give Perle a few pointers too.

He and his wife, Sylvia, planned a sit-down dinner for Perle, Margaret Truman, Ray Bolger, Ezio Pinza, Irving Berlin, Howard Lindsay, Buck Crouse, their wives, Bob and me. On that night a domestic crisis developed. Bobby began running a high fever and I refused to leave the apartment before the doctor examined him. Periodically, I'd call the Lyonses and assure them we'd be along.

By the time Bob and I arrived, dessert had been served. My greeting to Perle was "Have you ever had the measles?" She immediately realized what had detained us and said she'd have behaved in the same way.

We took to each other at once. When I asked if she'd take a curtain call on opening night, she shot back, "If I'm there, who'll stop me?"

Margaret Truman was sweet and unassuming. She telephoned me a couple of days later while I happened to be out. After I returned home, I looked over my messages. "Oh yes," the maid said. "Some nut kept calling claiming she was Margaret Truman."

I said that it probably was, since I'd recently met Margaret. Why hadn't she taken the number?

"Oh, I just thought it was one of your fans," she said, leaving me to ponder the implication of that.

Irving Berlin had again agreed to do the songs. To pull the production together Howard and Buck chose as producer Leland Hayward, whose response to any impossible dream was always "Well, what can we lose by trying?"

With that attitude, he persuaded the Radio Corporation of America to ante up the entire backing. He got George Abbott to direct, Jerry Robbins to choreograph, and Mainbocher—the couturier who had designed the Duchess of Windsor's trousseau—to give me a chi-chi image.

Offstage I'd long ago abandoned the chiffon with brown and white spectator shoes. I'd even given up tight black dresses with jet bugle beads for daytime wear. But I wasn't exactly crowding Mrs. Harrison Williams for her place on the list of best-dressed women of the year.

Mom and Pop in their courting days

Guess who is all gussied up for graduation from P.S.4 in Astoria, L.I.

The B-K Vacuum Booster Brake girls—Josie Traeger, far right, is still my closest friend. That's me second from left.

Girl Crazy 1930

"Sam and Delilah" drew a yelp of surprise opening night. Ten minutes later "I Got Rhythm"
really put me on the map.

I returned the same sentiments about Gershwin songs.

George White's *Scandals* 1931

Take a Chance 1932

THEATRE AND MUSIC COLLECTION OF THE MUSEUM OF THE CITY OF NEW YORK

In *Take a Chance*, I got another show-stopper, "Eadie Was a Lady." Maybe so, but grandma would have called her a "soiled dove."

Anything Goes 1934

Cole Porter wrote "Anything Goes" and four more hits for me.

"Blow, Gabriel, Blow" (left) is the kind of number a singer hopes for. In *Anything Goes*, I had it, as well as the title song, "You're the Top," and "I Get a Kick Out of You."

In 1934, I went to Hollywood—would you believe?—to play a con woman pretending to be Eddie Cantor's mother in *Kid Millions*.

Red, Hot and Blue! 1936

LESTER GLASSNER

Take my word for it. Bob Hope was new to Broadway when we introduced Porter's delightful "It's De-Lovely."

THEATRE AND MUSIC COLLECTION OF THE MUSEUM OF THE CITY OF NEW YORK

Red, Hot and Blue! almost turned co-star Jimmy Durante and me into comic strip characters. As I later learned, you gotta have a gimmick.

I tried Hollywood again for *Strike Me Pink* (1936), another Cantor opus, and the movie version of *Anything Goes* (1936), with Bing Crosby.

In *Alexander's Ragtime Band* (1938), I was still the girl who didn't get the guy, Ty Power—but I had some great Irving Berlin songs.

Cesar Romero and I were in Sonja Henie's *Happy Landing* (she's at right), so 20th Century tried to cook up a romance between us—but I scuttled the plan by playing jokes on Butch (Cesar to you).

Stars in Your Eyes 1939

THE PLAYBILL
FOR THE MAJESTIC THEATRE

Du Barry Was a Lady 1939

THE PLAYBILL

FORTY-SIXTH STREET THEATRE

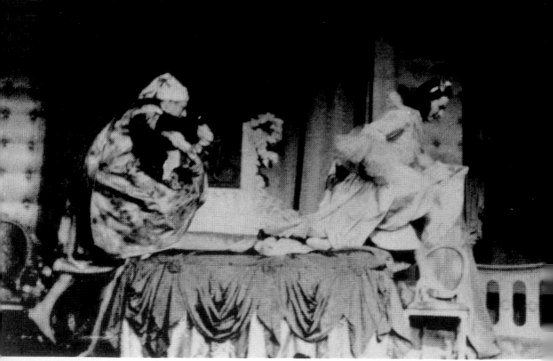

In *Du Barry*, Bert Lahr chased me so slowly that I accidentally passed him climbing over the bed. That bit got such a howl, we kept it in the show.

Panama Hattie 1940

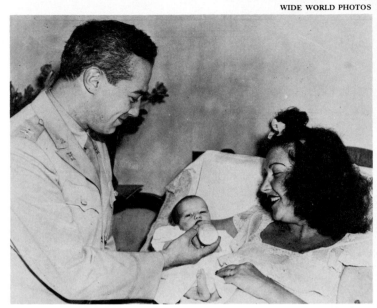

My husband Bob Levitt visited me and our new daughter in the hospital. Of my four marriages, the one to Bob is the only one I don't regret.

Something for the Boys 1943

Allen Jenkins and Paula Laurence were featured in my final Porter show. Paula and I were friendly until I tried to teach her stage etiquette.

THEATRE AND MUSIC COLLECTION OF THE MUSEUM OF THE CITY OF NEW YORK

Annie Get Your Gun 1946

Berlin's *Annie Get Your Gun* has wonderful songs and a good book. My lovesick "goon look" at Ray Middleton pinpointed the instant the audience decided the show was a hit.

This is my favorite photo of Ethel, Jr., little Bob and me.

The Duke and Duchess of Windsor gave Bob and me this photo inscribed "To Mr. and Mrs. Levitt who have raised a family—1947—'Doin' what comes natur'lly.'"

My daughter and I shared many things including look-alike shortie sunsuits.

CALL ME MADAM

Irving Berlin, Russell Nype and I chat before rehearsal. Russ hadn't yet got the crewcut that many men copied after he became the rage of New York.

SLIM AARONS

Playing the hostess with the mostes' was a welcome change after some of my frumpier roles.

On June 15, 1953, Mary Martin and I perched on a bare stage to sing our medley—and after that the staging of TV variety shows was never the same again.

My beloved Mom and Pop. We always rated tops with each other, and that's the way it will always be.

In 20th Century's *There's No Business Like Show Business* (1954), the only reason I didn't get the guy, Dan Dailey, was that I already had him, plus my kids—Mitzi Gaynor, Johnny Ray, Donald O'Connor and, eventually, daughter-in-law Marilyn Monroe.

Happy Hunting 1956

Gypsy 1959

Gypsy was the frosting on the cake. Jule Styne's and Stephen Sondheim's songs were tops and Arthur Laurents' book could have made it as a straight drama.

THEATRE AND MUSIC COLLECTION OF THE MUSEUM OF THE CITY OF NEW YORK

By contractual agreement, I missed a performance in June to fly to Colorado for my daughter's high school graduation.

Annie Get Your Gun (revival) 1966

My son developed an interest in directing so we took a trip around the world in order that he might study theatrical productions in various countries.

CBS

Hello, Dolly! 1970

Hard-boiled? Me? Look at my reaction while co-hosting the Mike Douglas Show when Mike surprised me with a visit from my grandchildren, Barbara Jean and Michael.

I established a whole new career doing concerts with symphony orchestras around the country after appearing with Arthur Fiedler and the Boston Pops Orchestra in July of 1976. This year I've already done Miami, Pittsburgh, Detroit, Kansas City, Richmond and San Francisco. I work as often as I want and yet I'm free as a bird.

My offstage evening dresses were made for me on Fifty-seventh Street at Wilma's, whose customers included Lana Turner, Betty Hutton and Alice Faye. Those gowns set me back between $400 and $500. Otherwise my dresses came off the rack. Usually I chose a solid blue or black at a cost of between $39.95 and $100. My hats— which were "in"—and my shoes were theatrical, to say the least.

I almost got off on the wrong foot with Main, as his friends called him. Going for my first fitting, I took Mom along thinking she'd find the place interesting, but he refused to allow her inside the fitting room. No outsider, he said, was allowed in his room when he was creating.

"But she's my mother," I said. Then I spied another elderly woman who had just entered. "If my mother can't come in, how is it this lady can?"

Said Main, "Because that is *my* mother."

Main had never done theatrical costumes before. His forte was understatement, but he understood that character costumes had to make an impact on those people perched in the second balcony. So he gave me a flame-colored lace over tulle, a black and white suit, a black velvet, and the dress I wore to present my credentials to the Grand Duke and Grand Duchess, which had a train I had to pick up and throw between my legs before I could move forward. "I don't mind a train," I remember telling him, "but you needn't have given me the Super Chief." Anyway, the costumes had a great deal to do with establishing a new image, as did my new upswept hair that ended in a poodle knot combined with some flattering bangs across my brow. Main didn't seem too impressed, because he asked me what I was going to do with my hair. I just looked him in the eye and said, "I'm going to wash it." He didn't mention the subject again.

Mr. Abbott and I understood each other at once. (I was discussing the fact that everyone calls him "Mr. Abbott" with an actress who had been on the most intimate terms possible with him. She assured me that, close as they were, there were only specific moments during which she felt free to call him "George," then she went back to "Mr. Abbott.") I'm a fast study, usually having my lines within two weeks. Unlike some people, who are afraid of getting stale, I give from the beginning. Mr. Abbott told me he especially liked that, since it jacked up the rest of the company, and as a director he could see what he was achieving.

The principals included Galina Talva, Pat Harrington, Alan Hewitt, Russell Nype and Paul Lukas.

Paul was a distinguished-looking man, an immaculate dresser. During the run of the show I was flabbergasted to learn that he'd take a Saturday night plane to Cleveland to visit a favorite tailor when he felt in need of new threads.

Paul had a great sense of humor. During the first few days of rehearsals he and I had lunch regularly. On the fifth day I put it to him straight, telling him that he couldn't go on grabbing the checks. "This isn't ladies and gentlemen," I explained. "We are co-workers." Paul shrugged and said to a friend who had just joined us, "You are about to see my greatest performance. I'm pretending to be unaware that Ethel is buying my luncheon. For an encore, I'll protest."

But beneath the suave, humorous exterior there was a troubled man. He was insecure about his voice and during the tryout period offered to resign because he was convinced he was ruining his number, "Lichtenburg," when in fact he talk-sang it charmingly. At some period before he began rehearsing *Call Me Madam*, he had undergone surgery for removal of some polyps from his vocal cords. Even though the doctors assured him the polyps were benign, nothing could convince him that they weren't malignant.

Somehow he had cultivated the friendship of a surgeon at Memorial Hospital and masochistically persuaded the doctor to let him watch the removal of cancerous larynxes. As time went on, Russell Nype and I always could tell when Paul had watched surgery that day. Because he would enter the theater and whisper, "I can't talk. My voice is gone." When I'd ask if by chance he'd been over to Memorial, he invariably had. Finally the surgeon and his wife came backstage to visit Paul. I managed to get the doctor aside to tell him what was happening and to beg him not to let Paul visit anymore—because there was nothing wrong with Paul's throat, but he was destroying himself with his fixation.

Of course the most enduring friendship grew up between Russell Nype, who played the Harvard type, and me. When I first met

Russell at rehearsal, I wasn't at all sure he was going to last the five days that Equity allowed the management to dismiss an actor without penalty.

Russell had long hair, somewhat wavy and thick. He had worn it that way in *Regina* with Jane Pickens. Although he couldn't see beyond his nose, he wasn't wearing his glasses, which made him very tentative about everything.

It was Buck and Howard who saved him. They took him aside and told him to go ahead and wear his specs. They also suggested that he get a crewcut. The result was sensational. After *Madam* finally opened in New York, the Duchess of Windsor took up Russell. And in a short time every other guy you saw on Madison Avenue was wearing big horn-rimmed glasses and a crewcut. Russell had created an image. That was both good and bad for him. Good because it stamped him on everyone's consciousness and bad because those parts don't come along every day.

In New Haven before our premiere I went to an Episcopal church for communion but arrived an hour early. I explained to the rector that I couldn't return later because of a scheduled rehearsal. He very kindly gave me communion alone. Naturally I wanted to express my gratitude, so I told him I'd like him to attend the theater as my guest. I said, "You gave me a free show and I'd like to give you one." Some people thought that was a strange offer to make—but fair is fair, I always say.

Our opening made it clear that the first act was in good shape, but we didn't have a strong second half. In the first I sang "The Hostess with the Mostes' on the Ball," "Washington Square Dance," "Can You Use Any Money Today?" and "The Best Thing for You Would Be Me." Paul sang-talked "Lichtenburg," and Russell stopped the show with "It's a Lovely Day Today."

In the second half I had "Mr. Monotony," which Irving had salvaged from a movie and later from *Miss Liberty*, plus a ponderous message song, "Free." Other than Russell's "Once upon a Time" and the infectious "They Like Ike," the rest of the musical numbers were reprises.

Neither of my songs went over. I told Irving that I'd gone along with "Mr. Monotony" against my better judgment because he liked it so much, but since the audience wasn't buying it neither was I.

Irving promptly retired to his room and turned out "Something to Dance About," which gave the second act the lift that was needed to prove to patrons they weren't mistaken to have come back for another act.

We still needed the kind of show-stopper that sends patrons out of the theater ready to stop complete strangers on the street to tell them to see this show. "Free" was burdening the audience with its preachments on liberty, while they craved a rousing number in the free and easy style of the rest of the production.

"What I'd like to do is a number with the kid," I told Irving. He went to his suite in the Taft Hotel, and the next night he called a meeting of Mr. Abbott, Howard, Buck, Leland Hayward, Russell and me.

One thing I noticed about the great songwriters such as Irving, George Gershwin and Cole Porter—they were always as nervous as neophytes when playing a song for its first listeners. Irving was actually perspiring. As he finished playing "You're Just in Love," he turned to me and asked, "Well, what do you think?"

And I said, "We'll never get off the stage."

Opening night in Boston, Russell and I stood in the wings mumbling our lyrics because we weren't too sure we'd mastered the tricky juxtaposition of the words. When we finished the number, the whole place exploded. There were six or seven encores. From that moment on there was no doubt we had a hit.

But Buck and Howard still weren't satisfied. They never stopped trying to add a joke, tidy up an exit, improve a punch line. I went along with the tinkering until the Thursday before our New York opening, when the show was supposed to be frozen—meaning no more changes. Still they continued making a change here and there until I faced them down, saying, "Boys, as of right now I am Miss Birdseye of 1950. I am frozen. Not a comma!"

Between ten A.M. and four P.M. the day tickets went on sale at the Imperial Theater in New York, $13,000 worth were pushed under

164

the wicket. By our opening on October 12, we had racked up the largest advance sale in the history of the American theater. Happily, my contract gave me 10 percent of all profits from the Broadway production, road companies, movie sale and subsidiary rights.

The general consensus was that *Madam* lived up to the out-of-town ballyhoo. If Irving's score lacked the range he had packed into *Annie Get Your Gun* and the book was less cohesive, *Madam* nevertheless was not only one of my strongest vehicles but launched Russell as a new type of juvenile.

General and Mrs. Eisenhower were in the audience to hear "They Like Ike," and the Duke and Duchess of Windsor were so enthusiastic that before long both Russell and I found ourselves caught up in the social whirl that centered around them.

After Jack Benny saw the show, he sat down and wrote me a fan letter on Sherry-Netherland stationery. I had it framed and it's still hanging on the wall of my apartment with other mementos:

SHERRY-NETHERLAND

Nov. 1950

Dear Ethel,

Last night when we left the theatre we were discussing your wonderful performance. Really, Ethel, you were better than ever. Your looks-delivery-timing so funny and yet with such class. And I left out your voice yet which also seemed to be better than ever. If you were a man I would *have* to dislike you.

Much love,
Jack

After Perle Mesta caught the show, she urged everyone to see it. I was invited to all of her parties in Washington, and she gave a few for me. Once when I was her guest, she instructed me on how to buzz the servants when I wanted my breakfast served. But next morning there were so many buttons I couldn't figure out how to reach the kitchen. I kept getting a dial tone. Since she was in her room talking, I didn't want to accidentally cut her off. So I finally put on my robe and slippers and went down to the kitchen to ask for tea and toast.

Not that Perle would have minded if I'd cut her off. She was an extremely down-to-earth person. One night at a party of hers we had to stand around for a long time. At the shank of the evening our feet began to hurt. So we surreptitiously hid our shoes. With our long dresses, nobody was the wiser and we were a lot more comfortable.

Ironically, I wasn't allowed to appear on the original-cast album of *Madam* put out by RCA-Victor. When RCA backed the show, it had been assumed that some kind of agreement could be worked out with Decca, for whom I had been recording exclusively. Instead Decca released an album of my songs. For "You're Just in Love" I teamed with Dick Haymes, a good singer, but hardly so perfectly cast as Russell. And "The Hostess with the Mostes' on the Ball" was missing altogether. It was reserved for RCA's "original-cast"—minus me—album. Dinah Shore did my songs, and for once my 10 percent of all profits was cold comfort for having someone else take my place.

I CAN TESTIFY from experience that absence does *not* make the heart grow fonder. Bob was traveling a lot while I was still in *Call Me Madam*, and we stood by helplessly while our marriage slowly deteriorated. Neither of us had any idea of what to do.

Whether he was carrying on with other women I can't say. I did realize that when he came home our relationship just wasn't the same. There was a strangeness between us.

I am possessive of those I love, and when things get rocky I must confess problems never bring out the best in me.

Nor did they in Bob. There were accusations, arguments, tears, terribly destructive exchanges in which we seemed to share a compulsion to hurt each other. Then there would be apologies and a reconciliation, followed by another estrangement.

It was so upsetting that I consulted the Reverend Pollard of St. Bartholomew's for personal guidance. Nothing helped. Reluctantly we separated rather than subject Little Ethel and Bobby to our hostility and quarreling.

Bob, I'm sure, had his charges against me and my behavior. From my point of view, he just seemed to go haywire. He was fired from his job with Hearst and went to Screen Gems. That didn't work out too successfully either. He began dating film star Linda Darnell, who, I understand, was as tragic as she was beautiful.

I never knew Linda, but once she confided to Dr. Damato that she would like to meet me. She said that, after all, she had met Bob after we were separated. She asked the doctor to arrange an introduction. He brought up the subject and asked how I'd respond if I happened to run into her at the Stork Club. "I'd kick her in the ass," I said. Dr. Damato told me years later that he had warned Linda that if she accidentally encountered me, for God's sake not to turn her back.

Not that I was sitting home brooding, no matter how unhappy I was over my second marital mishap. I was appearing frequently on radio with Tallulah Bankhead's *The Big Show*, and through the Duke and Duchess I met Charlie Cushing. Soon Charlie and I began seeing a lot of each other.

But even though Bob and I dated other people, neither of us really believed that our relationship had ended. As I look back, I can truthfully say it's my only marriage that I regret dissolving, because I still believe that we could have spent some happy days together in later years.

I can also say that he was the only guy I ever deeply loved. Not long ago I was telling a Hollywood writer who was a mutual friend of Bob's and mine that I really didn't understand and had never known exactly why Bob and I divorced. The writer said it was funny I should say that, because Bob had made the same comment to him a few years before.

After the wrangling, we established friendly relations again, but I think it shook him when I became seriously involved with Robert Six. Soon after that he remarried, but it didn't last. However, he was always a good father. He usually had the kids during the summer. In 1957 they spent their vacations with him in East Hampton. And in October, after they were back with me, he called to tell me he was marrying for a third time and to ask whether the children could attend his wedding. Of course, I agreed. I wished him happiness.

Then he kiddingly asked, "Won't you come to the wedding and sing 'Oh Promise Me'?"

"Come on, not at those prices," I told him, which he got a big kick out of.

Three months after the nuptials he and his bride and Paul Getty Jr.'s wife went out to his East Hampton house for the weekend, and he did this horrible thing. It wasn't an impulsive act. He had planned it. As I understand, he sent his wife and Mrs. Getty back to the city on Sunday and said he'd come in early next morning. After they were gone, he just lay down with a pillow under his head and took the sleeping pills. When they found him, he looked as if he were sleeping peacefully.

Bob was a wonderful, wonderful guy. He was also, while it lasted, a good husband. He had a great sense of humor and was always a good father. I don't regret a moment I spent with him. He had marvelous taste. As a matter of fact, when he died his jewelry came to me. I had the cuff links and studs I'd given him—crystal, onyx and diamonds—turned into a bracelet. I knew no one else would ever wear them. And the Omega watch he bought himself and had fitted with an irreplaceable handmade gold band is something I wear every day. It still has his initials on it. I left them because it seemed a nice thing to do.

As I said earlier, it's my only marriage I don't regret. The others were mistakes and some of them were beauts.

I mentioned my appearances on NBC Radio's *The Big Show* earlier too. The program was broadcast from six to seven-thirty P.M., EST. Tallulah Bankhead was the mistress of ceremonies. On their first program, Russell Nype, Paul Lukas and I did eight minutes of songs from *Call Me Madam*. For comic effect the writers arranged it so that Tallulah was called upon to fume at anybody taking up so much time on *her* program. When the applause died, she said, "Thank you, Ethel, and better luck next time. No, actually, dahling, it looks as if you've got another hit show that's certain to run on Broadway two years. Let's see now, you've had about *fifty* shows that have run two years each, haven't you, dahling?"

The routine went over so well I was asked back often. I never knew Tallulah socially. I don't think I was in her company more than three times. But professionally we were a mutual admiration society. A month after my first appearance, she telegraphed me, "DARLING ETHEL, MANY HAPPY RETURNS. WE HAVE MISSED YOU SO MUCH ON THE BIG SHOW. TAKE A DEEP BREATH AND COME BACK SOON. MY LOVE AND ADMIRATION. TALLULAH."

We were both people who didn't mince words. That's one of the things I loved about her. She said what she thought and that was it. There were no ifs, ands or buts.

I don't think I go as far as she did. She'd say anything about herself. You never knew whether it was true or just to shock. I remember her telling of going into a public ladies' room and discovering there was no toilet tissue. She looked underneath the booth and said to the lady in the next stall, "I beg your pardon, do you happen to have any toilet tissue in there?" The lady said no, she was sorry but she didn't. So Tallulah said, "Well, then, dahling, do you have two fives for a ten?"

One thing was true and surprising. When I did *The Big Show*, I always went to St. Barth's before rehearsal. When I'd get to NBC, Tallulah would always inquire about the services and would ask for the booklet for the day. That was a side of her I don't think many people saw.

Once we were kidding around and she asked me truthfully what I thought of her on *The Big Show*. I told her, "Toodle-ooh, you know what I think of you as an actress. I've always thought of you that way and I still do. On the level, you're a female John Barrymore." Now that wasn't just a wisecrack. I had great respect for her, and John Barrymore was one of the greatest actors who ever lived—but both of them tended to be a little casual about caring for their God-given talent.

C
H
A
P
T
E
R

XXII

ALTHOUGH I HAD MET the Duke and Duchess through Bob Levitt at the Hearsts, my friendship with them heated up after Bob and I separated. They were fun to be with. They naturally attracted exciting people, but I didn't treat them any different from Martha Neubert and her husband or Josie and Leo Traeger.

The Duchess and I really hit it off. I remember once she came in wearing this simple dress. On it she had a beautiful crossed-feather pin. One feather was solid rubies, the other was diamonds. It demanded some kind of comment and everyone made one. She liked mine best. I just said, "Oh, you and your costume jewelry!"

Shortly after *Madam* opened, the Duchess gave a little supper at Gogi's LaRue, which was a popular new spot. Ted Straeter led the orchestra there and the Duchess asked me to sing. So I got up and did "I Get a Kick Out of You." Next day I got notification from AGVA (American Guild of Variety Artists) threatening to fine or suspend me for doing a free appearance at the club. Imagine! I figured it was sort of a command performance. I mean if you're a guest of the Duke and Duchess of Windsor and the Duchess asks you to sing a song, are you going to spit in her eye?

Charlie Cushing was much older than I—a delightful guy, a wonderful man. He was a big investment banker. After Charlie and I started going together, the Duchess used to kid me that she and C. Z. Guest were going to sue me for alienation of Charlie's affections.

In trying to forget the problems of my wrecked marriage, I distracted myself with interesting people. And I did things I ordinarily wouldn't have considered doing when I was appearing in a show. One Saturday night after the performance, for instance, I caught a flight to Miami, where Charlie had a private plane meet me to take me to Palm Beach for a big bash. Then on Monday I flew to New York, did my show and felt a complete wreck. But those were fun days.

Although there was nothing serious between Charlie and me, he was wonderful to my children. I remember when Edith Baker gave a coming-out party for her granddaughter, I sent Ethel Jr. and Bobby ahead on Friday with their governess. And Charlie took them to the Piping Rock Country Club for lunch on Saturday. That night after the performance I was driven out for the party.

It was a lavish affair. They had a magnificent tent, and Meyer Davis' Orchestra played until all hours. My kids had never seen anything like it in their lives. When I got there, Bobby excitedly told me that workmen had uprooted trees to accommodate the limousines that were expected.

Charlie knew how much the kids liked pets. He gave them lots of birds, including this huge cage with two big cockatoos—gray with tails that never stopped. Ethel was especially fond of them.

On weekends all of us used to go out to Edith's place at Glen Cove. She had a palatial layout with a guest house so gorgeous the Duke and Duchess used to stay in it. Other weekends we'd go to Jimmy Donahue's in Jericho. Jimmy, a Woolworth heir, had bought Alfred Vanderbilt's mansion. Jimmy used to send limousines to get us and bring us back.

It was rumored—I don't know, because I never checked—that because conversations in Jimmy's magnificent dining room sometimes got racy all of the staff who waited on table had to be partially deaf. The trusted head butler who did the hiring saw to that. That was to prevent their overhearing what was said and telling other servants.

Servants, by the way, are often the biggest snobs of all and the worst gossips you can find.

I was very close to Jimmy. He adored me. When he was on the wagon, I never met a more refined, cultured man in my whole life. He never paid much in taxes, because he gave his money away. Every year, for instance, when Jane Pickens would raise money for children with muscular dystrophy or multiple sclerosis, Jimmy would double the amount she had raised.

He was a wonderful son to Jessie Donahue, who lived at 834 Fifth Avenue. Jessie had a vertigo condition that made it impossible to get about, but every night while he was in the city Jimmy would sit with her until after she had had her dinner, then he'd be on his merry way. Wonderful as he was, when he was drinking a Jekyll-Hyde quality emerged. Then, look out.

Jimmy would give the Duchess beautiful jewels, and the little Duke just closed his eyes to everything. I recall distinctly going to El Morocco one night. We sat in the little room. The Duchess was dancing with Jimmy and everyone else except the Duke. He and I danced, but the Duchess kept dancing with Jimmy until I got irked about the whole thing. Now talk about me and my plain language, I said to her, "Why don't you get off your ass and dance with your husband?" And she did. I didn't care what I said to her. I knew that basically she had the same kind of mind as all of us. Because she was the Duchess of Windsor she couldn't express herself in those terms, but she thought that way.

This is a pretty strange story, but Jimmy told it to me himself. I'm not making it up. One night while he was going with the Duchess they got to bickering. Jimmy had been drinking and she'd had her fill of Scotch. The little Duke had gone to bed. Jimmy and the Duchess got into a big fight, yelling and screaming and trading insults. Finally she looked at him and said, "And to think I gave up a king for a queen."

This is jumping ahead a bit. Jimmy had given me a beautiful party the night the revival of *Annie Get Your Gun* closed at the State Theater in 1966. He took over Goldie's restaurant for a black-tie dinner dance. Afterward, as a token of my appreciation, I had my jeweler make up some lovely gold cuff links shaped into his initials, J. D. They were stunning.

Then on a Thursday a friend of Jimmy's called. He asked if I was sitting down and told me Jimmy was dead. I was so shocked I could hardly believe it. I'd seen him on Tuesday and this was Thursday. What had killed him was a combination of alcohol and sleeping pills. I got permission from the family for the cuff links to be buried with him.

I went to the service and to the mausoleum. He was put in a crypt with a stained-glass window, and that day the sun shone through, creating the most beautiful atmosphere. I still miss Jimmy.

Jimmy was the first of my friends to be struck down by sleeping pills. Later there were so many others. Today if you went through my apartment with a fine-tooth comb the strongest sedative you'd find is Bufferin.

Anyone who read a newspaper in those days couldn't have missed the column items and stories about the friendship between the Duchess and Russell Nype. There is no doubt she had a mad crush on him. At the time, Russell was a young kid. He was flattered. Gifts from her used to come backstage frequently. I don't think they were expensive, but often before a matinee he'd say, "I got a box from the Duchess." And we'd all go out together after *Madam* and have lots of fun, but at the time Russell was seriously courting Diantha, his present wife. So even though the Duchess was hot for him, I don't think she actually had an affair with him.

Of course Russell and I became and remain the closest of friends. He and Diantha and their son, Rusty, are like family to me. Back in the days after Bob and I separated, we often had supper after the show. Sherman Billingsley was again sending champagne to my dressing room, and after the performance I'd say to Russell, "How about a bottle?" We must have drunk a swimming pool full of champagne in those days. In fact, during *Madam* my teeth became sensitive to hot and cold. I consulted a dentist and he said I had developed an acid condition from the champagne. That's when I switched to Almadén Chablis—which makes me such a cheap date today.

XXIII

ON OCTOBER 20, 1951, at L'Aiglon, our producer, Leland Hayward, gave a party celebrating *Call Me Madam*'s first anniversary on Broadway. Because Charlie Cushing was going to be playing in a golf tournament the next morning, he arranged for Milton "Doc" Holden to escort me. After the matinee on the day of the party Doc called to ask whether he could bring along a few friends. Since it wasn't a formal dinner, I didn't see why not.

When Doc picked me up at the Imperial Theater after the Saturday night show, he had several people with him. One was a six-foot, four-inch, 200-pound craggy-faced fellow from Denver. I noticed he was a snappy dresser and thought him attractive, but some dame clutched his arm, so I didn't pay too much attention. I'd never seen him around town before and it didn't occur to me that I'd see him again. But by the way Robert Six came on, he made it clear the woman with him was just a casual friend. He seemed to like me and he had the easy personality that I've since noticed has often been developed to mask a calculating nature.

At L'Aiglon, Leland had reserved a prominent table for Russell, Paul Lukas, me and other people connected with the show. Naturally, Six and his date were directed to one of the tables set aside for press, friends of friends and freeloaders.

Since the party celebrated a milestone for *Madam*, I, of course, was expected to be all over the place, charming friends from the press, RCA backers, and executives from 20th Century-Fox, the company that was dickering for film rights. Anybody who knows anything about these "anniversary parties" realizes they are publicity gimmicks designed to help sell another year's supply of tickets.

Anyway, Six's date was dancing with somebody else and he and I got to talking. I was surprised when he said that as president of Continental Airlines he spent approximately a week each month in town. We even commented on the fact that it was strange we'd never seen each other at the Stork, 21, El Morocco, LaRue or one of the other places around town. He told me how much he'd liked me in *Red, Hot and Blue, Annie Get Your Gun* and *Madam*, and I said the next time I vacationed in Glenwood Springs I'd have to fly Continental. It turned out we'd both separated from our spouses the previous May. Chitchat.

Don't ask me how it happened, but Six's date drifted off and he, Doc Holden and I left together. At the party every time I'd almost get a forkful of food to my mouth a reporter, autograph seeker or dance partner would interrupt. So I suggested that the three of us get something to eat. I guess Doc felt like a third wheel, because he said he was tired and asked to be excused. Then Six and I went to a Hamburger Heaven.

In the next three hours Six told me how he'd dropped out of high school in Stockton, California, gone to sea and worked as a bill collector before Lindbergh's solo flight across the Atlantic fired his interest in aviation. He'd operated something called the Valley Flying Service, a barnstorming scenic ride and charter service. It failed. During the Depression he'd spent a couple of years flying the Peking-Shanghai route for China National.

Returning to California, he became district circulation manager for the San Francisco *Chronicle* for another couple of years. Then he and another fellow opened a distributorship for Beechcraft serving the Northwest. In 1937 he left and bought into Varney Speed Lines, which had an airmail subsidy between El Paso, Texas, and Pueblo, Colorado.

He'd married Henriette Erhart, who was in the process of divorcing him when we met. Although he didn't say so, I later heard that her family's money had put him into the airline business. But even if he'd mentioned it, I doubt I'd have paid proper attention, because Six was an operator and knew how to turn on the charm. He was a diamond in the rough, not the kind of guy I ordinarily met. It was dawn when I got home.

Six came to my apartment for lunch before he left for Denver by way of Washington, D.C. He phoned from both places, and every time he came to New York he monopolized my time. I didn't think it was anything serious. I used to call him the "Whale" or "Jumbo," and I was still seeing Charlie Cushing as well as a couple of other guys. But the columnists began playing up our "romance." For example, Walter Winchell ran such items as: "Eth Merm's current dinner escort is Continental Airlines' biggie Bob Six of Denver. Sech muscles!" (Well, that's the way they wrote in those days.) Or he'd say I was out with the "Colorado Mint." Another columnist informed his readers: "More darn romance at the El Morocco—Ethel Merman and Bob Six, the airlines executive, close up the place regularly. It looks like a weddin' eventually."

Now I didn't object to this stuff. It was publicity for the show and fodder for the scrapbook Pop was still keeping for me. Six didn't keep scrapbooks (at least I don't think he did), but eventually I learned the items were just as useful to him in his business as they were in mine. I don't want to be crude about it, but what New York columnist ever wrote anything about where Bob Six hung out before he began dating me?

In April 1952 *Call Me Madam* closed after 644 performances. Although I had always refused to go on the road because I didn't want to leave the kids and I certainly wasn't going to have them growing up in hotels, I did agree to kick off the coast-to-coast tour in Washington, D.C.

It was to be a special occasion marking the reopening of the National Theater. Three years, nine months and five days earlier, the curtain had fallen for the last time on a production in that theater. Although Washington is the nation's capital, black patrons had never been allowed to sit with whites in theaters. In the altered social climate following World War II, Actors Equity had taken a stand prohibiting any of its members from performing in a play before a segregated audience in that city. Marcus Heiman, who held the lease on the National, rose up and informed the world that segregation was not the issue, but that he would not allow a union to run his business. A standoff developed and the theater closed.

Now it was being reopened as an integrated playhouse with all the attendant ceremonies. We were to open on May 5, and I was bowled over when Six told me he wanted to host a posh post-opening bash in my honor.

The following invitation went out to 150 distinguished guests:

IN HONOR OF
MISS ETHEL MERMAN
Mr. Robert Forman Six
Requests the Pleasure of Your Company
Monday Evening, the fifth of May at 11:30 o'clock

Chinese Room   Mayflower Hotel
Midnight to 4 A.M.   Black Tie
RSVP

Please Present This Card

The premiere was a festival of laughter and applause punctuated by bravos, although I must admit that General Eisenhower's rival for the Republican presidential nomination, Robert E. Taft, didn't find "They Like Ike" anything to cheer about. But everyone else seemed to.

Afterward there was Six's party for me. It was so studded with political stars that NBC had set up TV equipment in the lobby to cover the arrival of celebrated guests. Six had had the Chinese Room transformed into a French nightclub. Little hurricane lamps on each table and Lester Lanin's tinkling rhythms gave the place a lovely ambiance. Of course I eventually sang.

It was a memorable evening and by this time I was fairly certain that Six was someone special in my life. Now I've been around a lot. And even more than most actresses, I guess, I give the impression of being a strong person. I think I *am* strong. I can take care of myself professionally. But just because I can slam a comedy line or hold a note for the full chorus of a song—things that bring thousands of people to their feet cheering and sending waves of adoration across the footlights—that doesn't mean that I'm not as vulnerable as anyone else. You can't cuddle up to bravos, however thrilling they may be, or take them home with you. You can't confide in them, and they can't guide or comfort you. So I knew that I wanted my relationship with Six to continue.

What I didn't realize was that he wasn't interested in me as Ethel Zimmermann. He was interested in ETHEL MERMAN the public personality, the star. If I'd been wise, I'd have broken off with him and patched things up with Bob Levitt, who had his priorities right. Because what I didn't know then was that this party that touched me so much was written off as public relations by Continental Airlines. It was all publicity to put Six on the map. But even if I had known, I'm not sure that at that point it would have made any difference. With me, once the conquest is made, it takes a lot to shake my loyalty. But doubts about him were far from my mind in May of 1952. I thought I'd found my white knight, only he was riding a DC-3. I had a lot to learn.

To be a stand-by to a star, even though it pays several hundred dollars a week, may be the most frustrating assignment in the world. Worse, no one who is qualified to fill it really wants it.

This is not the same as being an understudy. An understudy usually has a minor role in the show and knows the lines, moves and business of two or three performers so that she or he can fill in if someone is absent.

A stand-by, in contrast, is someone who has played some leading roles—if not on Broadway, then in national companies or regional theater—but has yet to attract a large enough following to carry a show herself. However, she is hired upon the assumption that in case the star is ill she can step in and do a creditable job. In the case of Shirley MacLaine, who was a stand-by for the late Carol Haney, she did such a good job when she substituted for Carol that Hollywood producer Hal Wallis signed her up and made her a movie star.

During my years in the theater, Vivian Vance, Betty Garrett,

Nancy Andrews and Mary Jane Walsh started as understudies for me. In *Madam* Mary Jane became a stand-by, but left to marry and move to East Rochester, New York, to raise a family.

Her successor was a tall sexy blonde with a sardonic manner whose playing in revues, straight plays and musicals had won her a cult following. We knew we had an original when one of the first things she did after signing up was to get herself charged with indecent exposure in Central Park. The way she told it, she was out bicycle riding and got too warm. So she casually slipped off her blouse. Since she had a halter under it, she assumed she was properly attired, but a police officer didn't agree and she landed in the newspapers. That's Elaine Stritch's story.

But a few years later she got a lot of coverage by "absent-mindedly" writing her grocery list on the back of an invitation to a party for Princess Margaret and Lord Snowden. When the delivery boy returned the invitation, she asked him to escort her to the party and stole the spotlight. She has always been a smart press agent and maybe, just maybe, she realized what would happen when she removed her blouse.

I've always suspected that Stritch's glands work overtime, because she has enormous energy and drive. Now I don't like letting anyone else play my role. A role is a very personal thing to an actress. You don't want someone else fooling around with it any more than you do with your toothbrush. So unless I have laryngitis or something else that totally incapacitates me, I'm there.

Stritch suspected that—after showing up a half-hour before every performance for a few months, coming to my dressing room and noting my unbroken run of good health. "I gather you're well," she would say, and when I'd reply, "Never better," she'd turn on her heel and leave. Finally she took to calling and leaving word where she could be found between eight-thirty and eleven P.M.

Stritch got so tired waiting for me to get sick that she persuaded Leland Hayward to permit her to accept the role of the intellectual stripteaser in the revival of *Pal Joey*, which was scheduled to play previews in New York, omitting an out-of-town tryout.

Since she had only one number—"Zip"—and didn't make her entrance until ten-thirty, Stritch wanted to continue standing by for me in order to collect two salaries. That was fine with Leland, because she assured him that if I became ill Jule Styne, who was one of the producers of *Joey*, would let her understudy go on for her.

Everything seemed to be working out until Dick Rodgers, who wrote the score for *Joey*, looked at the production a couple of days before previews were to begin and insisted it should go to New Haven for a five-performance overhaul.

Stritch was frantic. Then, she estimated the driving time and decided she could check in with me, jump into her car and arrive in New Haven at the Shubert in time for her ten-thirty entrance. Matinees were something else, but she was so determined, she was willing to make two round trips between New York and New Haven on those days.

Christmas Day a blizzard closed highways. Stritch called Leland and persuaded him to waive the rules this once so that she could check with me from Grand Central at seven-thirty and catch the seven thirty-five train. I told her, Go. Then the train was delayed until seven-fifty, and she thought she'd blown her chance to open in *Pal Joey*. But upon arrival in New Haven she commandeered the first car she saw and gasped, "To the Shubert," arriving just in time to kick off her snow boots and shoot past her understudy, who was in full makeup standing in the wings. What's more, Stritch claims none of her subsequent performances in the role were ever as good.

The other four days she drove back and forth. From then on she collected two checks until *Madam* closed in New York, but she never did get to play Sally Adams in New York. On Memorial Day 1952 in Washington, D.C., when she had left *Joey* to take over my part in the national company of *Madam* Leland scheduled an extra matinee with Stritch and the rest of the people who were to tour, giving Russell Nype, Dick Eastham, who had replaced Paul Lukas, and me a chance to see the show.

The morning before that matinee I received a wire from Stritch: "WE WHO ARE ABOUT TO DIE SALUTE YOU." She was scared stiff and furious at the thought of us out front. In the first scene she was a little nervous, but after that she hit her stride and was brilliant.

That's why when I go to London these days and see her name in big lights I'm not at all surprised.

After I withdrew from the show, Leland Hayward sprung a lovely surprise. Having persuaded me to help launch the tour, he had ordered a set of new gowns to make the production look spanking fresh. Once my engagement was finished, Leland presented all of them to me. The red with yards and yards of lace came in handy immediately. Six wanted me to come to Denver to meet his friends and I decided the red job would be just the thing for a big party. It was too heavy to consider taking with me. So I sent it air freight. And I must say it created enough of a sensation to justify the thirty dollars shipping charges that it cost me. This was the kind of thing that really appealed to Six—it made me MERMAN.

Temporarily free of *Madam*, although I was scheduled to star in the film version, which was to begin shooting in late summer, I flew to Mexico City on June 7, 1952, for a quickie Mexican divorce. Finding the procedure complicated, I went on to Juarez, where a mutual consent decree was granted not more than thirty minutes after the petition was filed in the federal court. Looking back, I'm not sure I'm glad getting free was so easy. By this time, Bob Levitt and I were quite friendly when we met to discuss the kids' future. Maybe if I hadn't plunged into marriage, he and I could have gotten together again.

Certainly a cautious person might have hesitated about getting deeply involved with a man who asked her to marry him but insisted the ceremony would have to be kept secret for several months. Don't ask me why, but he did. To this day I don't understand why. All I know is that otherwise there would have been no marriage.

IN LATE AUGUST or the first week in September I finally went to Hollywood the way I'd always wanted to—as a star. Fourteen years had passed since I'd made that picture I promised you earlier I wouldn't mention again. (I don't count *Stage Door Canteen*, since it was made in New York and I only had one number.) This time Harry Brand, the head of publicity at 20th Century-Fox, turned his department loose making the town Merman conscious.

I checked in at the studio to find I was assigned Betty Grable's former dressing room, which meant the best on the lot. They also provided a house, a nursemaid for the kids and a chauffeur-driven car. It was unbelievable. Anything you wanted was given to you —down to a pedicure. Such treatment was undreamed of in the theater.

Producer Sol Siegel, director Walter Lang and cameraman Leon Shamroy were on hand to greet and promise me that everything would be done to make the film version an even more spectacular success than the stage show had been.

"Just give us Ethel Merman," Walter said, "the same way you do in front of the footlights, and leave the rest to us."

I was a little leery that the Technicolor process might put a damper on my movement. But not at all. Shamroy assured me there was no reason for film to be a celluloid straitjacket.

The cast included perky little Donald O'Connor in Russell Nype's part, Vera-Ellen as the Princess and George Sanders in the role originated by Paul Lukas.

George was sweet and believable and warm as toast as Cosmo Constantine, but he was a strange man, very hard to get to. Between takes he locked himself in his dressing room and that was it. He didn't seem to want to bother with anybody. Obviously he was a very unhappy man even then or he wouldn't have done what he did. You just don't wake up one morning and decide you're tired of living and kill yourself. But again, that's hindsight. Often, it doesn't occur to people that somebody who is behaving peculiarly is emotionally ill until it's too late.

After I'd seen the final cut of the film, it seemed wonderful to me, but I'd worked long enough to know nobody can predict how the critics will react. So I still remember the thrill I experienced reading Bosley Crowther's review in the New York *Times*. I think you'll understand why if I quote his first paragraph:

> Whatever pleasure Ethel Merman bestowed in *Call Me Madam* on the stage—and the evidence is that it was plenty as she played it on Broadway 644 times—may be counted a minor fraction of the pleasure she is sure to convey as the boss-lady of this gay-fandango in repeating it on the screen. . . . The wonderful Miss Merman is better than ever—in spades!

To put the icing on my cake, his final sentence read:

> There should really be no need for 3-D pictures when there are people like Miss Merman around.

In Miami, where *Call Me Madam* had its world premiere on March 12, 1953, I must admit I played cat and mouse with the press. The reporters wanted to know whether I was going to marry Six, who was in town, and I responded, "If I do marry him, it won't be here."

That was no lie. We'd wed three days earlier. Six and I had been visiting Frank O'Dwyer, the brother of the former mayor of New York, in El Centro, California. While there, we'd sneaked over to Mexicali, Mexico, for a simple ceremony. But since Six wanted to be a part of the premiere festivities in Miami, it was obvious to me that it wouldn't be a secret for long.

Sure enough, on June 5 the *Rocky Mountain News* heard the rumor that Six was dickering for the Churchill Owen estate in Cherry Hills Village near Denver. The reporter concluded that we were married. At first Six denied the report, claiming we were only partners in a Wyoming oil deal, but later in the day his office announced that we had been married two months earlier. I was elated. The story had broken, but nobody could blame me for talking out of turn. If I hadn't been so starry-eyed, I might have noticed that his representatives had managed to get in two plugs for Continental Airlines and some image-building by reference to Six's "extensive oil properties in Colorado, Wyoming and Utah" while I was said to be "making a movie" beginning in July. No name, just a movie. But when I'm in love, I'm oblivious to things like that.

Six and I honeymooned briefly at the Beverly Hills Hotel. In California I looked for a temporary rental and finally decided that Jean Simmons and Stewart Granger's house would be home for me and the kids while I was filming. Six would spend long weekends with us.

Meanwhile, Leland Hayward was assembling a two-hour TV production to be shown simultaneously on CBS- and NBC-TV. It was to celebrate the fiftieth anniversary of the founding of the Ford Motor Company. The talent already signed included Mary Martin, Edward R. Murrow, Marian Anderson, Burr Tillstrom's and Fran Allison's Kukla, Fran and Ollie, Wally Cox, Rudy Vallee, Eddie Fisher, Teddy Wilson, Howard Lindsay, Dorothy Stickney and Bill Lawrence of the New York *Times*. What Leland envisioned was for Mary and me to do a medley of our thirty-five big songs. We also did other things on the show, but the medley is what people remember.

I loved the idea. From the time Mary had sent Broadway spinning with "My Heart Belongs to Daddy" in *Leave It to Me*, I'd admired her. As she became more successful, people with verbal diarrhea had periodically spread the word we were feuding. The truth was that we admired and respected each other and welcomed this opportunity to work together.

In staging our segment of the show, Clark Jones, the director, placed Mary in front of a poster from *South Pacific* and me in front of one from *Call Me Madam*. From there we walked over to two stools set against a plain background and he just let us sing. The simplicity of the concept had such impact that everybody copied us. Every television variety show that you watched after our appearance had the star and guest sitting on two barstools singing medleys, but we did it first.

A funny thing happened the night of the show, which, by the way, was live. I remember that at one point Richard Halliday, Mary's late husband, brought this huge basket of flowers to my dressing room and said, "Ethel, you may look at this for three minutes. Then I have to take it to Mary, Marian Anderson, Dorothy Stickney and Fran Allison."

Because that's how the card read. What had happened was that one of Henry Ford II's new secretaries had goofed. Instead of sending a big basket of flowers to each girl, she had sent one basket and put all our names on the card.

That killed me. After the telecast, Mr. Ford gave a big party at the Sert Room of the Waldorf-Astoria. As soon as I got a chance I made my way to this man who had spent a mint on the show and this shindig at the Waldorf and I said to him, "You know, you're pretty chintzy." He looked startled. He didn't have any idea what I was talking about. "One bouquet for five ladies," I said. "How tacky can you be?" Would you believe that after all the money he'd laid out, he looked embarrassed. Well, he did.

The reaction to the show was fantastic. Across the country 60 million people watched. During the telecast customers at 21 stood in the lobby applauding the screen. The usually staid New York *Times* began its review by repeating, "Terrific! Terrific!" Decca released an album. One side read, "Mary Martin and Ethel Merman," the other "Ethel Merman and Mary Martin"; but however it read, it sold 200,000 copies the first ten days of release. Arthur Murray offered to donate $50,000 to the American Theatre Wing if we'd repeat our stint on his show. We refused. But twenty-four years later we decided to do it again.

I made a quick trip to Hollywood before flying Continental to Stapleton Field outside Denver, where my husband and reporters greeted me. We picked up my luggage, on which I'd paid eighty dollars in excess baggage charges, and set out for Troutdale in the Pines, a mountain lodge we'd rented for the summer. There I found Ethel Jr., Bobby, their governess, our black poodle Midnight, a parakeet and the two long-tailed cockatoos Charlie Cushing had given the kids. They'd all traveled by train, and outside Chicago the air conditioning had failed. Frustrated by the heat, the cockatoos tore out all the feathers from their long drooping tails. They were awful-looking, but Ethel Jr. didn't love them any less, insisting the tails would grow back, and I'll be darned if they didn't.

Six and the kids got on fine considering he'd never had children of his own and they were at an age when accepting a new father figure is difficult. Both Ethel Jr. and Bobby liked Colorado. Ethel naturally loved any place where there were chipmunks, black squirrels and all kinds of odd things running loose. And even Bobby, who leaned toward theater and music, enjoyed going when Six took him hunting and fishing.

When I married I had no intention of retiring. I still wanted to make movies and appear on television occasionally. I had given twenty years to the theater and had loved doing it. Now its demands were beyond what I was willing to give. During the seventeen months I had played in *Call Me Madam* I had had only ten days off. I knew I might eventually miss Broadway, but as a bride I felt my place was in Denver where Six was. I felt this so strongly I turned down *The Last Resorts*, a show for which Irving Berlin was to write the score. What was the point in being married if Six and I were to be separated three-quarters of the time?

I settled into the mountain lodge we'd rented until our new house was ready. It was a two-story stone job that I nicknamed "Uncle Tom's Cabin" in honor of its owner. Among its charms were a large living room, a big open fireplace and a patio that overlooked the mountain range. We were high up in Denver—the Mile-High City—so the air seemed crystalline compared to the smog of California and the smaze of New York.

There was a friendliness about the people that made me feel entirely at home. We belonged to both the Denver and the Cherry Hills country clubs. Almost immediately I was asked to head the Christmas Seal drive that year. And everyone was eager to entertain us in their homes.

There wasn't any night life to speak of, but I'd spent enough time at the Stork and El Morocco so I didn't mind. I made lots of casual acquaintances. A couple of girls—Helen Webb and Geraldine "Gerry" Coors, the ex-wife of Bill Coors, the beer tycoon—became real pals of mine. I still see them whenever either one comes to New York.

My greatest interest was in the twenty-eight-room house at 26 Sunset Drive, which we bought for $79,000 after some opposition. The Denver *Post* said the objections had nothing to do with the fact that I was Jewish (which I don't happen to be) or that I made my living on the wicked, wicked stage (which it isn't). The neighbors, according to the *Post*, just weren't crazy about having Six for a neighbor.

The expenditures for furnishings were small, since I had shipped out everything from my ten-room New York duplex and put it into storage until remodeling was completed. The improvements were minor—a modern counter for the kitchen, a special "Ike's Corner" in the library and a rumpus room for Ethel Jr. and Bobby. In addition to the furniture, I'd brought along my paintings, including the Dufy, Renoir and Monet.

One good thing seemed to follow another in those early days. Some first-person magazine pieces that Pete Martin and I put together for the *Saturday Evening Post* were published in hard cover. Later in the year Edward R. Murrow invaded the house with all his cables to show TV viewers how I'd settled down as a Cherry Hills matron. When his crew dirtied my aquamarine carpet in the huge living room, I screamed like any housewife until CBS paid for cleaning it.

I had hardly got my bearings when one of the organizations asked whether I'd do a concert at the Red Rock open-air amphitheater with the Denver Symphony Orchestra. It seemed like a friendly way to introduce myself. So Mom and Pop—he overcame his fright of flying—caught a plane and came to visit. In addition to other standards that I'd introduced, I sang "You're Just in Love" with Fred Nesbitt, a local baritone. Then for an encore we did "International Rag." It was quite thrilling performing before thousands of my neighbors under the stars in that beautiful natural theater.

A week later Charles Meeker Jr. and Franz Allers of the Texas State Fair Musicals and Edward K. Green of MCA visited Denver and made me a proposition. They wanted me to bring in my own show—Russell Nype, George Murphy, the Wiere Brothers and the Harmonica Rascals—for ten days at the Texas State Fair in Dallas. Six thought it was a great idea and I really got excited about working with Russell and George again.

I appealed to Roger Edens for special arrangements, including a good opener. He sent "I'm Just a Lady with a Song." It went:

Who am I
What am I doing here?
Am I where I don't belong?
Well, don't bother what my name is
My only claim to fame is
I'm just a lady with a song.
I don't know
Nothing from Op'ra
Op-e-ra is out of my class.
My voice is loud and throaty,
Resembles a coyote
The critics call it pure brass.
But singing songs is my business
And I sing where fate allows,
At Minsky's or the Palace
And here I am in Dallas

Competing with the pigs and cows.
Don't expect Jeanette MacDonald,
That would be dismally wrong.
But if you find my songs are right for you,
I'll stay and sing all night for you.
I'm just a lady
Whose voice is good and graty
I'm just a lady with a song.

After that I went to Hollywood for the *Colgate Comedy Hour* with my old pal Jimmy Durante. But apparently nobody had learned anything from my success on the Ford jubilee show. Because when I sang "I Got Rhythm," they loused it up with sight gags—crystal shattering, pictures falling, blah, blah, blah.

I wasn't particularly upset, because my real interest lay in getting my home set up. I really believed this marriage was going to be a happy one. Six was an extroverted guy who knew how to pay a girl a compliment. He took an interest in remodeling our new home and, surprisingly to me, encouraged me to accept short-term engagements. It seemed to me I had managed to combine the best of two worlds.

The Owen mansion at 26 Sunset Drive had been built in 1927. It was a graystone Tudor, a beautiful thing. Inside there was a lot of hand-carved oak. The people before us had used a beige scheme, but I had the walls redone in turquoise and brightened up the place with lots of colorful chintz.

I dearly loved the acres and acres of landscaping and to this day I regret selling it. At the end everything was split down the middle. I sometimes wish I'd bought Six's half and used the house as a summer place. There's no more beautiful spot in the world than Colorado. And Lord knows, the house was big enough for plenty of guests. The only problem would have been help. Who wants to work today? So maybe it's just as well I let it go.

I was surprised how much I enjoyed living just an ordinary, normal life where I didn't have to worry about saving my strength for an evening performance and where I felt like hopping out of bed before eight in the morning to see my kids off to school and Six off to the office.

I never made any pretense of being a cook. Oh, I could manage eggs in an emergency, but I received a lot of satisfaction planning menus, seeing that the laundry got sent out and keeping an eye on household expenses. Luckily Denver is barbecue country and Six had learned to simmer a barbecue sauce about the same time he learned to handle guns. Of course the cook could have done everything, but it was a wonderful ego booster when my friends visited and told Six how delicious some specialty he'd whipped up was. We had two grills outside, and whenever weather permitted, barbecuing added to the occasion.

If anyone asked me whether I didn't hanker for a new Broadway show, I could honestly give them a flat no. For the first time in my adult life I wasn't pregnant, ill or expected at the theater. Unless you've spent the greater part of two decades under those conditions, you can't understand what a luxury that freedom can be.

Early in 1954 Bobby, Ethel Jr., Six and I flew to Hawaii for a three-week vacation. Upon our return I began preparing to repeat the role of Reno Sweeney in the television version of *Anything Goes*. Jule Styne, the songwriter and producer, had persuaded Leland Hayward, then an executive at NBC-TV, to present a tab version of it on the *Colgate Comedy Hour*. They signed Frank Sinatra and Bert Lahr for the Gaxton and Moore roles. Then the book was cut to an hour and set in the 1920s, with flappers and bootleggers giving it a mildly campy air. Since Billy Gaxton hadn't stressed his singing, three of Cole's standards from other shows were added for Frank. It was twenty years since I'd created the role, but everything melded together, resulting in one of the first successful book musicals ever done in the then-new medium.

My other professional activity that year was returning to 20th Century-Fox to capitalize on the success of *Call Me Madam* with a vaudeville story, *There's No Business Like Show Business*. Irving Berlin supplied the score and Sol Siegel and Walter Lang were back in the same capacities they'd filled in bringing *Madam* to the screen. Dan Dailey played my husband. Our kids were Mitzi Gaynor, Donald

O'Connor and Johnny Ray. There was a love interest between Donald and Marilyn Monroe. But with all due respect to Marilyn, nobody could understand this combination. Mitzi and Donald would have made much more sense, but Marilyn was just too much glamour for Donald. It was like Eddie Fisher and Elizabeth Taylor in real life. The chemistry wasn't right. Casting Johnny Ray as the son who entered the priesthood didn't ring true either. Mitzi, on the other hand, was well cast. She called me "Mom" in the picture and "Mom" off the set. She and I had one of the new numbers Irving composed for the show, "A Sailor's Not a Sailor Till a Sailor's Been Tattooed." It went over pretty well. When the film had its Denver premiere, Mitzi and her husband, Jack Bean, came to stay with us. After that when I'd go to Hollywood she always gave a party for me at her home on Arden Drive. But time passes and you grow apart. I haven't seen her very often in recent years.

Somehow *There's No Business Like Show Business* didn't work out as well as *Madam*. Maybe it's because the story included all the predictable situations that film musicals always used, maybe it was because it hadn't been perfected on Broadway. In any case, I didn't make another film for almost ten years.

In between engagements, I just enjoyed having my home and entertaining. I also loved jumping into my four-seater Thunderbird— the first of its kind in Denver—with its Colorado license number 6, to dash to the supermarket or meet a friend for luncheon. In the beginning, of course, I was something of an oddity around the neighborhood. Ethel Jr. came home from bicycle riding one day and told me that while she and another child were tooling around the girl said, "I hear Ethel Merman lives around here." Ethel Jr. replied, "Yeah, she's my mom." I asked what her friend had said. "Nothing," Ethel Jr. told me. "She just fell off her bicycle."

Well, nobody was falling off bicycles anymore because of my presence. I'd more or less settled in. Syndicated columnist Leonard Lyons came to Colorado, where his son Warren was to appear in a show the kids were putting on at the Silver Spur Ranch camp. On the way he stopped off to see us and wrote a column setting down

his impression of life with the Sixes. It gives you an idea of the way
we lived then:

> There was a Madison Ave. sunset—that is, charcoal-gray
> clouds in a pink sky—when the plane landed in Denver.
> And time too for reunions with old friends, the Palmer
> Hoyts and the Robert Sixes. Mrs. Six is Ethel Merman—
> or, as she prefers it, Ethel Merman is Mrs. Six.
>
> The reigning star of Broadway's musicals is an accepted
> responsible member of the local community. "Look at
> me," she said, "chairman of the Easter Seal Drive, Com-
> munity Chest—dogs, cats, squirrels—the works." She led
> me on a tour of the large house, and was proud in showing
> the children's rooms and their large playroom. "Me?" she
> said. "When I was their age I slept in a hall in Astoria."
>
> She likes living here, she said, and likes the life in the
> West. "No nightclubs, and in bed early," she said. "Night
> life? There are parties at people's homes. Nice people.
> They invite me because I'm Bob's wife, different from
> New York—where it's 'Come-and-bring-your-piano-
> player.' Nice people." Six is head of Continental Airways.
> They'd met at the first anniversary party of *Call Me
> Madam*. Miss Merman had forgotten that her percentage
> deal with the show made her co-host of the party. "I kept
> hollerin', 'Drink up, everybody.' "
>
> Six, who is 6 ft. 2, had his gloves on and was busy at
> the charcoal broiler in the garden. In the distance were
> ranges of Rockies. "And wait'll you see how Ethel cooks,"
> said Six. "She made the soup." It was Soup Argentine,
> and she beamed at our approval. Then she rang the ser-
> vants' bell, and shouted, "Somebody's in the candy store."
>
> We had barbecued chicken and rice and beans, and
> she'd shopped for the strawberry tarts. Six, she said,
> hadn't asked her to retire from Broadway. "She can do a
> show any time she wants to," he said. But he'll not com-
> mute to New York. Hollywood, only three hours away by
> air, is easier. They'd been visiting in Hollywood a few
> days earlier, and returned only for the minor surgery she
> needed. Her recovery was speedy and complete.

"We sailed to Catalina, the Bogarts and us," said Ethel. "We just anchored there, and signaled to each other. Signaled. Bogey'd yell across the water. 'Hey, Ethel, got a loaf of bread?' Then he'd come over in his little putt-putt boat for the bread. Yes, bread."

We entered the living room, and she played her newest Decca album, "Memories—from the Gay 90's to the Roaring 20's." Her eyes had a starry, faraway look as she rocked to the rhythm of the songs. She hummed along to "He Was Her Man and He Done Her Wrong," then said, "Get this corny write-off," and joined in the finish of the song. Six beamed proudly. "It's sing-along music," he said. "Makes for community singing, with Ethel as the bouncing ball."

Dusk was settling over the Rockies, and it was time to leave. The last songs of the album were George M. Cohan's "45 Minutes from Broadway." Ethel sang along, but the transplanted Broadway star sang it "45 Hours from Broadway." Then it ended, with the record and the hostess singing "Give My Regards to Broadway," and the Sixes drove me to the airport.

In a corner of the room I'd noticed two copies of *Variety*. And as we drove through Ethel Merman's new home-city, Denver, I remembered a story about Lilyan Tashman, who had said that stardom palled and expressed a wish to get far away from all show business. "I want to retire to a faraway desert island," Miss Tashman had sighed. "A beautiful desert island, with a stretch of sea and sand and moonlight—just enough moonlight to read *Variety* by."

That was Leonard Lyons' impression. For a while I thought I'd found a peaceful, happy existence. On the surface it looked as if everything were working out great. It was wonderful for a while. Then secretly I began to be troubled by certain things.

XXV

LET ME EXPLAIN the facts of life as any female star—stage, screen, nightclub or television—knows them. Most of us enjoy an earning capacity that even highly paid executives can hardly hope to equal. So stars expect to share expenses with their husbands. During World War II, for instance, I contributed the major portion toward running our home because Bob Levitt was not a rich man and his army pay could not begin to cover expenses. But I loved him dearly and didn't mind doing it.

With Six, even though headlines blared, "MERMAN MARRIES MIL-LIONAIRE," I expected to contribute a fair share. Why not? I was earning big money from TV and films. I'd collected approximately $6000 weekly during the run of *Call Me Madam* and $150,000 for the film, plus my Dallas earnings. Presumably, if I decided to return to Broadway, I would make as much as if not more than in *Madam*. So fair is fair. I figured if I wanted luxuries I ought to pay for them.

I continued to feel that way until the early part of 1956, when I began sensing a change in Six. I wasn't accepting as many engagements, so that I could be in Denver with the children and him more of the time. But he would go to New York on business, which was all right. I could understand that. The trouble was that he would promise to phone at a certain hour. I'd rush home to wait for the call and it wouldn't come.

First I'd worry. Then I'd get upset. What was I doing sitting there in a big house twiddling my thumbs? Then I'd get irritated. So I'd try tracking him down. Because he was traveling on the edge of the jet set, I had a pretty good idea of the places he might be. But when I'd call him at the Ritz Towers he'd get angry and hang up on me. That was my punishment. Well, who needed that? I'd gone along with him as long as I was treated properly, but when I began to be mistreated I thought the devil with this.

To begin at the beginning, when we bought "Six Acres," the down payment was $10,000. He was to put up his five grand and I was to match it. When that time came, he asked me to ante up the entire amount. In return he gave me a promissory note for his share, payable on a certain date. It seemed a strange way for a "millionaire" to behave, but I thought possibly his ready cash was tied up. The due date for the note came and went. Long after, at my insistence, he met his obligation with a show of bad grace.

That was only the beginning. Every month I was presented with a breakdown of expenses: "E.M.S.'s share . . . R.F.S.'s share." That's the way I was billed. The four indoor servants were paid by him and me. Somehow the gardener, Bryant Felderwerth, became my total responsibility. Or the bill from a little pharmacy located in Englewood, Colorado, was sent by Six's secretary, who broke it down so that I owed $142.64 and Six $2.58.

My children never flew to California on Continental that I wasn't billed for them. If we traveled with one child, I was expected to pick up two-thirds of the expenses. If we traveled with both children, I paid three-quarters of our expenditures.

My records show page after page, month after month how this went on. I was being drained. Six was a very selfish man. Looking back, I don't think he was capable of loving all out. I took as much as I could, and then I began to ask myself why I should pay to create my own misery. If I hadn't been paying, maybe I could have swallowed his absences, thoughtlessness and greed; but when I was paying, that was a horse of a different color.

I had friends in Denver, but not a lot. The children were busy. I missed Mom and Pop terribly. But I think the capper came on February 14, 1956, when I received voucher number 15194 from Continental Airlines, Inc., Stapleton Airfield, Denver, Colorado. Under description of expenses incurred was the following notation: "To charge you for the moth flakes for storing rug, received in 1953 until February 10, 1956."

That same day I wrote out check number 15981, clearing myself of my indebtedness—seventy-three cents.

I still refused to recognize my mistake. That spring, since Six was spending more than half his time in New York, I thought it might help our marriage if I was there. I signed to play the Tallulah Bankhead part in George Kelly's old Broadway play *Reflected Glory* on *G.E. Theater* and a lonely horseplayer in *Honest in the Rain* on the *U.S. Steel Hour*. I'd always wanted to take a stab at straight acting, but truthfully I wasn't satisfied with these efforts on TV.

When Lindsay and Crouse approached me about the possibility of doing a new musical, I talked it over with Six. He was all for it, saying we could invest through our corporation, Mersix, Inc., and that since he was purchasing new planes for Continental he'd be in New York and London more than Denver anyway. A rough draft of the first act arrived the first week in August. It was promising enough for me to enroll Bobby in Hackley School at Tarrytown, New York. Ethel Jr. wanted to remain at Cherry Creek High.

On August 20, I appeared in San Francisco at the Cow Palace to entertain the Republican National Convention. Next morning at eight A.M. I flew back to Denver to get ready to go East. I'd taken an apartment at the Park Lane Hotel in New York, complete with a library that Six used as an office, and I wanted to take along such personal things as my paintings and linens to make the place homelike.

Happy Hunting was a jeep among limousines. You had to tend to business, shifting gears and feeding the gas to keep it moving when the going got rough, but if you didn't mind the bumpy ride, it got you there. Howard Lindsay and Buck Crouse's book was based on the notion that a diamond-in-the rough rich woman (me), miffed at not being invited to the Grace Kelly–Prince Rainier wedding, decided to buy her daughter (Virginia Gibson) a titled husband (Fernando Lamas), but fell in love with him herself, which, happily, left the daughter free to marry the Philadelphia lawyer (Gordon Polk) she really loved.

As an idea it seemed as promising as *Call Me Madam*. It was topical and offered me a chance to be funny and sing a lot. But the plotting and jokes turned out to be strictly pre-Depression vintage, and some of the situations, as the critics eventually pointed out, owed a good deal to *Auntie Mame* and another Broadway play, *The Happiest Millionaire*. The music was composed by a dentist named Harold Karr and the lyrics were by Matt Dubey. I had a lot of numbers. One of them, "Mutual Admiration Society," caught on and aided in promoting the show—which needed all the help it could get.

The other songs, like the plot, were jerry-built and shopworn. Abe Burrows directed. One of the chorus singers, who played a small part, later made quite a name for herself as an actress—Estelle Parsons.

We opened December 6, 1956, and ran 412 performances. Now here I go again sounding as if I'm patting myself on the back, but most critics attributed the fact that so many people were willing to shove $8.05 each under the ticket wicket to my efforts. In *The New Yorker* Wolcott Gibbs summed up by writing: "Against these chilling handicaps (for some reason, practically all the most villainous jokes and a good many of the more nerveless songs are visited on her), Miss Merman still manages to produce her customary miracle and convulse her admirers continuously. It's a great gift and, as I've said, quite inscrutable to me." And, in a large part, to me.

I wish we could draw the curtain at this point. We can't, so here goes. *Happy Hunting* rivaled *Sadie Thompson* as my most miserable theatrical experience. I had never before encountered a clique who seemed intent on trying to blow the show apart. Fernando Lamas, the leading man, proved particularly difficult. His experience in

Hollywood led him to expect the management to provide everything. Soon after we opened, Herman Bernstein, our company manager, came to me with bills for a contour chair, highball glasses and other niceties for his dressing room. Lamas had charged them to management. Herman asked, "What do we do about this?" As a part of management, I said, "We don't do anything."

That was only one of many small hassles. During a love song I was seated in a chair. Lamas was standing near me. Gradually he moved backward, upstaging me, hoping I'd turn to look at him so the audience would see only the back of my head. No way. I just sat there looking at the spot where he ought to have been and let him sing. If that was the way he wanted the scene played, that's the way I'd do it.

He killed my laughs by stepping on my lines. For my final curtain call he obstructed my entrance. When the stage manager gave him notes requesting that he keep out of my path, he ignored the orders and finally told the stage manager to stop sending them. I appealed to Equity, and the union reprimanded him for unprofessional behavior.

Another cast member, Gene Wesson, suddenly appeared on stage one night with dyed gray hair. He'd tested for the role of John Barrymore in *Too Much, Too Soon* and refused to restore his hair to its natural color because he was convinced he'd begin filming the moment a girl was signed to play Diana Barrymore. The fact that gray hair made him seem miscast in *Happy Hunting* appeared to be unimportant to him.

Then, one way or another—and I have my suspicions how—our problems found their way into Sheila Graham's Hollywood column. Miss Graham wrote that offstage Lamas and I had not spoken for many months but that relations had now deteriorated to the point where Lamas rubbed off my kisses in full view of audiences. She also added that Wesson blamed me for his being fired.

Abe Burrows solved the kissing bit for me (if possible, I wanted to kiss Lamas even less than he wanted to be kissed) by restaging the scene so I merely hugged him.

Miss Graham also reported that Lamas had been attempting to leave the show to appear with his wife, Arlene Dahl, in a nightclub act. But after *Variety* revealed that management was ready to offer Lamas his release, nothing more was heard of that.

Then on September 4 some mysterious column planter persuaded Dorothy Kilgallen that I had had a difference of opinion about the tempo of the title song with the new orchestra conductor, Irving Actman. Supposedly it had resulted in my standing center stage beating out time for Actman.

Intrigued, Shirley Eder, another columnist, sought out Actman and quoted him: "Ethel's been wonderful to me! She's the greatest woman I know. If I ever find out how those rumors of our being unfriendly started, I'll sue. I swear I will. No one could be better to me than Ethel Merman. I love her and everybody loves her."

Not everyone loved me, but I appreciated the sentiment. I also appreciated little gestures that let me know how other co-workers felt. In the midst of charges and countercharges that swirled around me, a small package was delivered to my dressing room. Inside was a gold St. Christopher's medal. With it was the following note:

September 24, 1957

Dear Ethel,

   This is in observance of nothing at all in particular— but I *do* wish to say that this engagement with you has been the most rewarding and completely happy experience I've had in the theater in a lifetime, and I anticipate nothing nicer in the hereafter. May St. Christopher protect you always.

Love,
Bill

Bill was Bill Fields, white-haired and stately, who was our press agent. Although he was too gentlemanly to refer to the siege against me, he obviously wanted to boost my morale whether it needed it or not.

Closing on November 30, 1957, we had grossed $3,200,000 on the $500,000 investment. Profitable or not, needless to say, *Happy Hunting* was not my favorite show.

Relations with Six had improved during the Broadway run. Partly, I think, because he enjoyed the reflected glory. Also because

I made a point of defining myself in wifely terms in interviews. "When I slam the dressing-room door behind me, I retire from show business," I told one writer. "I am just Mrs. Robert Six until the next performance." It helped too that I was busy and not sitting alone in a twenty-eight-room house.

When *Happy Hunting* closed, I became my own marriage counselor and decided to keep busy accepting frequent TV appearances on both coasts with such performers as Perry Como, Eddie Fisher and Dinah Shore.

After a special with Frank Sinatra, Mike Todd gave a surprise birthday party for his wife, Elizabeth Taylor. Mike and Liz drove up from Palm Springs. She arrived wearing a babushka, blouse and skirt, but nothing could detract from her beauty.

I remember as if it were yesterday how Mike at one point in the evening reached into his pocket and pulled out a diamond and emerald earring, one of the most beautiful I'd ever seen. It was typical of him that it wasn't wrapped. He handed it to Liz, saying, "Now if you like it, the other one is yours."

She liked it. So he dug around in his pocket until he came up with the mate. A fantastic man!

It was the last time I was ever to see him alive. That summer his plane hit a mountain peak near Grants, New Mexico, and he was gone. I couldn't believe that anyone so much larger than life could pass. And I thought of him every time I wore a pair of earrings he had given me while I was starring in *Something for the Boys*. Each was a gold star holding a star. On the back of one was engraved "To Ethel Merman"; on the other, "SFB, 1943." Yes, they went in the robbery too, but one thing the thieves couldn't take were my memories of this great showman.

I think Mike was the love of Liz's life, just as Bob Levitt was of mine. I remember after Mike's death, at the time Liz had married Eddie Fisher, I went with them to MCA's private screening room to see *Bell, Book and Candle* and *The Last Hurrah*. In *The Last Hurrah* there was a scene in which Spencer Tracy was shown in a casket. Liz just went. She began to sob and ran into the powder room. After she'd been there quite a while, Eddie asked me to see whether she was all right. I found her completely destroyed. I ran cold water to wet towels and patted her eyes to ease them. Then, I have to admit, I did a sneaky thing. I'd always wondered whether those thick velvety eyelashes were her own. So I looked. And I can assure you— they're all hers.

In 1958, even though I kept busy in television I realized this wasn't helping my relationship with Six. It was cold potatoes. One day I received a call from Arthur Laurents, who wanted to use Gypsy Rose Lee's memoirs as the basis for a show. The conversation went something like this:

"I want to do a show. But I don't want to do the usual Ethel Merman musical," he said.

"Neither do I. I want to act."

"How far are you willing to go?"

"As far as you want me to," I told him. "Nobody's ever given me the chance before."

That's how I came to appear in the role that I consider the pinnacle of my career. I loved the idea of doing a role like this from the moment Laurents described the character. He sent me a draft of the script and I knew immediately that Mamma Rose was an actress's dream. Ever since Josh Logan had given me the little trophy inscribed "To "Sarah Bernhardt Jr." I had known I could act. Now I'd have a chance to prove it. In most musicals there is a hairline story, a thin plot and thinner characterizations. *Gypsy* was a full-fledged play. It could have dispensed with the music. I didn't think twice before giving my word.

David Merrick and Leland Hayward were to produce. They agreed to make me a partner, receiving 5 percent until initial costs were recouped and 7 percent of the gross thereafter. They were also to pay my living expenses, which were to exceed no more than 1 percent of the gross.

Jerome Robbins, who had been a chorus boy in *Stars in Your Eyes* and choreographer of *Call Me Madam*, was to direct and do the dances. Jule Styne had signed to compose the music and Stephen Sondheim the lyrics.

The boys' intent, of course, was to produce a drama-with-music, not a musical comedy. They alternated a panorama of small-time show business with the life struggles of Mamma Rose and her two offspring—Baby June, later June Havoc, and Baby Louise or Gypsy Rose Lee.

Around Christmas we all went to Jule Styne's apartment on East Sixty-third Street. We sat on the floor while Jule played and Steve Sondheim sang the songs for us. I burst into tears. Jule had written some big hits, but these were dramatic songs with dimension. He was reaching out, stretching himself just as I wanted to do. I had eight songs. Not one was included to give me a show-stopper. Not one was intended to have a sock ending. Seven of them were placed so that we intentionally killed the applause, which would have broken the mood. On the first song, I exited after "But not Rose." Blackout. Period. In the kitchen scene we worked against applause. Every number was like that. I was all for it because doing it that way made the impact of the whole production so much stronger. But on "Rose's Turn" at a certain point, Sandra Church, who played Louise (Gypsy), appeared upstage while I was beating my brains out. And I said, "Look, I have to have a finish for this. I've worked too hard. I demand I have a finish—'for me, for me, for MEEEE!' Vooooom! Then let her come in."

In most of my shows I'd had a big build-up for my entrance. In *Gypsy* I came stalking down the aisle like a "jungle mother," wearing my old coat with the big collar and the belt way down below my waist and the funny hat with the big bow. I was carrying my dog, Chowsie, swinging the big old pocketbook and looking most unattractive as I interrupted rehearsal, shouting, "Sing out, Louise!" It was new and it was terrific and it immediately told you what kind of a person Mamma Rose was. I don't say this just because I created her, but Mamma Rose is the most memorable character ever portrayed in any musical, with all due respect to Nellie Forbush, Liza Doolittle, or any of the rest.

We started rehearsing on February 11, 1959. Sandra Church was the original Louise, Lane Bradbury was June and Mort Marshall was Mr. Goldstone. Maria Karnilova, Faith Dane and Chotzi Foley played three tough strippers—Tessie Tura, Mazeppa and Electra.

Various people were considered for Herbie. Among them were

Victor Jory, Robert Alda, Wendell Corey and Lew Parker. Any of them could have played the part well. But there was one guy born to do it—Jack Klugman. I was there the day he read for the role. He'd never been in a musical and wasn't sure he could do it. At that audition he kept stumbling and finally told us to get someone else. I knew he could do it. So I got up there and told him, "Come on, Jack. I know you can cut it." Then I began to sing our duet "Small World." He said later that I showed such confidence in him he felt he had to come through for me. By the time we finished the song, he had the part. If there ever was a Herbie, he was it. He was rough and had such thrust. We were so right together.

We arrived in Philadelphia with enough material for a show and a half. Opening night, April 11, the final curtain fell around one A.M. Some of Arthur Laurents' beautiful play had to be condensed. Other bits went, including Jack's solo, "Nice She Ain't." It was decided to extend the out-of-town engagement for a week's further polishing. Sometimes tempers flared. But to my surprise, the *Inquirer* ran a story about trouble between Jerry Robbins and me. Winchell carried an item to the effect that I'd walked out of a meeting with the producers saying, "I've had it." Dorothy Kilgallen predicted that my "backstage battles" with Jerry "threatened to become more colorful than those between Dolores Gray and Michael Kidd about *Destry.*"

All false, totally false, but those are the things that get printed about you when you are in the public eye. There is no way of stopping them. Any action you take only spreads rumors further.

Along with Josh Logan and George Abbott, Jerry was one of my favorite directors. I called him "Teacher." Learning "Rose's Turn," my soliloquy, I followed in back of him as he walked through the number, copying his moves and gestures. He also taught me to sit still and get my effects. I'd never been presented to better advantage. I loved working with him and if I ever do a straight play, he's one director I'd trust.

In the view of the older generation though, I was crazy to get involved in the show. They felt the book was too serious and the girls not pretty enough. And what the hell was Ethel Merman doing playing a character named Rose when the title of the show was *Gypsy?*

After the tryout in Philadelphia, Gypsy came backstage and said, "You made me cry."

I was pleased, because many people thought Rose was selfish and self-centered. But the way I saw it was that she wanted everything for her two girls. It wasn't that *she* wanted to be a star. She says in "Rose's Turn," "It was for you, June . . . It wasn't for me, Herbie." Only after the kids didn't need her anymore did she say that now it was her turn—"You either got it or you ain't"—but that was because she was very upset. Mamma Rose sacrificed her whole life, gave up the love of her life for Louise and June. That's why when I played her, I got sympathy. People cried.

For our New York opening on May 21 Gypsy sent me a huge bouquet with a card reading, "Dear Ethel, How mother would have loved seeing you tonight. Love, Gypsy."

When Gypsy came backstage, she informed a reporter, "I told Ethel to drink lots of milk and stay healthy. She's going to be my annuity." Gypsy probably didn't notice that her bouquet along with everyone else's was sitting in the hall. I'm allergic to flowers, much as I enjoy them. They're the worst way to keep me in trim.

Among scores of telegrams, there were two memorable ones:

LOVE AND KISSES FROM GUESS WHO? NOT FERNANDO LAMAS.
NOT GENE WESSON. HOWARD AND BUCK.

The other might have given me shivers if I had possessed psychic powers. It read:

DEAREST ETHEL, GLAD YOU ARE BACK AND IF YOU NEED AN
UNDERSTUDY I KNOW WHERE YOU CAN GET ONE. GREAT
GOOD LUCK FOR THE BIGGEST HIT EVER. LOVE, FREDDIE BRIS-
SON.

He was married to Rosalind Russell.

The night of the Broadway opening Benay Venuta was such a nervous wreck I had to get away from her. "I'm all sweat," columnist Louis Sobol reported her saying in the lobby. "You'd think it was my opening." When Louis inquired about my nerves, Benay said, "Ethel? Do you know what she was doing a couple of hours ago? Sitting at home polishing the jewelry that she was going to wear after the opening. She's got no nerves."

Over the years I'd had some flattering things said about my talent, but nothing like what my work as Mamma Rose brought. Tom Donnelly of the Washington *Daily News* called the character "a four dimensional portrait. Lynn Fontanne, Helen Hayes, Judith Anderson and Dame Edith Evans will have to move over," he said.

Newsweek's man wrote, "Even if *Gypsy* were not the slickest and most satisfying musical of the 1958–1959 season, which it resoundingly is, the show would be memorable for the emergence of Ethel Merman as one of the first ladies of the stage, with or without music."

In June the theater critics honored me for giving the best performance by an actress in a musical comedy. But when it came time to pass out the Tonys, the American Theatre Wing ignored *Gypsy*. My friend Mary Martin won for Maria von Trapp in *The Sound of Music*. When Cheryl Crawford attempted to offer me condolences, I cracked her up by shrugging it off with "How are you going to buck a nun?"

Since the Wing had split the award for best musical between *Fiorello* and *The Sound of Music*, a lot of people got up in arms at the committee for not splitting the one for best performance by an actress in a musical. I didn't care too much. I'd never depended on awards anyway. You know in your heart how satisfied you are with your work. And I'd been so confident about *Gypsy* that when I came to New York to negotiate the contract in December of 1958 I had signed a year's lease for a home away from home at the Park Lane Hotel.

It never struck me more forcefully than during the second half of 1959 how little the public knows of what is really happening in the life of a public personality, in spite of all the press coverage. On the surface I had every reason to be happy. I was playing my favorite role in a show that was grossing $82,000 a week, and every night waves of enthusiasm and love came rolling over the footlights at me from the audience.

My daughter had been elected to the National Honor Society and was planning to attend Colorado College in Colorado Springs. I had had the foresight to have a clause written into my contract giving me the right to be absent the night of June 3 to attend her graduation from Cherry Creek High School. In order to make it, Bobby and I caught a plane to Chicago. There we switched to another one and sat up all night in order to arrive in time for the ceremonies. Afterward, we repeated the happy ordeal so that I could be on stage the next night. While we were all together, Six and I promised the kids to take them to Montego Bay in Jamaica for their Christmas vacations. I had reason to feel that "Everything's Coming Up Roses" could still be my theme song.

I think that it was about that time that Ethel surprised me by asking whether she could call herself Six instead of Levitt. Then a year later, Bobby decided he'd call himself Six too. They wanted us all to be one family. After the kids began going by the name of Six, people assumed my then husband had adopted them, but he never did.

In reality, everything was about to go wrong. In mid-August I came off the stage after "Mamma's Turn" with an odd feeling in my throat. I could talk, but it felt as if I had a scrim over my larnyx. Even though I'd done two shows that day, a group of us went someplace in Greenwich Village to hear a Dixieland jazz band.

When I woke up the following morning, I didn't hurt or feel bad, but I had this thing, this funny feeling. I arranged to see Dr. Stuart Craig, a great throat man. He took one look at me and said, "You'll be out of the show a week. You have burst a blood vessel in your throat."

I told him he was balmy. He didn't agree. He just phoned a larnyx specialist in my presence and said he was sending me over to be examined. No details. I went to the specialist, who examined me and said, "Miss Merman, you have burst a blood vessel in your throat."

I wanted to know what I could do about it. There was no treatment, he said. I wasn't to sing or talk loud, and I wasn't to whisper either, since that caused the worst strain. I was to murmur when I had to talk. Mostly, I was to rest my voice.

My understudy, Jane Romano, went on for me and did a good job. Bill Fields alerted some of the press, who gave her the Cinderella treatment. But somebody forgot to explain to her that without Bill's drum beating none of those feature writers and columnists would have been in the audience to witness her performance. She read the notices and instead of being grateful she demanded an increase in her salary. The management refused to grant it and Jane left the show. I was sorry to see her go, but I still expected that she would eventually make a hit. Unhappily, not long after she developed leukemia and passed on while still quite young.

While I was appearing in *Gypsy*, something I'd looked forward to for years materialized. I began working with Roger Edens again. In November of 1959 NBC signed him to produce a TV special, *Ethel Merman on Broadway*.

The thinking at the network was that they were riding a sure thing. I was at the peak of my Broadway success. Roger was, I felt, the man who best understood how to use my talent to obtain maximum effect. They chose for our director Gregg Garrison, a man who had directed and is still directing some of the most imaginative musical shows on television. They gave me not one but three leading men—Tab Hunter, Tom Poston and Fess Parker. All were very hot then. We had to be a smash. Right?

Wrong! We laid a giant dinosaur's egg. Everybody had a different reason for how he felt, but nobody liked us. They said we crammed too much material into the hour. The audience heard only snippets of my hits instead of full songs. The chemistry of the casting was wrong. We really didn't have an idea for a show. Our idea was too sophisticated, blah, blah, blah.

The point is that in show business it takes more than hard work, experience and talent. You can have the best intentions, a good idea, all the know-how, *but* if you don't have luck nothing else helps. That's why when I'm asked how to succeed in show business I always say I haven't the foggiest.

WHEN BOBBY AND I had flown to Denver for Ethel's graduation, Six and I had promised to take the kids to Montego Bay for Christmas. In the meantime, things began falling apart. We began disagreeing more and more frequently.

Even though we'd decided to go our separate ways, we agreed to spend the Christmas holidays in Jamaica for Ethel and Bobby's sakes. I will say this for Six: however unhappy he made me, he was decent enough not to spoil the holiday for my children. I don't think either of us enjoyed the vacation, but that wasn't the point.

Still, there had been some talk of a reconciliation. Then in early March of 1960, Six sent me a letter and clipping from Doris Lilly's column in the New York *Post*. A paragraph in the column read:

> If Bob Six and Ethel Merman get back together it will surprise a lot of people. Bob is in Honolulu having dinner with a beautiful lady and between courses sends flowers to another beauty in business. Meantime, Ethel has been seen around with a youthful theatrical director.

Knowing what I knew, I thought Six was a little off base. So I let him have it, but good. On March fourth, I sent him the following letter, which ended all talk of reconciliation:

Dear Robert—

How can you possibly have the colossal nerve to send me a clipping together with a letter from HONOLULU while you're shacking up with a broad there, and criticize me for taking a bottle of champagne on to a party from Morocco—this being the same broad you've been shacking up with all over the country?

You said in your letter to me—"you can take it from here"—well, you can do the same.

I should have signed it "The Airline Widow."

The following Christmas, I used my vacation to fly to Mexico for a quick divorce. Then on my way back I stopped off in Denver to visit my daughter, who was now Mrs. William Geary. At college she had met and married a wonderful young fellow and had decided what she wanted was to become a housewife. Christmas Day she was radiant. She cooked the kind of old-fashioned Christmas dinner I'd have had no idea how to go about preparing.

I suppose, given hindsight, I should have been more concerned about my brilliant daughter as early as the Christmas we spent in Jamaica. She was so filled with plans. She was going to accomplish everything. One day it was one thing and the next day it was another. She was going to be an actress (I have a recording of her performance in a college production of *Brigadoon* that I flew out to see), a teacher or a veterinarian. It was too much to keep track of. I attributed her frequently switched plans to high spirits, enthusiasm and the eagerness that all kids go through as they mature. It never occurred to me that these might be signals of deep confusion. I thought that day in Denver how wonderful it was that she had outgrown them. She had met Bill and now seemed happy in her new role as wife and mother-to-be.

In July, with a month's vacation coming to me, Bobby, Benay Venuta and I set out for my first long European vacation. The Rover people donated a chauffeur-driven car for us and a station wagon for our luggage. Benay wanted to see museums and churches. I was more interested in shopping and sampling the night life. Bobby

wanted to do everything, so we had a ball everywhere we went—
London, Paris, Capri, Rome, Florence, Venice, you name it.

Before my trip to Europe, I'd been active campaigning and singing
at fund-raising benefits for Richard Nixon. But when John Kennedy
was elected and Frank Sinatra asked me to entertain at the inaugural
festivities, I agreed immediately. To me that was like a command
performance. You don't say no to the President of the United States
any more than you do to the Queen of England or the Duke and
Duchess of Windsor. And, as I said at the time, I felt I owed it to
the Democrats to help raise funds to pay off their campaign expenses—since I'd done whatever I could to put them in debt in the
first place.

On January 20, 1961, David Merrick canceled performances of
Becket and *Gypsy* so that Sir Laurence Olivier and Anthony Quinn,
the stars of *Becket*, and Milton Rosenstock, my conductor, and I
could fly to Washington for the inaugural festivities.

I have to say right here that I know there are a lot of stories about
the terrible things David Merrick is supposed to have done to people
who have worked for him. But I take people as I find them and
David has always behaved in the most generous and considerate
fashion in our dealings. Once, in fact, a researcher from a major
weekly magazine called to talk to me about him for a cover story the
editors were doing. She kept digging for mean things David might
have done. Since I had only good memories to recall, none of my
anecdotes were included in their report.

Anyway on January 20, at LaGuardia Airport, Larry, Tony, Milton and I boarded the President's plane, *The Caroline*, and flew to
Washington.

We were taken to a little hotel on the outskirts where our evening
clothes were deposited and we went on to rehearsal at the Armory.
A blizzard had whirled in by the time we were to return to the hotel
to bathe and dress. We set out anyway, covering only three blocks in
an hour. There was nothing to do but turn around and go back or
miss the program.

I'll never forget. I was wearing a winter suit—wool skirt, match-
ing coat with fur lining and a simple blouse. That night I went on-

stage in that outfit. What an experience! Everyone seemed filled with hope, and I still remember the young President's handsome face as I sang "Everything's Coming Up Roses" to him.

Later Joe Kennedy took over one of the fashionable restaurants in Washington. Almost everyone but Larry, Tony, Milton Rosenstock and me was formally attired. I certainly stood out among the women in my tweeds.

After the party we managed to get back to the hotel very late. Around noon the next day my phone rang. It was Larry. "Ethel, come on. Get out of bed," he said. "There are no planes running. We'll have to take a train."

We made the train, but it was so crowded that people were sitting on their valises in the aisles. Just outside Newark, in the Jersey meadows, the train got stalled for an hour. The managements of our shows kept our audiences informed about our progress and most people waited.

The curtain didn't go up on *Gypsy* until almost a quarter to ten. I just ran into my dressing room, slapped on a little makeup, voom, voom, voom—and was onstage. What a twenty-four hours that had been!

A month later to the day, I notified the Merrick office that my understudy would have to appear at the afternoon and evening performances because I was flying to Denver to see Ethel Jr. and my new granddaughter, Barbara Jean. I arrived at Idlewild (now John F. Kennedy) Airport and was notified that there would be a delay in departure time of several hours. So I hopped back into a taxi and hurried to the Imperial Theater, where I went on for the matinee.

When I arrived at Penrose Hospital and saw that beautiful baby girl, I couldn't contain myself. I got on the telephone to all my friends to say that from now on they could "Call me Grandma." Of course I had some photographs made, and anyone who exhibited real interest in the baby received a picture of her.

Then on November 10, 1962, I was doubly blessed when Bill and Ethel presented me with a grandson, Michael, a sturdy little fellow who reminded me of the days when his mother and Bobby were the same age.

C
H
A
P
T
E
R

XXVII

WITH ETHEL JR. MARRIED, Bobby at Hackley School and me with no serious romantic or domestic entanglements at the time *Gypsy*'s run ended, I agreed to make my first national tour. Why not? I wasn't elated about it, but I didn't dread it either.

It meant putting my furniture in storage and carrying all of my clothes in wardrobe trunks. Emotionally this period has to rate as a low point in my life. During the nine months I was on tour, I had no residence except the hotel at which I happened to be staying. For the first time in my life I had no permanent address.

On *Gypsy*'s closing night in New York when Jack Klugman and I sang "Together Wherever You Go," the audience demanded more. And for once I broke professional discipline. I held up my hand to silence them and asked, "Do you really want more?" The clamor was deafening. "Okay, boys, let's take it from the top," I told the orchestra—and that's what we did.

Our tour opened in Rochester on March 29, 1961, and we played Detroit, Cleveland, Boston, Toronto, then Chicago for ten weeks, and San Francisco and Los Angeles for eight each. I found Julienne Marie, who had replaced Sandra Church as Louise, much more professionally compatible; and Betty Bruce, who had been in *Something for the Boys*, was the new Tessie Tura and also my stand-by. She'd studied ballet as a child and had danced with the Metropolitan

Opera corps de ballet before coming to Broadway. She did a fast balletlike tap routine with twirls and beautiful movement. She was a very funny gal and we became pretty good cronies—which was nice, because with so strenuous a role I had no time for social life. Except for Sunday layoffs I followed a routine I'd devised. I found I needed a lot of sleep, so I'd switch off the phone, go to bed and wake up when my body told me it was rested. I never accepted a cocktail or dinner date and until after the performance I never took so much as a glass of wine.

In Boston a couple of important things occurred. During our three-week stand at the Colonial, we broke the ten-year box-office record and I met a gal who became one of my best friends. Her name was Temple Texas. She was a tall, willowy blond beauty who had been a show girl, an actress and a press agent. Now the funny thing is, she had been *my* press agent during *Gypsy*'s New York engagement, but I'd never met her. Frank Goodman, in whose office she worked, had the cockamamie idea that I didn't get along with other women. So after Temple set up the interviews, she let Frank and the other men in his office deal with me.

Well, while *Gypsy* was in Boston, Rosemary Clooney arrived in town for an engagement. Joe Schribman, Rosie's manager, and Temple, Joe's wife-to-be, came along with her. Rosie called me on a Saturday night and I invited all three of them up to my suite at the Ritz-Carlton. We had a wonderful time swapping stories and tipping a few until seven in the morning.

To give you some idea of my condition by the time they were leaving I went into the bathroom and picked up a Ritz-Carlton bath mat. I brought it out and draped it over Rosie's shoulders, assuring her she'd never find a chicer monogrammed stole.

Temple and I immediately found we had lots in common. In fact, after I broke up with Bob Six she dated him and I started going around with her ex–boy friend Steve Masters. When we got to be real pals, I tried to get her to exchange notes on the guys, but she wouldn't open her mouth.

Her escapades made me laugh a lot. And my totally organized life struck her as hilariously eccentric. In Boston, for example, I rented a two-bedroom suite. One was used for sleeping, the other for storing my wardrobe trunks. On the outside of each trunk, I'd itemized its contents:

Day Clothes:
Gray cocktail dress
Black cocktail dress
Red floral print, etc., etc., etc.
Drawer 1:
Blue accessories
White accessories, etc., etc., etc.

Each trunk was itemized in this way. I guess it was my secretarial training. After all, all my clothes were in those trunks, so to me the only sensible thing was to index the contents so that when I wanted to locate a scarf I could just consult the chart. But Temple found it unreal to be so systematic.

After she married Joe Schribman and there were children, I admired the way she reared them. Her attitude was that she refused to change her lifestyle to fit theirs. They were going to have to conform to hers. So when she had a party, the kids joined the festivities. If she was up until four A.M., the kids stayed up too. That way they slept until Temple was ready to awaken. Now people may not think that's the way to rear children, but I can testify that Temple's turned out fine.

One night in Los Angeles at about two A.M. little Owen, who was just two at the time, was sitting there looking very sleepy. I thought that this damn party couldn't be very enjoyable for him, so I sat him up on the bar and sang some songs from the score of *Gypsy* for him.

Temple is a warm, giving person, and I'll never forget the night that she and Joe and my date and I were dining at Dominick's on Beverly Boulevard. Our table was just this side of the gentlemen's room. During dinner Joe excused himself and was gone quite a long time. Suddenly we heard a thud. My escort ran into the rest room to find Joe on the floor.

We drove to Temple and Joe's home and Joe lay on the couch in the library until the ambulance arrived, but I'll never forget Temple.

This was an ex–show girl who had been around. But as Joe lay there, she just kind of walked around the grounds as if none of the rest of us were there. I heard her say, "Please don't let him die. He's a good man. Please let him live." It was all very quiet, almost under her breath, as if she were talking into the night.

At the hospital tests were made and it was discovered that Joe hadn't had a heart attack. He was allergic to alcohol. Now he's fully recovered. But I'll never forget seeing that tall blond sophisticated show girl so desperate, so vulnerable.

A few years later she passed through a personal crisis. She developed cirrhosis of the liver. For the next year she was hospitalized and bedridden. Her weight dropped to a hundred pounds. I was one of the few people she allowed to see her. Frankly, I didn't think she was going to live. Neither did she. But every time I went to Los Angeles, I visited her as often as I possibly could. Gradually her liver began to repair itself and she began regaining her health. Her first night out was when she attended my concert at the Dorothy Chandler Pavilion in Los Angeles. Now, happily, like her husband, she is fully recovered.

In Boston too I received a memento that I'll always cherish. It reads:

August 16, 1961

Dear Miss Merman—

May I tell you what infinite pleasure you gave me when I saw *Gypsy* last weekend. I have always been one of your most ardent fans, ever since *Annie*, and it was such a joy to sit once more at your feet and watch your incredibly simple and selective performance—not a superfluous gesture or elaboration. Yet you sway us with absolute certainty to whatever mood you wish to convey. I certainly compare your art to that of Edith Evans in our country. America is indeed lucky to claim you—and delight in your success.

Please don't feel you have to respond to this most inadequate line, I had to thank you.

Most sincerely,
John Gielgud

Even though I hadn't looked forward to the tour, each city brought its own surprises and increased my happiness in having undertaken it. After ten weeks in Chicago we jumped to San Francisco, where I was greeted by a five-minute standing ovation before I even opened my mouth. That response continued night after night for eight weeks. It was truly fabulous, especially in light of what was going on within my body.

I was in the bedroom of my suite at the Mark Hopkins Hotel, getting ready to visit the hairdresser for a shampoo and set. I decided to take along a sweater because I knew the air conditioning kept the salon chilly. I leaned down to take a sweater out of the lower drawer of my dresser. As I was coming up I heard something go *skurrrrcchh* and found I could hardly straighten up. I was in pain, but I kept my hair appointment.

By the time I arrived at the theater, I was in such agony I barely remember doing the performance that evening. Afterward Richard Grayson, the company manager, volunteered to take me to Dr. Morton, an osteopath on Sutter Street. Dr. Morton diagnosed my problem as locked vertebrae and gave me a treatment. The next morning I went back for another treatment before the Saturday matinee. I was uncomfortable but able to work.

By Sunday I had recovered sufficiently so that I went to Sausalito for a day's outing, but the next morning I could hardly pull myself out of bed. I went to see Dr. Morton again and he referred me to Dr. Edward Kelly, an osteopathic surgeon.

Dr. Kelly X-rayed my back and informed me that I was suffering from a herniated disc that caused irritation of the nerve root in my spine. He advised leaving the show and entering St. Francis Hospital, where they would place me in traction.

I couldn't do it. Why couldn't I do it? Because I'm a star and there is another side to stardom in addition to what the public sees. There's the obligation. This show was included in a subscription series that had sold out in part because of the drawing power of my name. Whether I hurt or not, I felt I had to go on. I couldn't let my co-workers down any more than I could let the audience down. I explained the problem to Dr. Kelly, who injected me with a combination of Xylocaine, Pontocaine, Cortisone and Hydeltrasol to relieve the pain. I was able to go out there and sing and smile and wheedle and actually forget personal discomfort as I concentrated on Mamma Rose's problems. Afterward I was extremely uncomfortable again.

Dr. Kelly in turn referred me to Dr. Malvern, a physiotherapist, who prescribed office therapy and portable traction. Since I insisted on performing six nights and two afternoons a week, Dr. Malvern had me come to his office every morning for treatment, then sent me home to bed, where I was placed in traction with stacks of pillows under my legs. I remained in that position until five in the afternoon, at which time I received a spinal injection. It was timed to dull the pain until eleven-fifteen, allowing me to finish my performance before the effects of the drugs wore off. I took the shots daily from September 19 through September 30. In that way I was able to go on stage and uphold the tradition that the show must go on, that the subscription audiences must not be disappointed.

During the San Francisco engagement David Merrick approached me about appearing in *Hello, Dolly!*, the Jerry Herman–Michael Stewart musicalization of Thornton Wilder's *The Matchmaker*, and I turned him down flat. As I told Radie Harris, who had flown to San Francisco to see the show, I felt grateful for what the theater had given me, but I also felt that I had given a lot in return. I had reached the point where I wanted to do as I pleased without having to worry about keeping a performance crisp.

Just before *Gypsy* closed in San Francisco, my son and I were walking down Geary Street and passed a shop in which I spotted a painting of some tomatoes and mushrooms that I liked. Bobby thought it was awful. But my birthday was coming up and the next day this beautifully wrapped package was delivered to me at the Mark Hopkins. Inside was the painting. The enclosed card read, "Dear Mom, Remember *you* liked it. Happy birthday. Bobby."

In other words, he still thought it stunk, but he would humor me.

For my opening in Los Angeles on October 3 Mom and Pop flew out from New York. Although the pain from the herniated disc had subsided, I experienced another kind of pain inflicted by well-meaning admirers who persisted in wanting to know why in God's name I wasn't appearing in the motion picture version of *Gypsy*.

My answer was always the same. "It's very simple. Nobody asked me." What I didn't say was that I had heard there was a deal between Freddie Brisson and Jack Warner. Freddie had bought the screen rights to the Broadway hit *A Majority of One* for his wife, Rosalind Russell, and had agreed to let Warner Brothers produce it if the studio let Roz play my role in *Gypsy*.

So I lost the part, just as I'd lost *Panama Hattie*, *DuBarry Was a Lady* and *Annie Get Your Gun*. I understand that Bette Davis, a dame who doesn't mince words any more than I do, has cited me several times as an example of a star who had been overlooked after creating a role.

It was a particular disappointment losing Mamma Rose, since she is my favorite role. Still, I had the satisfaction of knowing that I had helped create something that had become so important that a movie company was willing to pay millions of dollars to bring it to the screen. Nor do I think that the movie people did her justice. They made her too beautiful, too chic. The critics felt that too. In fact I received more good publicity by not doing the picture than I'd probably have got had I played the part.

The tour of *Gypsy* ended in St. Louis around Christmas, having grossed $2,473,626.61.

I had intended to play Rose in London during the spring of 1962, but at the last minute Jack Klugman found it impossible to go, and Julienne Marie's husband (the writer, before she married James Earl Jones) wouldn't allow her to leave the country. I didn't want to attempt a production with a British cast, so I signed to make my Las Vegas debut.

Before I could get my act together, I received another offer. If Jack Warner and Mervyn LeRoy didn't think I was widely enough known for *Gypsy*, producer-director Stanley Kramer thought I'd do perfectly as a leading slapstick comedienne in *It's a Mad, Mad, Mad, Mad World*. For the cast Kramer signed up practically all the comedians in films, about ninety in all, including Jimmy Durante, Milton Berle, Sid Caesar, Buster Keaton, Terry-Thomas, Phil Silvers,

Buddy Hackett, Mickey Rooney, Jonathan Winters, Edward Everett Horton, Dick Shawn, Eddie "Rochester" Anderson, Carl Reiner, Marvin Kaplan, Jerry Lewis, Paul Ford, Dorothy Provine, Edie Adams, Peter Falk, Jim Backus, Barry Chase, Ben Blue, Arnold Stang, the Three Stooges, Don Knotts, Andy Devine, Joe E. Brown and even Spencer Tracy.

In writing the script, William and Tania Rose used the device of several greedy groups trying to outwit and outrace one another to reach a cache of $350,000 in stolen funds. On this plot line, the Roses and Kramer effortlessly worked in countless classic slapstick bits that they had lifted from the greatest silent comedies, and they managed to come out with a picture that made a comment upon human greed.

I played Dorothy Provine's battle-ax mother, Mrs. Marcus. I was so overladen with costume jewelry that I clanked when I walked. And I used my white purse as a lethal weapon—almost. All in all, Mrs. Marcus was a wickedly funny shrew who would not have been out of place in Charlie Chaplin's *Monsieur Verdoux*.

What particularly appealed to me about the project was that it gave me a chance to demonstrate a side of my talent that generally had been overshadowed by my sustained high notes. Then, in case anyone concluded that I'd suddenly lost my voice, I agreed that spring to perform an Irving Berlin medley on the Academy Awards telecast.

It's a Mad, Mad, Mad, Mad World was shot in Cinerama on location near Palm Springs. During the five months of filming, temperatures often reached 120 degrees. But Kramer did a wonderful thing. He secured a freight-car-length trailer that had no sides but had a wide top to provide shade. He placed chairs in the shaded area so that we could go there to escape the sun and enjoy a bit of cross ventilation. He also had a little boy constantly making the rounds with buckets of iced juice for us to drink and pails of ice to put on our wrists and brows.

People claim that comedians are melancholy loners when they're not in the spotlight. That's true of some of them. Sid Caesar and Phil Silvers tend to be quiet introspective fellows. Worriers. On the other hand, all you had to say was "I like those shoes" to send Jonathan Winters into a fifteen-minute monologue on everything from horseshoes to gumshoes. Mickey Rooney is also an extrovert and, of course, Milton Berle.

In the picture I wore three or four strands of beads around my neck. Miltie was the chief target when I started wielding my pocketbook. After a couple of days he came to me and asked, "Ethel, what have you got in that big purse?"

It just so happened that I had a set of replacement beads that I carried at all times in case the ones I was wearing got broken. I showed him.

"I thought so," Miltie said. "Feel this."

I felt his head. There was a huge bump. He had me frantic, believing I'd given him a minor concussion. I was practically hysterical and apologizing all over the place until I learned the truth—it was a growth he'd had since he was a baby.

In this picture I was tossed around like a volleyball and ended up dumped in an ashcan, but I enjoyed every minute of it. I'm a girl who enjoys a challenge, and there were plenty of those in holding my own against many of the great funnymen of our time.

Naturally, like any picture made under trying conditions, *It's a Mad, Mad, Mad, Mad World* ran over schedule, so I had to postpone until October my Las Vegas debut at the Flamingo—my first club work since appearing at the Casino in the Park in 1930. Only now I was getting $40,000 a week, which was great, since I don't gamble and could bank whatever was left after taxes.

Judy Garland and Mitzi Gaynor flew in with forty friends to attend the premiere. There were flowers enough to give me three allergy attacks if I'd kept them in my dressing room and hundreds of telegrams, including Van Johnson's traditional well-wishes: "HOPE YOUR OPENING IS AS BIG AS SOPHIE TUCKER'S."

During my engagement, attendance records were broken. I should have been happy. I recorded a live album under a new contract for Reprise, but I didn't enjoy it. I thought maybe it was just that I didn't find the Las Vegas atmosphere congenial. So over the next couple of years I played various spots from Harrah's in Lake Tahoe to the Casanova Room of the Deauville in Miami Beach; from the Persian Room in New York to various rooms in New Orleans, Chicago and Sydney, Australia. I wanted to like club work because it offered unusual freedom. Also my salary was high and I could more or less choose the periods when I wanted to lay off.

I had no personal obligations to a husband. Ethel Jr. had a family of her own and was continuing her education as a special student. Bobby was involved in preparing for a theatrical career as a director. Mom and Pop were self-reliant. There was no reason for me to do anything I didn't enjoy, and I found no satisfaction working to the hard-drinking, half-listening expense-account crowds. God knows, they were generous with their applause, sometimes so generous that I wondered whether they ever heard the end of any song. It wasn't the quantity but the quality of their response that disturbed me.

That summer I took out *The Ethel Merman Show*, playing tents for seven weeks, opening in Rochester, New York, with Davis and Reis, a record-pantomime act; Czony and Claire, ballroom dancers; the Elkins Sisters and the Wanderers. We followed Rochester with Washington, D.C., and Atlanta. I received $185,000 plus a percentage, out of which I had to pay the other acts. But once again I might as well have been back on Broadway. My private life halted at five P.M. That's when I rolled up my hair, soaked in my bubble bath and relaxed in preparation for the evening show. At six P.M. I always had a medium rare steak, a baked potato and a salad. Then I did my own theatrical makeup in my hotel room so that upon arrival at the theater I had only to slip into my first costume.

One thing did tickle me. In Atlanta on opening night Alderman Rodney Cooke presented me with the key to the city. Flashbulbs popped and it was quite a scene. But when the ceremony was over, Mr. Cooke began to pack up the key.

"Oh, don't I get to keep it?" I asked with a straight face.

He lamely explained that it was the only one the city had, but he promised to have one made for me.

"So much for Southern hospitality," I cracked.

Well, the next night the Mayor himself showed up backstage with a huge floral key made up of chrysanthemums and orchids. It was comparable to presenting me with a common cold, but I'd given them such a rough time the evening before, so I accepted it graciously.

Upon finishing the summer-theater tent tour, I joined Bobby in Europe, where he was spending the summer visiting some of the famous theatrical producing companies before he enrolled in Carnegie Tech to study directing.

People at the time were forever asking me how I felt about the fact that both of my children had decided to enter the theater. I thought it was swell. Ethel leaned toward the academic side, planning to teach creative dramatics. Bobby, as I've said, hoped to direct. Naturally I'd have tried to talk either of them out of it if I'd thought one untalented. I'd also have opposed a singing career for either. The theater is difficult enough when a youngster is trying to establish himself against competition from contemporaries. It's impossible when he or she faces comparison to a successful parent.

Anyway, we met at the Edinburgh Festival, saw the productions, and returned to the United States by way of the Stratford Festival in Canada. When I came back to New York, I announced I'd like a shot at Lady Macbeth. You'd have thought from the reaction I said I wanted to hitch a ride to the moon. And I must admit I was half kidding—but only half. After all, isn't Lady Macbeth only Mamma Rose's unmusical sister?

With my vacation over, I went to Hollywood to do the Lucille Ball and Red Skelton television shows. After taping the Skelton show, I learned that Barbra Streisand was guesting on the Judy Garland program.

Judy was a pal of mine. I often visited in her home when I was in Hollywood. Roger Edens was as close to her as he was to me and over the years we managed some great singalongs. I remember one night at Bert Friedlob's house on Beverly Drive, Roger was playing the piano and Judy and I were singing. Suddenly this dame said to me, "My God, how old can you be to remember the lyrics to all these *old* songs?"

Judy sort of looked at me and I looked at Judy. Then I said,

"Look, dear, I know the lyrics to 'The Star-Spangled Banner,' but I wasn't around when it was written." That ended her case. Judy loved my doing that.

That reminds me of something I always felt about Judy. Anyone who knew her only through the headlines must have thought her personal life was hell. "Poor soul," people would say.

Poor soul nothing. Judy had a wonderful sense of humor. There might have been quite a lot of melodrama in her life, but what saved her was that she always saw the funny side of her troubles. There was a wide streak of the clown in her.

I remember once she was a little off the wall and had to be institutionalized. I saw her not long after her release and nobody enjoyed telling of the whimsical blow fate had struck her more than she did. It seems that when those in charge felt she was ready for release, she got all packed to leave. But before she could check out, she had to have one final visit with the top doctor.

He was on the telephone when she arrived, but waved her to a seat. His call went on for quite a long time and this little fly kept buzzing around Judy's head. She made a couple of grabs at it and missed. It came right back. Judy grabbed again and almost fell out of the chair.

Now apparently the doctor didn't see the fly, because when he got off the phone he gently but firmly escorted her back to her room. Judy tried to explain, but there was no way he was going to release her. By the time they got to her quarters, she was completely hysterical and had to spend another day there before she could convince anyone there really had been a fly.

To most people such an episode would have been a tragedy. Not to Judy. She made a wonderful story out of it. In fact, she always got a lot of mileage out of her "victim" humor.

Judy was a very thoughtful girl. Over the years, I seldom made an appearance that I didn't receive a congratulatory telegram from her on opening night—when she didn't show up in person.

Of course, like everybody else, I'd been bowled over by Barbra Streisand's talent when she exploded on Broadway with her "Miss Marmelstein" number in *I Can Get It for You Wholesale*. We met and kept vaguely in touch with each other. Upon the birth of Barbra and

Elliot Gould's son, Jason, I sent him a silver frame. So we were friends.

Hearing that I was in the area, Judy's director suggested that I do a surprise walk-on with these other two belters. I did, and the reaction of the studio audience was so terrific that Jim Aubrey, who was then head of programming at CBS-TV, bumped the scheduled segment and substituted ours.

Whenever I happened to be in Hollywood, I saw quite a lot of Ernest Gann, a novelist and screenwriter, who had, among others, *The High and the Mighty* and *Twilight for the Gods* to his credit. Our friendship was nothing serious. To tell the truth, after my divorce from Bob Six I'd become a little gun-shy. That had been a costly mistake in more ways than one. Ernie Gann had a nice sense of humor. I enjoyed his company and he seemed to like being with me. That was about as involved as I wanted to get.

Then Ernie and I went to a party at Temple and Joe Schribman's on November 30. Ernest Borgnine, who was being divorced by Katy Jurado, was there. Right away Borgnine began paying a lot of attention to me. I thought he seemed pleasant, but I wasn't any more interested in him than I was in Ernie Gann. I'd never seen Borgnine in *Marty*, his big hit, and he hadn't seen me in *Gypsy* as far as I know, nor any of my other Broadway shows.

Next day Borgnine began calling. We started going out a lot, but I was due back in New York to fulfill an engagement at the Plaza. Then I intended to spend Christmas with Mom and Pop and Bobby. Borgnine definitely didn't fit into my plans.

I'd hardly arrived in Manhattan when calls started coming from the West Coast. Then suddenly Borgnine turned up in person. He gave me a big rush and on the day after Christmas he proposed. Don't ask me what I was thinking about when I said yes. There's no rational explanation for my behavior. But I agreed to marry him.

From the reaction of the press, you would have thought that war had been declared. Headlines! "MERMAN-BORGNINE TO WED."

Nobody could believe it. Least of all me. When anyone is brave enough to ask me, I admit that it seems as if I hadn't learned anything from my previous failures. In the first place I wasn't any better acquainted with Ernest Borgnine that I had been with Bill Smith. Yet I told a reporter that a half-hour after we met I felt as if I'd known him all my life, that he was somebody I could rely upon.

If tried, the only defense I could cook up would be temporary insanity. I certainly wasn't marrying him for his looks. Nor was I in need of suitors. In fact, when Ernie Gann heard about the engagement, he sent me a cute telegram: "YOU'RE MARRYING THE WRONG ERNIE."

The only explanation I can make is that as long as I had been around, I was—and still am—Ethel Agnes Zimmermann. I still have a tendency to believe what people tell me, until I have reason not to. For all the experiences I've had and for all the bold brassy dames I've played, I guess I'm still a little naive. I say what I mean and mean what I say and I expect the same from others. That's probably why I've gotten into some of the messes I have.

Now that doesn't let me off the hook. Even though Borgnine came on as sympathetic and understanding, I wasn't some inexperienced schoolgirl. I'd been around a few years. I might not have seen him on the screen, but I knew he'd had two hectic marriages. I should have been wary of any man who'd explain the failure of his first marriage by saying, "I won the Oscar, but Rhoda started wearing the dark glasses."

Especially since he quickly married actress Katy Jurado, who was no shrinking violet. Rhoda had lasted nine years, but by the time Borgnine and Miss Jurado had been wed a couple of years they were in a fight to the finish on the streets of Rome. Once he chased her all over town in a cab and carried her struggling and screaming into the hotel where they were staying.

I'll give the man credit. He'd have made a wonderful hypnotist. How else would I have been foolish enough to tell reporters this was the first time I'd really been in love? But I plead guilty.

After getting engaged, I gave up my Park Lane apartment and shipped my furniture and paintings to California. It was as if I hadn't learned anything from doing the same thing for Bob Six, even though that experience had cost me a bundle.

The funny thing was that I had hardly completed all these

moves when I began to be troubled by doubts. Little things began bothering me. But with all the commotion of working, getting my loved ones settled and planning the wedding, I avoided facing the fact that the smartest thing I could do would be to back out. I might even have done so if it hadn't been for the bridal shower. Gypsy Rose Lee, Vivian Vance, Lucille Ball and a lot of other friends held it in my honor. I don't remember what most of the presents were. But when I opened Lucy's gift I wanted to cry. There were itsy-bitsy sheets engraved EMB. There were princess- and typewriter-size sheets engraved ETHEL MERMAN BORGNINE. When you are in deep conflict about something, sometimes the most trivial thing can tip the scales. It doesn't really make any sense, but I thought then that the only person in the whole world who can use these is me. So on June 26, 1964, Ernest Borgnine and I were married.

XXVIII

My Marriage to Ernest Borgnine

C
H
A
P
T
E
R

To TELL THE TRUTH, the marriage was over before the honeymoon began. Several years later Borgnine was still putting out the story that he had spent $10,000 on our honeymoon—what with thirty-six violinists, all the flowers and a cruise to Japan. The facts are that he got free round-trip tickets for two to the Orient for some personal appearance he had made in San Francisco.

Thirty-eight days after the ceremony, the press carried the story that Borgnine and I had split up. When a reporter asked the reason, I told him, "I'm a lover, not a fighter."

Borgnine sued and I countersued in Santa Monica. The decree was granted to me on grounds of extreme cruelty. I had already returned the gold necklace he had given me. I asked no alimony or support. The only thing I requested was that he pay the charges for shipping my furniture and paintings back to New York, since I'd stood the expense of bringing them to California.

Borgnine was in a hurry to get married again. So he hopped down to Juarez, Mexico, on July 7, 1965, where he married Donna Rancourt. Their first child was born one month later on August 5, 1965, and my divorce became final in November of 1965. He swore that this time it was for keeps, but later during *their* divorce proceedings

231

she claimed she'd spent $15,000 on armed guards. He's married again since then.

As for me, I've never been able to discuss details of those thirty-eight days with even my closest friend. Nor have I wasted time or emotion thinking about them. I just feel lucky to have been able to "walk" away from the marriage. Some things in life aren't even worth regretting. You're better off passing them like a freight train passes a hobo.

I can't plead that I didn't have time to think over the marriage plans and reconsider, because in February of 1964 I went to London for several weeks. There Bernard Delafonte presented me in cabaret at the Talk of the Town. I had done a Royal Variety performance at the Palladium in 1955, when I'd been in England with Bob Six on a business trip. But that was all very impromptu. I didn't even have my orchestrations with me. So I just sang "There's No Business Like Show Business" to close the show.

I wondered whether the British reporters would stir up resentment against me for waiting thirty-four years before appearing in their country. But I need not have given it a thought. Love poured forth. Before my premiere some lovely white heather, a four-leaf clover and other good luck charms arrived in the mail—seldom with a return address so I might be able to send a thank-you note.

Opening night at the Talk of the Town, the audience was with me from the moment I began striding through the aisles among the tables to reach the stage. During the hour I sang for them, they gave the introduction to almost every song a wave of applause. That's the British. They may have a reputation for reserve, but when they are with a performer there's no doubt about it. By the time I reached "You Can't Get a Man with a Gun," most of them were standing on chairs cheering, crying, applauding.

The British press, which I've heard can sometimes be cruel, was pretty good too. The *Daily Express* headed its review "WHAM! IT'S ETHEL!" and went on: "It's rather like being clobbered by Sonny Liston." The *Sunday Telegraph* summed up their notice: "One is never in doubt from the start to finish that here is something that the

London stage has regrettably never known." My favorite quote came from Kenneth Tynan in the *Sunday Observer:*

> Style is the effortless projection of substance, the hammer that releases the chime, the seamless blending of instrument with purpose; and Merman, with her background of classic shows written for her by Gershwin, Cole Porter and Irving Berlin, is the strutting incarnation of style in American musicals. . . .
>
> Miss Merman celebrates herself and us; sans pathos or rabble-rousing. The big room rocks to her; we rise to her indomitable simplicity and wonder, as our palms steam with applause, what there ever was about Callas that we deemed worthier of our tears.

Parents who had collected my recordings or seen my movies brought their kids to the Talk of the Town to see me, and the correspondent of the New York *Times* observed that I'd done "what no other entertainer has managed since the Beatles and the rock 'n' roll groups came on the scene. She has bridged the generation gap."

A few days later headlines reported the Beatles led the revelry at a party in my honor at the Kensington High Street flat of singer Alma Cogan. I had dropped by to meet the famous musical revolutionaries, but was asleep in my suite at the Dorchester by the time Alma's irate neighbors began threatening to call the police. In fact, I'd had to leave before George Harrison arrived. But I did especially enjoy Ringo Starr, who has a very off-beat personality.

At times I think I was a little more than the Dorchester Hotel had bargained for. As I've said, I love tea. So when I'm on tour I carry an immersion rod so that I can have a cup of tea even if room service is closed. When Betty Bruce heard I was going to England she went to Hammacher Schlemmer and bought this transformer that altered the current. Well, the first time I plugged everything in, all the lights on the eighth floor in the very swank Dorchester Hotel went out. So I called the engineer. He came up and explained that I had the wrong converter. I needed one that changed both current and voltage.

I remember saying to him, "Well, what will I do? I want my tea."
He told me to pop around to the ironmonger.

"I beg your pardon," I said. But he eventually made me understand that I must go to a hardware store. I finally got the right contraption, but the story got around that I'd blown the master fuse at the Dorchester.

One of the interviewers inquired why I didn't use room service. I explained I had some fancy mules and some very, very nice negligees, peignoirs or whatever you care to call them. But I also had an old flannel robe, which I adored, and some comfy slippers.

The problem? If I called room service for tea, the man who served arrived wearing white gloves and a cutaway with silver buttons. How was I going to feel in my old flannel with my hair up in curlers and cold cream on my face? Wouldn't he look better than I did?

I've another little secret that I never told before. When I travel I can't carry detergent to get the tea stain out of the mug. So I used to take a hotel towel and go voom, voom, voom to clean the cup. The towel got all brown and I felt embarrassed about the maid. But I finally solved that. I bought a brown mug.

While I was at the Talk of the Town, I also headlined a popular TV variety show, *Val Parnell's Sunday Night at the Palladium*. I had a rehearsal the morning of the telecast and was running late. I got out of the bathtub and hurriedly dried myself. I hadn't dressed, but I went to the sink and picked up a new tube of mascara. Nothing would come out. I pressed hard and suddenly out came a whole mess that hit me in the stomach and in the pubic region. My first thought was Oh my God, it's waterproof! That made me do the worst thing I could have. I applied soap and water, which merely smeared it all over my stomach. The more I scrubbed the blacker I became.

It was getting later and later, so I took gobs of Kleenex to wipe off all the mascara I could and threw the tissue in the toilet, voom, voom, voom. Then I saw the toilet bowl was turning black. Well I didn't want the maid coming in and seeing that. She wouldn't know what it was. And it was so hard to remove. What would she think?

So late or not, I got down on my hands and knees with soap and a washcloth and scrubbed the toilet bowl.

After returning to the United States for my upcoming marital mishap, I announced that I would now concentrate on television and movies. Since I had a month with nothing to do before marrying Borgnine, I accepted an offer from Ross Hunter in Hollywood, who was producing *The Art of Love*, written by Carl Reiner, and featuring Dick Van Dyke, Angie Dickinson, Elke Sommer, James Garner and Reiner in the cast. It was a featherweight comedy that sank like lead. I played a madam. I had lots of gowns and some outrageous wigs, including a pistachio-colored one. On the wall of my office there was a photo of me in a feathered headpiece. That photo is about all that remains of the picture—except for an occasional disinterment for TV. They gave the photo to me after filming was finished. When my friend Morty Sussman, who designs my clothes, was furnishing his new apartment on East Sixty-fifth Street, I decided it was just the touch his guest bathroom needed.

After word got out that my marriage was already kaput, David Merrick immediately called to persuade me to appear in *Hello, Dolly!* since I was returning to New York. But I couldn't see it.

Instead I decided to play the Hilton in Sydney, Australia. The only problem was that I needed an accompanist. I decided to inquire of Roger Edens whether he knew of anyone who was available, since Roger understood my style so completely.

Over the years, if I had to do a television show, Roger and I would work long distance. Roger played beautiful piano, but he sang like a *mink*. Just terrible. What he would do over the phone was to decide on which numbers I would sing. He'd make arrangements. Then he'd go to some studio, lock himself in a room with a piano, and he'd make a recording of the song just the way he wanted me to deliver it. I mean timewise, with retards, changes of tempo—the works. He would send me the record. I'd play it over and over again. By the time I had to do the show, I knew it backward.

To my surprise, at the time I called Roger about a pianist he asked how long the Hilton engagement would run. When I said two weeks, he informed me he had nothing pressing on his schedule and volunteered to do it. Those two weeks were as much fun as those times we had worked together in *Girl Crazy* and at the Casino in the Park thirty years before.

After we closed, we came home by way of the Orient. Roger refused to accept any salary for working with me. But he owned a collection of hands—paintings, glass, sculpture, you name it—and as a token of my appreciation, in Bangkok, I found a big beautiful carved hand which I bought and had shipped to him.

My trips to London, Australia and the Orient increased my interest in seeing more of the world. Bobby, who was nineteen and full of curiosity, made a perfect traveling companion for a trip around the world. Since he had a job as a director at a summer theater and I was committed to tape a segment of the Dean Martin show, we booked passage from Los Angeles in the middle of August.

As we boarded the plane, Muzak was playing "I Got Rhythm." Bobby nudged me and whispered, "They're playing your song, Mom."

At Anchorage the plane landed for refueling to make the jump across the pond to Tokyo. As we took off, Musak seemed to have developed a macabre sense of humor, because it was playing "How Deep Is the Ocean?"

Beginning August 20, we spent two days visiting temples, gardens, good restaurants, geisha houses and the Kabuki theater in Tokyo. In each city we hired a car, a chauffeur and an English-speaking guide, making it convenient to see a lot in a short time.

From Tokyo we went to Kyoto, then on to Osaka and Hong Kong. On August 27 we arrived in Bangkok, then on to the Ashoka in New Delhi. I loved it there. When we came down to the dining room for luncheon, all the waiters were dressed in little white coats, white trousers, white gloves and orange terrycloth turbans. At one end of the dining room was a velvet-draped stage on which a small orchestra—mostly violins and violas—kept playing songs from *South Pacific* over and over. After Bobby and I finished dining, the maitre d' asked my son, "Did your mother enjoy her music?"

"Oh very much," Bobby told him. They thought I was Mary Martin.

Following stops in Agra and Jaipur, we arrived in Bombay, where Bobby not only couldn't see Bombay, he couldn't leave the bathroom. I wandered around shopping and sightseeing and managed to get something to cure his dysentery so that he would be in shape to fly to Moscow the next day.

In Moscow Bobby was eager to attend the Moscow Art Theater. Luckily for me, Joan Plowright was staying at the hotel and was able to dig up an extra ticket so I could see Larry Olivier, who was in the city in *Othello*. After the final curtain he gave a beautiful speech. When we went backstage, I said, "Gee, you speak beautiful Russian."

He shook his head. "Not a word."

He'd learned it all phonetically.

Two days later Bobby and I boarded a flight to Leningrad. Russian planes, of course, have no first class or tourist sections. Nor are there any individual seat lamps. There is a kind of dull gray light that envelops the whole plane. After we got settled, I looked around and decided my eyes were playing tricks on me. A few feet away was a man I could have sworn was the socialite photographer Jerry Zerbe, who had taken my picture hundreds of times at El Morocco and elsewhere. I wasn't imagining things. It was Jerry. He was going to Leningrad to do some photography for a book he was working on.

During our entire trip Leningrad was the only spot where our travel agent goofed. We arrived on Wednesday night to learn that the Hermitage was closed on Thursday. Since we were staying only one day, we missed seeing the paintings. But we did get to see *My Fair Lady* in Russian, which was very interesting.

We traveled by train from Leningrad to Helsinki, and it was the only part of our trip that I would willingly have missed. Along the way there were these towers on which guards with guns were stationed. I began to feel fidgety. The train stopped at intervals and uniformed men with guns searched all the compartments to see that nobody was being smuggled across the border. That spooked me.

Otherwise I loved seeing so much of the world in three weeks and four days, but I must also admit that near the end of our trip I was eager to get home. Of course Bobby was ready to go on another three weeks, and the following April we did go to Stratford to the Canadian Shakespeare Festival.

I WAS CONCENTRATING on one-shot appearances during the latter part of 1965 and the beginning of 1966 when I received a telephone call. The squeaky voice on the other end of the line was immediately recognizable. "Wouldn't it be wonderful to do a twentieth-anniversary revival of *Annie Get Your Gun?*" Irving Berlin asked. "How does that strike you?"

It struck me right between the eyes. When I do a show I almost take the veil, and I wasn't sure I wanted to live that kind of life at this point. I asked Irving to give me time to think. What finally sold me on the idea was that a whole new generation (including Bobby, who was now a production assistant at the American Shakespeare Festival in Stratford, Connecticut) had been toddlers when the original production closed. I liked the idea of letting them see it. The only limitation I imposed was that this was to be a short-term engagement. I felt I'd paid my dues to the theater and I wanted to please myself and do as I pleased without always being aware of my obligation to the audience.

It was, if I may say so, a spectacular revival. Irving wrote a new number, "Old Fashioned Wedding," for the show. When he played it for me the first time, it was only half as long as it eventually became. I told him that it was just beautiful but that he had to finish it. So he lengthened it and it became a show-stopper.

Jack Sydow did a wonderful job directing and Danny Daniels elaborated on the original dances. Harry Bellaver, who had played Sitting Bull twenty years before, acted the same part again and was, if anything, better the second time around. Benay Venuta played Dolly Tate and a newcomer, Jerry Orbach, was our Charlie Davenport. For Frank Butler, producer Richard Rodgers signed a curly-haired blue-eyed young man who seemed to have a big career ahead of him. His name was Bruce Yarnell.

The only sour note came from a young critic on *Women's Wear Daily* who made a big fuss about the difference in Bruce's and my ages. The critic was certainly entitled to his opinion, but I suspect he was more interested in drawing attention to himself than evaluating the show. In any case, audiences weren't bothered by the age gap, either during the Toronto tryout or the New York engagement.

The review appeared shortly after Sybil Burton, free of Richard, had married Jordan Christopher. So when a columnist inquired whether our age difference bothered him, Bruce gave her a wicked grin and said, "We just say, Why let Sybil and Jordan have all the fun?"

Unhappily, a few years later Bruce's career was cut short by a fatal plane accident.

My understudy in the show, Eileen Rogers, was beautiful, talented, ambitious and funny. On the day before our opening in Toronto, she asked Dick Rodgers to be excused from rehearsal to go out to buy flowers for my dressing room. Dick told her, "You don't want to do that. Ethel's allergic to flowers."

Eileen nodded. "I know. I want to get her a hundred and fifty carnations."

Eileen doesn't worry about who's playing what now. At the time she and her husband, Bill Thompson, had been trying to have children for a number of years. It was a far more important goal than achieving stardom. Luckily, after we closed, Eileen became pregnant and produced a wonderful little boy. Then about a year and a half or two years later she gave birth to another son. I used to visit her family in Plandome, Long Island, and she was completely content as a wife and the mother of two beautiful sons. A wonderful gal.

Eileen never sent me any flowers, but on opening night at the New York State Theater, Lincoln Center, a package from Tiffany's was delivered to my dressing room. Inside was a miniature gold blossom. On Irving's personal stationery were the following lines:

> A sweet-smelling rose
> Starts a run in the nose,
> So a metal
> Petal
> For Etel.

Some people, including Irving, liked the revival even better than the original production. For me there was a special thrill in having a vehicle in which I'd originated the leading role two decades earlier prove itself again. In fact, Bruce, Harry, Benay, Eileen and the whole company proved so congenial and we had so much fun I agreed to extend the engagement for an additional eight weeks.

From the time of my last divorce in 1965 through 1967, I saw a great deal of Jimmie Van Heusen, who had written such hits as "Swinging on a Star," "Love and Marriage," "All the Way," "High Hopes" and "Call Me Irresponsible," to name only the award winners. Jimmie loved to go places and have fun. He was great to be with. Of course the columnists tried to make something of it. Once after Louis Sobol saw us together on several different occasions within a few days, he asked when we were going to become Mr. and Mrs. Jimmie just smiled and I said to Louis, "What! Spoil a great friendship? And all the fun we're having?"

And we did have fun. Jimmie was a guy like Sinatra who enjoyed traveling in a pack. There was nothing pretentious about him though. He lived in a dumpy little apartment between Eighth and Ninth Avenues on Fifty-seventh Street, even though his home in California was a big beautiful place. And he never liked fancy restaurants. We used to go to Patsy's on Fifty-sixth Street all the time.

Jimmie didn't care how many guests he took out to dinner. He was a very attentive fellow, always sending flowers and everything. I loved Jimmie in a funny way, but there was never any mention of marriage between us. That was the remotest thing from his mind and mine.

Once again after the closing of *Annie Get Your Gun* I turned to television. But I broadened out to include situation comedies and adventure shows, appearing with Lucille Ball and Vivian Vance on the Lucy shows, in Marlo Thomas' *That Girl* and *Batman;* and eventually in Durango, Mexico, I even had a guest shot on a *Tarzan* segment as a missionary.

Whenever I was in California, I of course tried to see a lot of Ethel Jr. and her family. I was concerned about her. She didn't seem able to decide what her niche in life was going to be. She was still a baby herself, taking care of two babies. She had great difficulty in coping. It was too much for her. One day she was all enthused about continuing her education, and shortly after she would be talking about a career in show business. There is no denying that she was a troubled girl.

Naturally this didn't make for a very placid relationship with her husband, and they divorced. Nor did psychiatry seem to be of much aid in guiding her to more mature behavior. To the contrary. I tried to help. But like most daughters, Ethel Jr. resented what she thought of as my interference. And like most mothers, I was reluctant to face the fact that she was a very sick girl. I suppose I just closed my eyes and kept hoping for the best.

I was relieved when one of the doctors put her on medication which made her seem much more like her natural self. He also encouraged her to return to Colorado College and to pursue her ambition eventually to teach creative dramatics to children.

In August of 1967 she called Bill and arranged for Barbara Jean and Michael to visit her. After worrying so much about her, I was elated that she had made such progress, as was Bill. So I was totally unprepared for the telephone call that I received on August 23 telling me that my beautiful, intelligent and high-spirited daughter had been found dead at a Green Mountains cabin, where she and her children were staying. Everything had been fine when Barbara Jean and Michael were put to bed, but when they attempted to awaken their mother in the morning they couldn't rouse her.

Thank God that I have always been of a religious nature, because even in my anguish and despair I held on to the thought that one day I would see my darling again. It was because of my faith that I was able to function at all.

Benay Venuta accompanied me on the plane that took me to Colorado Springs. Benay had known Ethel Jr. since Ethel was a baby. Benay's children and my children had played together as youngsters. Benay came along to comfort me, but on the plane she drowned her grief, so that I more or less ended up looking after her. Which may have been a blessing, since it gave me something to occupy myself with other than Ethel's passing.

I never saw Ethel Jr. after she went to sleep and never woke up. I wanted to remember her as she had been—so alive and vibrant. I only asked for a lock of her hair to go with my memories of happier days.

My son arrived and took over making the final arrangements. We decided that she should be cremated and that I would purchase a room in the Evergreen Shrine of Rest, where eventually all of us would be reunited.

The building is almost a hundred feet high. There are four rooms around the chapel. Each has stained-glass windows to allow in the sunlight, and soft music fills the air continuously.

To enter Ethel's room you have to pass through a bronze New Orleans–type filigree gate, which is always locked. There is an altar on which stands an urn in the center. Ethel's bronze name plaque is on the marble wall behind the urn and there is a bench with a pink velvet corduroy seat upon which the family or friends can sit to meditate and pray.

For a long time after her passing I kept by my bedside Ethel's curl attached to a smiling photograph taken at a time when she expected to conquer the world. Now I don't go in for the occult or any of that kind of thing, but I do believe that all of us will be reunited eventually. That conviction reinforced my faith and comforted me.

One thing I want to set straight. Some newspapers stories originally listed the cause of death as "drugs." This should have read "medication," since drugs have come to mean something illicit. Ethel's were medically prescribed. But prescribed or not, they interacted dangerously when mixed with alcohol. Also, maybe because of her father's suicide, some people mistakenly spread the story that Ethel took her own life. This is untrue. She left no notes when she retired that night, nor any indication that she didn't expect to awaken and go on with her life. This was not a time of despair. After a stormy journey, Ethel had reached the calm. She was planning to teach creative dramatics. She was looking forward. She felt strong enough to take responsibility for her children. No mother contemplating such an act would have brought her children to her and then have left them behind.

For a short time after Ethel died, I accepted no professional engagements, but prayer and the support of the daily message from Unity Village gradually brought me to accept what I could not change and helped me realize that Ethel Jr. had been ill and is now better off and happier where she is. Although immediately after her death I could not fully accept that concept and shrank from the idea of work, I agreed to appear on the Ed Sullivan show. It was then that I realized that, along with my grandchildren and travel, work was some of my most effective therapy.

The summer after Ethel's death in 1968, I leased a house on St. Martin for the month of June, thinking it would provide a wonderful vacation for Barbara Jean and Michael. Everything was fine until we reached San Juan, where I learned we were to transfer from our jet to a propeller plane. No way. The airlines assured me there would be another jet flight next morning. We checked into a hotel, where we spent two days waiting for such a plane. Since our luggage had been checked through, both evenings, our stockings and undergarments had to be washed, but I didn't mind. It gave me something to do.

We arrived on St. Martin to find the house I'd rented, located fifteen miles from town, without either a telephone or radio reception. Just complete isolation—except for the mosquitoes. There were so many of those we had to spray our pillows with repellent, which worked better on us than on them.

The first night, the kids came creeping into my bedroom, saying, "Grandma, can we get in bed with you?"

Could they! I was scared too. As I lay there looking through the beaded curtains at the moonlit yard, even the bushes seemed to take on human shape. Then all of a sudden the curtains parted. I expected someone to stand up with knife in hand. Just at that instant a huge dark body landed on the bed. It was a Labrador retriever the owner had left behind to protect us. We lasted less than a week.

After trying Seaview, Fire Island, one summer, Kennebunkport, Maine, and a couple of other spots, the three of us returned to St. Martin. First we visited Disney World in Orlando, Florida, where Barbara Jean and Michael wanted to see everything—voom, voom, voom—and eat everything in sight. I have to admit I was also impressed. I wrote Mom and Pop this was "the most fantastic place" I'd ever seen. It was twice the size of Manhattan, much cleaner and full of surprises. We'd allowed four days but could have stayed a week before taking off for St. Martin. This time we stayed at a lovely place called Mary's Fancy, which had a lot of well-landscaped grounds, a pool, donkeys to ride—everything kids like.

I loved those summers with my grandchildren. Maybe I spoiled them, but what grandmother doesn't? I don't know which I enjoyed most—looking forward to those summers then, or looking back on them now.

IN LATE JULY OF 1968 Russell Nype, Richard Eastham and I played *Call Me Madam* at the St. Louis Municipal Opera for a week. Then we went on the Kenley Circuit, a group of theaters located in Columbus, Warren and Dayton, Ohio. They are run by John Kenley and members of his family. John not only knows how to please his audiences but also the performers who work for him. Everything is first class. So arrangements had been made for me to have a chauffeur and limousine at my disposal throughout the engagement. But when Russell arrived, he was driving a sporty little two-seater 1955 T-Bird. I told John to save himself some money and cancel the chauffeur. I thought it would be a lot more fun making the hops with Russ.

At each stand I always had accommodations with a kitchen so that I could have cream cheese, yogurt, crackers and tea in case I wanted a snack after all the spots in town had closed.

Naturally I'd have supplies left at the end of the week, and it seemed silly to throw them out and then go to a supermarket to replenish my supply when we arrived at our next date. The jumps weren't long. I didn't see any reason not to take the stuff with me. So I fixed up this tote bag. On top I kept the milk, crackers and whatever I had on hand. Underneath I stashed my jewels—which were real in those days. When we'd stop for lunch, I'd take the bag along and set it in the booth with me. Russell said people would think I was one of those New York bag ladies; but whatever they thought, yogurt and soda crackers were a wonderful camouflage for several hundred thousand dollars' worth of jewels.

Later in 1968 and 1969 Russell, Dick Eastham and I revived *Call Me Madam* a number of times, including a winter engagement in Miami. While we were there, Carola Mandel invited Russell and me to Palm Beach to attend a luncheon in honor of our old pal the Duchess of Windsor. During luncheon, Russell told me later, the Duchess looked at me across the table and noticed I'd abandoned my ruffled look for simpler lines since the days when we had first become friendly. "My," she said to Russell, "Ethel's awfully Peck and Peck these days, isn't she?"

"Boy," as I always called the Duke, was not among the luncheon guests. He had a golf date; but after we'd finished eating, the Duchess called the club and had him come over to see us.

Over the years Russell, Diantha and their children have remained close to me. Usually I spend a couple of weeks visiting them in their big house in Kennebunkport. Maine's a wonderful place, and the Nypes make it even better.

Diantha and I go antiquing, and there always seems to be something doing at the country club. In winter, if Russ is on tour or playing a dinner theater, Diantha and I often dine together. They make me feel a part of the family.

So it was natural in 1970 that when David Merrick asked me for the thirteenth time to appear in *Hello, Dolly!* and I accepted that I should suggest that Russell play Cornelius. Even then I only agreed to do it for three months, but the company and management were so pleasant that I ended up staying nine months.

I was the eighth Dolly to play in the New York company. Carol Channing, Ginger Rogers, Betty Grable, Martha Raye, Pearl Bailey, Phyllis Diller and Bibi Osterwald preceded me. People wondered whether I didn't feel strange following the other girls. The answer is no. Some people prefer steak, others veal or shrimp or ham. The way I look at it, each of us had her individual strong points. There is no single correct way to interpret Dolly any more than there is to play, say, Lady Macbeth. And that, by the way, is a role I've always hankered to play.

As for myself, my Dolly was bound to be different. Jerry Herman had originally written the score with me in mind. After I turned David Merrick down, Jerry removed two numbers. When I agreed to play the part, those songs—"World, Take Me Back" and "Love, Look in My Window"—were restored to the score.

I didn't open *Dolly*, but I closed her after 2844 performances. And Mr. Merrick was kind enough to say in a 1971 *Reader's Digest* article that without me he wasn't sure that *Dolly* would have broken *My Fair Lady*'s record, which was then the longest-running musical ever to be presented on Broadway. I'm sure he'd have found a way, since he's a modern Barnum. In fact, at one point he even tried to persuade Jack Benny to play Dolly Levi to George Burns's Horace Vandergelder. I must admit it did please me to have so demanding a showman go on record to wit: "She is the most thoroughly professional star I've ever done business with. She's out there every single performance, dedicated, making a show really work."

Would that be a bad epitaph?

It was during 1959 that I began turning into a landmark of sorts, although it took me almost a dozen years really to make it.

When I was getting ready to sign for *Gypsy*, Six, who was quite an operator, said to my financial adviser, "Of course, she'll be able to write off her apartment and living expenses."

Now Irving Katz, who is one of the smartest tax men in the country, said, "It's possible."

Possible! Six demanded to know what Irving meant. Because as head of Continental Airlines Six knew that every time he left Denver, he deducted whatever he spent.

So Irving explained that as a tax dodge, a lot of people had maintained modest legal residences in one state while they worked and lived in another. As I understand it, the IRS got wise to what was going on and came up with something called the "tax home." Now if people were on a job indefinitely, the IRS claimed that where they worked was considered their tax home. Irving told Six that a number of recent decisions of this kind made my undertaking tricky.

Six wasn't buying that. He asked to be sent copies of the decisions. Apparently he showed them to his lawyers, who agreed, because from then on Six was a pussycat with Irving.

The way Irving worked out the problem was to suggest that I sign a year's contract. The producers yelled blue murder. What about protecting the investors and making a reasonable profit? So it worked out that I had a run-of-the-play contract—not to exceed two years. That way, the government couldn't claim my employment was indefinite. The producers also agreed to pay my traveling and living expenses. Everything seemed fine when Six and I filed a joint return in 1959.

But on April 8, 1963, the IRS notified us that $32,949.11 for New York expenses had been disallowed. For a couple of reasons, Irving advised paying the claim plus interest of $6,560.48 and suing for a refund. In the first place, it stopped further interest from accruing. It also kept us out of Tax Court and in District Court, where we could have requested a jury.

After some delay and a lot of changes in my personal life, in February of 1971 the ruling went against us. A U.S. Appeals Court ruled that in spite of my family, my contribution to expenses and the huge house, "it is the job and not the taxpayer's pattern of living which must require the traveling expense."

Naturally we appealed and on November 13, 1971, I was on the front page of the *Wall Street Journal*. In part, the story read:

> The Second Circuit Appeals Court recently told the District Court to look again and ignore the "tax home" hocus-pocus. What mattered was whether Miss Merman's expenses were compelled by her business affairs. The key question, the higher court said, was whether her New York stint was indefinite enough that "a reasonable person in her position would pull up stakes and make her permanent residence in New York"; if it was, then keeping her residence in Colorado was a personal matter.
>
> *"When an assignment is truly temporary, it would be unreasonable to expect a taxpayer to move his home," the court said. His expenses are thus forced by the "exigencies of business."*

After I'd won, a lot of people who had sort of given up because of the "tax home" gimmick took heart and sued for relief—and mine became a kind of landmark case.

Mom suffered a heart attack in 1971 after I closed in *Dolly*. She, who had always looked after the rest of us, now needed looking after. When I mentioned the problem of getting a full-time nurse to Pop, he asked whether I remembered the wonderful office nurse Kathryn Shreve, who had worked for a Dr. Schmidt who had once taken care of him and Mom. I got Kathryn's number in New Jersey and called. She said she was sorry, but she wasn't available. An hour later she called back and said she had always been fond of Mom and Pop and she'd take the job. There was only one problem—she had a dog. I was so happy to get her, I told her, "I don't care if it's a Great Dane, just come."

Kathryn couldn't have been more devoted to Mom and Pop if she were their own child. In April of 1973 Mom suffered a massive stroke. For eight and a half months Pop and I went to the hospital every day. At one point I was scheduled for a record session with London Records to cut one of my albums with Stanley Black and the London Festival Orchestra and Chorus. So I had to hop a jet and cut the sides. Otherwise I visited Mom every day until her death on January 14, 1974. Now she rests in Colorado Springs along with my daughter, Ethel.

Kathryn stayed on to care for Pop in the apartment. Pop was becoming frailer, but his main problem was that he was legally blind. As he said shortly after his ninety-seventh birthday, "I'm lucky, Ethel, to be ninety-seven and still have all my marbles." He was also lucky to have the wonderful care Kathryn gave him. My parents loved Kathryn and she them, but naturally she needed time to herself occasionally. One day a week Beverly Douglas, a friend of Kathryn's from Kenilworth, New Jersey, came to New York to relieve her. On Saturdays another friend, Ona Lucille Hill, came to Pop's apartment and kept him company. This enabled Kathryn to shop, sleep and do personal errands.

During the summer Kathryn took Pop to her home in Kenilworth, where he could sit outside, smell the flowers and take an interest in the squirrels and rabbits, even though they were only a blur as far as he was concerned.

It was wonderful for him. In New York he was too proud and fastidious to go out to dinner anymore because of his difficulty locating the food on his plate and getting it to his mouth. That meant he was confined to his apartment day after day. The only break in the monotony occurred when he has his daily Scotch and received such loyal friends as Madeleine Gaxton, Dick Kieling, Dorothy Strelsin, Bob Lucas, Mickey McMillin, Erik Palm, Tom Hendee, Joe Messina, Dr. Damato and, until their deaths, Jack Peninger and Dorothy Fields.

In Kenilworth Pop had made friends with the couples who live next door and across the street, as well as with Kathryn's and Lucy's families. Somebody was always popping in to talk with Pop. On rainy days, if nothing else, Kathryn could load him into her car and take him for a drive.

Even though Pop was away all summer, I wouldn't allow the hotel to sublet his apartment. I paid the upkeep so he always had a home to return to. Some people might think that was a little extravagant. But I feel this way: A shroud has no pockets.

Both Kathryn and Lucy were so good to Pop that they have become almost like sisters to me. Lucy's crazy about show business. As a teenager she used to dance in the aisles when Sinatra and the swing bands appeared at the Paramount Theater on Broadway. She once had almost a hundred huge scrapbooks devoted to her prime favorites—Irene Dunne, Jeanette MacDonald and her favorite of favorites, Nelson Eddy.

Since she's known me, she has taken up keeping my scrapbooks just as Pop used to do. Of course I'm no competition to her real favorite, who replaced Nelson Eddy after his death, Raymond Burr. Lucy has collected articles on Burr not only from newspapers and magazines printed in this country, but from all over the globe. When she got a batch of stories from Swedish papers, I bought a Swedish-American dictionary for her and she worked for weeks laboriously writing out word-for-word translations. She's spent over $5000 on photos—candid and production shots—covering Burr's entire career, beginning with his student days at the Pasadena Playhouse, through Broadway, films and TV. The dream of her life is to meet him.

With Pop in such good hands, I was free to pick and choose dates that I wanted to do, ranging from a salute to Irving Berlin on an Oscar telecast, to an appearance in London at the Palladium.

I did make one appearance I had no control over. Jerry Herman called to ask me to sing "my" numbers from *Dolly* on Merv Griffin's talk show. Merv introduced his guests, including Ralph Edwards. Ralph had been a hit in radio and television with such things as *Truth or Consequences* and *This Is Your Life* for forty years. Merv said Ralph was going to talk about how his staff fooled the subjects of *This Is Your Life*. "For instance," Merv asked, "how do you surprise your subjects?"

I wondered too. Well, Ralph held up a paper-covered book he carried and said it was easy. He just tried to get them in some situation where they were likely to be unsuspecting. "For instance, I could say to you, 'Merv Griffin, this is your life.' Or 'Jerry Herman, this is your life.' " He started tearing the wrapper off the book and said, "But what I'm really going to say is 'Ethel Merman, queen of musical comedy, this *is* your life!' "

I just collapsed. It destroyed me. All those memories came rushing back. I dissolved. I cried so hard it took them eight minutes to get me pulled together and across the hall from Merv's studio to the one where Ralph's audience was waiting.

Josie Traeger and Leo, Temple Texas, Perle Mesta, Benay Venuta, Goldie Hawkins, Barbara Jean and Michael and Bill Geary appeared one after another. The only one who missed it was Pop. He was just too frail to make the trip to California.

Some people used to say the program was framed, but I'm here to tell you it wasn't. For me it was an emotional bath that left me cleansed and raring to get on with the rest of my life.

One thing about television, it puts you in touch with the public. Since I've been doing it, people stop me in the street to say they love me, or in drugstores or taxis—anywhere. And I know it's sincere, because what do they have to gain by saying so if they don't mean it.

What's more, it gives me a jolt, a goose, to know that I'm contributing to the enjoyment of millions of people.

How had they arranged *This Is Your Life?* Through my agent at the time, Milton Goldman. Which brings me to agents. Every entertainer needs an agent, although some only have lawyers. My accountant is Irving Katz. He's wonderful about reading the fine print. So is my lawyer, Royal Blakeman. Often Irving even goes further than that. When *I Love My Wife* opened, I was approached to record "Everyone Today Is Turning On." I might have done it. It has an attractive melody, but Irving pointed out that it promoted all the permissiveness I'm against.

But to get back to agents. I know agents. I have hired them and fired them. Over the years I've had many. Lou Irwin, who helped me get started in the business, and George Rosenberg, who was instrumental in securing proper handling for me in my later pictures. I've been with big agencies, where they've treated me like a football, tossing me from one representative to another. I've also been with one-man agencies. I had an agent—you should excuse the expression—who couldn't get me booked into the men's room. People thought I'd retired. I had another who negotiated a big engagement in the East and forgot to tell me. Needless to say the deal went out the window and so did the agent. In 1972 a fellow who was representing me called and excitedly told me that there was a part for me on *The Odd Couple* television show, which co-starred Jack Klugman, who had played my boy friend in *Gypsy.*

I was elated. "What's the role?"

"Jack's mother."

"His mother?"

"Oh, it's wonderful."

"You've got to be crackers!" I said, and that was the end of him.

Now I have two wonderful representatives—Robert Gardiner and Gus Schirmer.

First let me tell you about Gus, who is actually more my personal manager than an agent. He is the son of the famous music publisher and a go-getter in his own right. Before becoming a manager he packaged companies for summer theaters and produced. He's a warm friend and an aggressive representative. I first knew him about ten years ago when he had a garden apartment on Sixty-second Street in New York. Lots of us used to drop in at his place on Sunday nights. He served a gourmet dinner and showed a movie afterward. Then he signed a lot of high-powered Hollywood clients and transferred to the West Coast.

I saw him whenever I happened to be out West, and the more we talked the clearer it became to me that we thought along the same lines. Since I was unhappy with my current representative, I said to him, "Come on, Gus, let's see what you can do for me." That was two years ago, and since then, with his connections, I have had more spots of the kind I enjoy doing than I can handle.

He thought I'd be good at and enjoy doing game shows—*The Match Game, Hollywood Squares*—and he was right. I've often appeared on talk shows—Merv Griffin, Beverly Sills, Johnny Carson, Mike Douglas, Dinah Shore and occasionally on *Today.*

I've worked such variety shows as *The Muppets* and the Bobby Vinton show and such specials as the Steve Lawrence–Eydie Gormé Cole Porter special, the Ted Knight special and *The Big Event.* Some of the specials haven't fared too happily with the critics, but Gus has always seen to it that the producer and director presented me so that I came off smelling like a rose—which, in addition to seeing that you work, is what a manager is supposed to do.

Gus knows I love traveling. So he arranges that. In April of 1976 he set me for the Easter Seal telethon in Honolulu. My friends Rose Marie, Richard Deacon, Jessica Walters and a young man from Chicago named John Kent, who was an Easter Seal poster child around 1970, were part of the group flown over to entertain and raise pledges.

John is twenty-seven years old and most handsome. He was born with foreshortened legs and arms, but he hasn't let it stand in his way in developing a terrific personality or in becoming a smart lawyer. He brought with him the girl he was going to marry. We suggested that the ceremony be performed on the telethon. But the powers that be nixed the idea on the grounds that it would seem too commercial.

So we decided to give John his wedding anyway. We bought a bridal gown for his betrothed, a white shirt and trousers with a red sash for him, and special leis for both. I was living in a penthouse suite atop the Ala Moana Hotel, and on Saturday morning everyone assembled for the wedding. The minister read the first minute of the ceremony, then stopped, and I sang a cappella "They Say That Falling in Love Is Wonderful." Then the minister finished the ceremony and pronounced them man and wife. Of course I cried. It was a wedding, wasn't it?

The Kents and I became good friends and I still hear from them. When I made an appearance in Chicago in late 1976, of course I arranged for them to be in the audience.

In November Gus booked me for two shows to be done in England—*The Muppets* and the Steve Lawrence–Eydie Gormé Cole Porter special.

The Muppets, which was shot first, turned out, in my opinion, to be one of the best television programs I've ever done. The comedy was low key. But the writers and the director caught my personality nicely. Any number of people have told me I have never been better presented on TV. I must admit I fell in love with Kermit the frog, Fozzie and Miss Piggy and all the rest. When we sat around singing "Mutual Admiration Society," I really meant it.

Before beginning to tape with Steve and Eydie, I flew to Berlin to visit Barbara Jean, who was fifteen and a participant in the Student Exchange Program. I checked into the Kepinski Hotel from Thursday through Saturday. Barbara Jean stayed with me, even taking her grandma to the airport on Sunday. Initially she had been a bit homesick, but by the time I arrived she loved Berlin. She speaks fluent German, and during my stay she showed me every nook and corner from the zoo in the center of the city to the Berlin Wall—always by bus. We visited the Schmokel family, who were the first of her three hosts during her year-long stay, and went to a rathskeller seating more than 1600 people that belongs to Mr. Schmokel's parents. The remainder of the time we shopped and dined, and I submitted to one unscheduled interview when a reporter showed up in the lobby of the hotel to ask me such probing questions as whether I sang and if I had ever met Cole Porter.

Back in London for the Porter special, I was happy to find that Gus Schirmer and Dorothy Strelsin were in town. Dorothy had once been one of Leonard Sillman's *New Faces*. She married very well, but since her husband's death I think that in spite of all her money she's itching to go back to work.

Dorothy informed me that she was giving a Thanksgiving dinner for twenty-four friends at the Athenaeum Hotel. To make it typically American she ordered turkey, candied sweet potatoes with marshmallows on top, cranberry sauce, pumpkin pie—the works. It's one Thanksgiving I'll never forget. The chef served boiled Irish potatoes with marshmallows over them, *heated* cranberry sauce, and something he called apple-pumpkin pie. Of course Thanksgiving is a holiday that doesn't have much meaning outside the U.S., but that chef can rest assured that there never has been—and probably never will be—another menu like his.

Gus had a new project in mind. CBS was interested in using me in a series. Gus knew me well enough not to suggest tying myself down to a weekly grind, but had arranged that a young actor named Austin Pendleton would be the continuing character and I would appear only every third or fourth show with the billing "And starring Miss Ethel Merman as Dolly Rogers."

The idea was for me to play a musical comedy actress who receives custody of her young grandson when his parents are sent to prison for a tax fraud conviction. In the script, I am about to take off on a thirteen-week tour of *Mame*, so I foist the kid off on my bachelor son (Pendleton).

You may have seen the pilot on CBS in June of 1977. It was called "You're Gonna Love It Here." The pilot turned out okay, but lacked the zing to make the fall schedule.

My other agent is Robert Gardiner. He books me for concerts only, a form I thoroughly enjoy. All I need are my voice, my orchestrations and the expertise of my conductor, Eric Knight, in familiarizing the various orchestras with my approach. Bob says he can book Eric and me as often as I want to work, and with Eric to keep everything flowing smoothly that will be often.

I worked with Arthur Fiedler and the Boston Pops in May 1975, when the show was taped. The audience tore down the house; but how good do you have to be to get a standing ovation when you work with a Fiedler? Anyway, it was successful enough so that it was held to be aired on PBS during the Bicentennial in July 1976. However flip I may be about Fiedler, audience response was so exciting the night of the show that I choked up and was almost unable to finish my thank you to the patrons.

Another special night occurred in Hershey, Pennsylvania, when I narrated *Peter and the Wolf* with the Pittsburgh Symphony, giving Gene Shalit of the *Today* show an opportunity to fulfill his secret desire to conduct. ·

Since then I've worked with symphony orchestras in Nashville, Wichita, Seattle, Dallas, Chautauqua, Winnipeg, Oklahoma City, Detroit, Pittsburgh, and at the Hollywood Bowl in Los Angeles. As a matter of fact, Gus and Bob between them have kept me so busy I've hardly had time for my needlepoint.

One day in the fall of 1976 my telephone rang. It was Arnold Weissberger, the famous theatrical lawyer who is also Chairman of the Board of the Friends of the Theater and Museum Collection of the Museum of the City of New York. Arnold had an idea. Would I consider appearing with Mary Martin in a one-night benefit, *Together on Broadway*, in which we would be honored and would in turn raise funds for the museum's theater and music collection?

Why not? When I began doing concerts, I had approached Mary about some joint appearances. That was only a short time after her husband's death, and she'd frankly told me that she didn't feel up to performing. I told Arnold that if he could persuade her to work, I was more than willing.

Mary and I have always been members of a reciprocal admiration club. Some people have tried to turn us against each other, but neither of us has ever let them get away with it.

As you have no doubt gathered by now, I'm a kind of take-charge type. I like to look after myself. If I want anything, I buzz out and get it. I enjoy keeping a part of my time for myself alone. And if anyone shoves me, I'll shove back.

Mary is just the opposite. Not that she is without convictions or bland. Her way is just quieter. Nobody pushes her around, because she always sees to it that she has someone looking after her interests. When Richard was alive, he arranged everything. After he passed, Ben Washer, who had been a top-flight Broadway press agent, stepped in and took over. Ben had been a friend of both and had handled the press for some of their productions. Now, like Richard, he is within Mary's beck and call twenty-four hours a day. He advises her, sees that traveling and living arrangements are taken care of and escorts her wherever she goes. So Mary's life runs smoothly. As a co-worker, she is so considerate that it would be almost impossible not to get along with her.

She has by delegating responsibility retained a lovable fey quality (Is it any wonder that Peter Pan is her favorite role?) to which audiences respond. She also has it in real life. One evening two escorts brought her to my apartment before we went out to dinner. In the course of conversation she announced she was very proud of the brave thing she had done that day. We all waited to hear what it was. What she had done was to board a public bus and ride to her destination.

In order to really appreciate that story, you have to remember that one matinee afternoon during the Broadway run of *South Pacific*, Richard was indisposed and could not accompany her to the theater as he always did. The apartment doorman secured a taxi for Mary, and when she got in she told the driver that she wanted to go to *South Pacific*. Pressed for the name of the theater, Mary, who had been playing in the show for a year, couldn't recall it. In all that time, she'd just never bothered to look, depending upon Richard to get her there.

I assume Arnold arranged for Mary's appearance, because before long Anna Sosenko, the benefit producer who lighted, advised and developed The Incomparable Hildegarde, was on the phone demanding publicity stills and setting up press conferences for the evening, which had been set for Sunday, May 15, 1977. Seats were priced from $25 to $150, with the $150-ticket holders privileged to attend the after-theater gala.

A single ad in the New York *Times* brought an avalanche of ticket orders. Forty thousand dollars' worth of checks had to be returned. Celebrities who had neglected to get their ticket orders in tried pulling every string to get seats. Even Lauren Bacall had to stand by until almost curtain time to receive her locations.

In an interview, Mary had said she never heard applause at a premiere. I told her she'd better hear it on May fifteenth, since there wasn't going to be any second night. So she had a little battery of reflectors clamped along the lower edge of the balcony to bounce the sound back on stage.

Me? When Donald Sadler, our director, asked what kind of clown business I intended to work up for our entrance, I told him none. I'd just acknowledge the applause. And that was some welcome. Now I'd expected a nice reception, but what we received was beyond imagination.

That night I learned the meaning of a love-in. The audience on May 15, 1977, took me right back to October 14, 1930, and *Girl Crazy* when I startled them with "Sam and Delilah" and "I Got Rhythm."

When Mary, wearing her sailor suit from *South Pacific*, and I in Mamma Rose's ratty old furs, bed-blanket coat and funny hat jumped through two huge paper hoops to the strains of "Send in the Clowns," a number that belonged to neither of us, a roar of greeting came blasting across the footlights.

During the remainder of the evening the star-studded audience gave Mary and me repeated ovations. There was such an outpouring of love, I felt as if they were unconsciously repaying us for all the years we'd sacrificed our social lives to give performances and shown up when we were ill or someone near and dear to us was ailing. Whatever the reasons, the love was there.

In the New York *Post*, Martin Gottfried underplayed it, writing, "Mary and Ethel restore magic to Broadway." Walter Kerr's piece in the New York *Times* was headlined "THE MERMAN-MARTIN MAGIC BLAZES IN BENEFIT 2-ALARM FIRE OF GENIUS."

Ethel Merman is the bonfire and Mary Martin is the smoke. They go very nicely together, if you're in a mood to burn up the town! . . .

The scorcher, as you scarcely need to be told, was Merman, too hot for Fahrenheit to measure, too bright to be stared at without a pair of those goggles that riveters wear. . . . It was Ethel the Everready who opened up first (and second, and third, and after that I lost count).

I always think of her as standing still and belting. I don't know why. I'm sure she did stand still once while she was first singing "Let's Be Buddies" in whatever triumphant show that was. But at the Broadway she was an itch that couldn't be scratched, a brushfire claiming a whole mountainside, a pop and a snap and a crackle that kept her rocking from side to side like a metronome on wheels, slipping without warning into a fiercely infectious jig-step for "Doin' What Comes Natur'lly," throwing her substantial but untamable body around as easily as she tossed breathtaking keyshifts to the winds, and—I guess I still don't believe it—unleashing "Everything's Coming Up Roses" like a freshly tapped gusher with the sound soaring high in the air, straight up and off into eternity. Incredible.

A CERTAIN ELUSIVENESS

Speaking of eternity, there is an afterlife. During one of her subsequent appearances, Miss Merman was momentarily interrupted by the appearance of a trumpeter choosing to play Gabriel in the song featuring that archangel's name. The trumpeter ripped off a few calls, judgment-day calls. "Do you hear that playing?" Miss Merman asked with an instant pick-up, and in earnest (one of the finest things she does, again and again, is to take rhetorical questions such as "Why doesn't alcohol thrill me at all?" seriously, so that she can ride upward on a wave of exhilaration). Gabriel's stand-in kept blowing. Miss Merman began swinging. Guess who won? The thing is, with Gabriel now definitely outclassed, they're going to need her up there. And if they need her, she'll oblige, so we're all set.

Mr. Kerr was equally enthusiastic about Mary's smoky magic. Near the end of the review he noted something worth adding to my already long quote:

They work together most remarkably, without sentimentality or undue deference. Obviously each has a healthy respect for the other, obviously the strains of "Friendship" that float from the pit during the overture aren't inappropriate. They're pros and they can either do it or they can't, and they were up there to show that they could. Not even a "Hello, Dolly!" with two crimson dollies descending two mauve staircases—and with a chorus line that waggishly included Joel Grey, Yul Brynner, Burgess Meredith and the like—got out of hand. Sleek, sure, robust, finally rip-roaring. Ditto the duo-medley of "I" songs, with the pair harmonizing on "Red, Red Robin" and doing counterpoint with "Indian Love Call" and "Tea for Two" (Martin yodeling and Merman munching on the fox-trot).

It's Tuesday morning now. I hear music and there's no one there . . .

Of course I'd received the usual telegrams and flowers on opening night. Among them was one from the president of Lamston's chain stores. On the *Today* show, when asked whether my mind ever wandered during a long run, I said, "Sure. Sometimes when I'm singing a ballad I'm really thinking, I've got to get over to Lamston's and down to Macy's." The president wired to thank me.

On Tuesday morning, when Walter Kerr was hearing music, I was receiving a daintily wrapped huge package. Upon opening it, I found hair rollers, rain bonnets, nail files, fingernail polish, combs with flowers attached, shower caps—all kinds of goodies. On top was a card. It read: "FROM YOUR FRIENDS AT LAMSTON'S."

I'd intended to take it easy that day, but I got all dolled up and shot over to the Lamston's where I regularly shop to spend the afternoon kibitzing with the salesladies.

I knew again how much the love that flows over the footlights and spills into the streets means to me. Over the span of years I've collected a lot. And I also knew then that as long as I have my voice I'll go on drawing on it.

The only serious blight to my happiness during 1977 lay in the reminders that Pop's iron constitution was beginning to fail. I realized that there was no way he could make that big one-hundredth birthday party he'd always looked forward to. In his ninety-eighth year, his health began to decline alarmingly. Although he spent the summer in New Jersey with Kathryn, they cut their stay short in the fall and returned to the city, where Pop was admitted to Roosevelt Hospital.

In spite of the best care, his body failed to respond. After several weeks, his doctor advised converting Pop's apartment into a tiny hospital, with twenty-four-hour nursing care, and we brought him home.

I visited him several times daily. Sometimes he was too miserable to respond. But on other days he'd make a supreme effort to reassure me. He'd tell jokes, kid me about wanting his cut of the profits from this book, or we'd sing "Alice Blue Gown" and other favorites of his, with Pop recalling all the lyrics. More often, though, tears would course down his cheeks and he'd talk about joining Mom.

He left me on December 22, 1977. Even though I had been preparing myself for the inevitable, when he passed it was almost impossible for me to accept. Then I realized that I was being selfish in wanting to keep him. This was the best thing for him. There would be no more suffering, and in my heart of hearts I could take comfort in the conviction that he was happy with Mom and Ethel Jr.—and that one day we'd all be together again.

So I steeled myself, tried to look on the bright side and continued the work in which Pop had always taken so much pride.

Because of all the success I've enjoyed, I'm often asked to advise young people who want to go into the theater. But truthfully, I don't feel that I have the secret. I'd like to say, Work hard, never give up, keep trying, that's the secret. But that's not true. In my case things have pretty much been handed to me.

I'll pat myself on the back and admit I have talent. Beyond that, I just happened to be in the right place at the right time.

When they were casting *Girl Crazy*, I was singing up a storm at the Brooklyn Paramount. Vinton Freedley saw me and took me to George Gershwin. Gershwin gave me "I Got Rhythm." Now how far wrong can you go with that? Or "Sam and Delilah"? Once I had the attention, all I had to do was deliver.

I do think you have to make that big dent to begin with.

I don't want to sound pretentious, but in a funny way I feel I'm the last of a kind. I don't mean that there aren't some girls out there somewhere who are just as talented as I was. But even if they are, where will they find the shows like *Girl Crazy, Anything Goes, Annie Get Your Gun, Call Me Madam* and *Gypsy?* They just don't produce those vehicles anymore.

I feel very fortunate. I wouldn't change one thing about my professional life and I make it a point not to dwell on my mistakes. I've got everything I need for the rest of my life, and I'm still going strong. Everything's coming up roses—for me.

APPENDIX

Legitimate Stage Musicals

1930   **GIRL CRAZY**

Book by Guy Bolton and John McGowan; music by George Gershwin; lyrics by Ira Gershwin; produced by Alex A. Aarons and Vinton Freedley; staged by Alexander Leftwich; dances by George Hale; settings by Donald Oenslager; costumes by Kiviette. Opened at the Alvin Theater, October 14, 1930. 272 performances.

Cast:

Danny Churchill	Allen Kearns
Molly Gray	Ginger Rogers
Pete	Clyde Veaux
Lank Sanders	Carlton Macy
Gieber Goldfarb	Willie Howard
Flora James	Eunice Healy
Patsy West	Peggy O'Connor
Kate Fothergill	Ethel Merman
Slick Fothergill	William Kent
Sam Mason	Donald Foster
Tess Parker	Olive Brady
Jake Howell	Lew Parker
Eagle Rock	Chief Rivers
Hotel Proprietor	Jack Classon
Lariat Joe	Starr Jones

Sergeant of Police	Norman Curtis
The Foursome	Marshall Smith, Ray Johnson, Del Porter, Dwight Snyder

Antonio and Renee DeMarco
Red Nichols and his orchestra; Roger Edens at the piano

Ladies of the ensemble: Lillian Ostrom, Kay Downer, Gertrude Lowe, Norma Butler, Gloria Beaumont, Kathryn Cathcart, Julia Pirie, Vivian Porter, Ruth Gordon, Mary Mascher, Virginia May, Marion Harcke, Muriel La Count, Lillian Loray, Elsie Neal, Faye Greene, Nondas Wayne, Ruth Timmons, LaVern Evans, Betty Morton, Bobby Loyd, Vivian Keefer, Dorothy Donnelly, Jane Lane, Gene Brady, Lillian Garson, Marvyn Ray, Thomasine Haye, Dorothy Gordon, Leila Laney, Paulette Winston, Rena Landeau, Kathy Schauer

Gentlemen of the ensemble: Bob Gebhardt, Bob Derden, Hazard Newberry, Bob Burton, Harry Griffin, Jack Fago, James Notarro, Starr Jones, Norman Curtis, John Sciortino, Jack Classon, Kendall Northrop, Mickie Forbs, Jack Barrett, Arthur Craig, Dick Nealy

Orchestra directed by Earl Busby

MUSICAL NUMBERS

Act I:

Bidin' My Time	The Foursome
The Lonesome Cowboy	Cowpunchers
Could You Use Me	Ginger Rogers and Allen Kearns
Bronco Busters	Dudeens and Cowboys
Barbary Coast	Peggy O'Connor, Eunice Healy, Olive Brady, Chorus
Specialty	Eunice Healy
Embraceable You	Ginger Rogers and Allen Kearns
Finaletto	Willie Howard, William Kent
Sam and Delilah	Ethel Merman
I Got Rhythm	Ethel Merman and Chorus

Act II:

Land of the Gay Caballero	Ensemble
Specialty Dance	The DeMarcos
But Not for Me	Ginger Rogers and Willie Howard
Treat Me Rough	William Kent and Chorus
Boy, What Love Has Done to Me	Ethel Merman
Cactus Time in Arizona	Ginger Rogers and Chorus

GEORGE WHITE'S SCANDALS
(Eleventh Edition)

Sketches by George White, Lew Brown, Irving Caesar; songs by Lew
Brown and Ray Henderson; produced and staged by George White; set-
tings by Joseph Urban; costumes by Charles LeMaire. Opened at the
Apollo Theater, September 14, 1931. 202 performances.

Cast:

Rudy Vallee   Ross McLean
Everett Marshall   Hazel Boffinger
Ethel Barrymore Colt   Lois Eckhart
Peggy Moseley   Willie and Eugene Howard
Alice Frohman   Gale Quadruplets
Joanna Allen   Barbara Blair
Ethel Merman   Jane Alden
Ray Bolger   Joan Abbott
Loomis Sisters   Fred Manatt

and

THE MOST BEAUTIFUL SHOW GIRLS ON THE STAGE

Hazel Boffinger, Pearl Bradley, Lois Eckhart, Joanna Allen, Peggy Mose-
ley, Renee Johnson, Cornelia Rogers, Mae Slattery, Jacqueline Feeley, Inez
DuPlessis, Anne Morgan, Peggy Ring, Julia Gorman, Mary Ann Carr, Pa-
tricia Howard, Margaret Heller, Hazel Nevin, Alice Faye, Marian Thomp-
son, Adelaide Raleigh, Ethel Lawrence, Joan English, Myra Gerald, Beth
Foth, Betty Allen, Dorothy Daly, Patsy Clarke, Gay Delis, Rose Collins,
Dorothy Keene, Gloria Mossman, Hilda Knight, Gloria Pierre, Florence
Johnson, Gay Hill

Orchestra directed by Al Goodman

MUSICAL NUMBERS

Act I:

The Marvelous Empire State   Ray Bolger
Life Is Just a Bowl of Cherries   Ethel Merman
Beginning of Love   Loomis Sisters
The Thrill Is Gone   Everett Marshall
This Is the Missus   Rudy Vallee
Ladies and Gentlemen, That's Love   Ethel Merman
That's Why Darkies Were Born   Everett Marshall

Act II:

Song of the Foreign Legion	Everett Marshall
Here It Is	Joan Abbott
My Song	Rudy Vallee and Ethel Merman
Back from Hollywood	Barbara Blair, Julia Gorman, Hilda Knight, Betty Allen
The Good Old Days	Rudy Vallee, Willie Howard, Ethel Merman
The Wonder Bar	Entire Company

1932   HUMPTY DUMPTY

Book by B. G. DeSylva and Laurence Schwab; additional dialogue by Sid Silvers; songs by Nacio Herb Brown and Richard A. Whiting; produced by Laurence Schwab and B. G. DeSylva; staged by Laurence Schwab; dances by George Hale; settings by Cleon Throckmorton and Charles LeMaire; costumes by Kiviette. Opened at the Nixon Theater, Pittsburgh, September 26, 1932. Closed in Pittsburgh.

Cast:

Sam Moscow	Lou Holtz
Rebecca Moscowitz	Lisa Silvert
Louis Mosco	Sid Silvers
Consuelo	Doris Groday
D. W. Croffuth	Douglas Wood
Martin Sully	Eddie Foy, Jr.
Michael Sully	J. C. Nugent
Gerald Townsend	William Lynn
Irene Parker	June Knight
Wanda Brill	Ethel Merman
Bonelli	Walter Armen
Peter Knox	Harry T. Shannon
Jay Gordon	Oscar Ragland
Miss Jersey City	Sara Jane
Dancer	Vernon Biddle
Show Girl	Toni Chase
Actress	Edith Speare
Steve	O. J. Banasse
The Diamond Boys	Tom, Harold, Hugh Diamond

Mary and Bobby	Mary and Bobby Day
The Admirals	Thomas Ladd, Jack Armstrong, Budd Kelhner, Paul Pegue
The Ritz Quartette	Edward Delbridge, Neil Evans, Chet Bree, William H. Stamm

Dancers: Gene Brady, Jean Carson, Dody Donnelly, Madeline Dunbar, Mitzi Garner, Billy Green, Frances Gordon, Marion Herson, Juliette Jenner, Dorothy Kal, Irene Kelly, Evelyn Laurie, Frances McHugh, Florence Mallee, Mary Joan Martin, Peggy Moseley, Ann McKenney, Bernice O'Neal, Blanche Poston, Julia Pirie, Adelaide Raleigh, Llona Sears, Marie Vannerman, Leona Wallace, Mildred Webb, Betty Allen

Orchestra under the direction of Lou Silvers

TAKE A CHANCE

Book by B. G. DeSylva and Laurence Schwab; additional dialogue by Sid Silvers; songs by Nacio Herb Brown and Richard Whiting; additional songs by Vincent Youmans; produced by Laurence Schwab and B. G. DeSylva; staged by Edgar MacGregor; musical numbers staged by Bobby Connolly; settings by Cleon Throckmorton; costumes by Kiviette and Charles Le-Maire. Opened at the Apollo Theater, November 26, 1932. 243 performances.

Cast:

Duke Stanley	Jack Haley
Louie Webb	Sid Silvers
Toni Ray	June Knight
Wanda Brill	Ethel Merman
Kenneth Raleigh	Jack Whiting
Andrew Raleigh	Douglas Wood
Consuelo Raleigh	Mitzi Mayfair
Mike Caruso	Robert Gleckler
Thelma Green	Josephine Dunn
A Butler	George Pauncefort
The Ritz Quartette	William H. Stamm, Edward Delbridge, Neil Evans, Chet Bree
The Admirals	Tommy Ladd, Jack Armstrong, Budd Kehlner, Paul Pegue

Actors and Actresses in Kenneth Raleigh's Revue "Humpty Dumpty": Oscar Ragland, Sara Jane, John Grant, Louise Seidel, Lee Beggs, Al Downing, Andrew and Louise Carr

Dancers: Louise Allen, Gerry Billings, Lucille Brodin, Flo Brooks, Jean Carson, Marian Dixon, Helen Fairweather, Emily Fitzpatrick, Arline Garfield, Frances Gordon, Ethel Green, Marion Herson, Julie Jenner, Dorothy Kal, Gloria Kelly, Paula King, Jane Lane, Evelyn Laurie, Florence Mallee, Anna Marie McKenney, Frances McHugh, Dorothy Morgan, Julia Pirie, Blanche Poston, Adelaide Raleigh, Mildred Webb, James Ardell, Henry King, Clark Leston, Edward Shane

Orchestra under the direction of Max Meth; Sam Gurski's Recording Orchestra

MUSICAL NUMBERS

Act I:

The Life of the Party	Nightclub Girls and Guests
Should I Be Sweet	June Knight
So Do I	Jack Whiting, June Knight, Guests
I Got Religion	Ethel Merman
She's Nuts About Me	Jack Haley
Tickled Pink	Jack Whiting and Girls
Turn Out the Lights	Sid Silvers, Jack Haley, Jack Whiting, Girls
Charity	Guests
I Long to Belong to You	Jack Whiting and June Knight
Rise and Shine	Ethel Merman and Ensemble

Act II:

Tonight Is Opening Night	Ensemble
Smoothie	Jack Haley and Ethel Merman
Eadie Was a Lady	Ethel Merman and Ensemble
Should I Be Sweet (Revue Version)	June Knight and Girls

1934   ANYTHING GOES

Book by P. G. Wodehouse and Guy Bolton; revised by Howard Lindsay and Russel Crouse; music and lyrics by Cole Porter; produced by Vinton

272

Freedley, Inc.; staged by Howard Lindsay; dances by Robert Alton; settings by Donald Oenslager; gowns by Jenkins. Opened at the Alvin Theater, November 21, 1934. 420 performances.

Cast:

Bartender	George E. Mack
Elisha J. Whitney	Paul Everton
Billy Crocker	William Gaxton
Bellboy	Irving Pincus
Reno Sweeney	Ethel Merman
Reporter	Edward Delbridge
First Cameraman	Chet Bree
Second Cameraman	Neal Evans
Sir Evelyn Oakleigh	Leslie Barrie
Hope Harcourt	Bettina Hall
Mrs. Wadsworth T. Harcourt	Helen Raymond
Bishop Dodson	Pacie Ripple
Ching	Richard Wang
Ling	Charlie Fang
Snooks	Drucilla Strain
Steward	William Stamm
Assistant Purser	Val Vestoff
First Federal Man	Harry Wilson
Second Federal Man	Arthur Imperato
Mrs. Wentworth	May Abbey
Mrs. Frick	Florence Earle
Reverend Dr. Moon	Victor Moore
Bonnie Letour	Vera Dunn
Chief Officer	Houston Richards
Ship's Drunk	William Barry
Mr. Swift	Maurice Elliott
Little Boy	Billy Curtis
Captain	John C. King
Babe	Vivian Vance
The Foursome	Marshall Smith, Ray Johnson, Dwight Snyder, Del Porter
The Ritz Quartette	Chet Bree, Bill Stamm, Neal Evans, Ed Delbridge
The Alvin Quartette	Arthur Imperato, David Glidden, Richard Nealy, Stuart Fraser
Ship's Orchestra	The Stylists

Reno's Angels: Ruth Bond, Norma Butler, Enes Early, Marjorie Fisher, Ruth Gomley, Irene Hamlin, Renee Johnson, Irene Kelly, Leoda Knapp, Doris Maye, Lillian Ostrom, Jackie Paige, Mary Philips, Cornelia Rogers, Frances Stewart, Ruth Shaw, Eleanore Sheridan

Musical direction by Earl Busby

MUSICAL NUMBERS

Act I:

I Get a Kick Out of You	Ethel Merman and William Gaxton
Bon Voyage	Ensemble
All Through the Night	Bettina Hall and William Gaxton
Sailor's Chanty	The Foursome
Where Are the Men?	Vera Dunn, Angels, Petty Officers, Girls
You're the Top	Ethel Merman and William Gaxton
Anything Goes	Ethel Merman, Foursome, Ensemble

Act II:

Public Enemy Number One	Passengers
Blow, Gabriel, Blow	Ethel Merman and Ensemble
Be Like a Bluebird	Victor Moore
All Through the Night (Reprise)	Bettina Hall and William Gaxton
Buddy, Beware	Ethel Merman
I Get a Kick Out of You (Reprise)	Ethel Merman
The Gypsy in Me	Bettina Hall and Girls
Finale	Entire Company

1 9 3 6   RED, HOT AND BLUE

Book by Howard Lindsay and Russel Crouse; music and lyrics by Cole Porter; produced by Vinton Freedley; staged by Howard Lindsay; choreographed by George Hale; settings by Donald Oenslager; costumes by Constance Ripley. Opened at the Alvin Theater, October 29, 1936. 183 performances.

Cast:

Reporters	Geoffrey Errett, Karl Kohrs, Bill Houston, Norman Lind, Vivian Vance, Betty Allen
Deputy Warden	Lew Parker
Warden of Larks Nest Prison	Forrest Orr
"Nails" O'Reilly Duquesne	Ethel Merman
"Policy" Pinkle	Jimmy Durante
Vivian	Vivian Vance
Anne Westcott	Dorothy Vernon
Grace	Grace Hartman
Lucille	Lucille Johnson
Cecile	Cecile Carey
Kay	Kay Picture
Irene	Ethelyne Holt
Betty	Betty Allen
"Fingers"	Paul Hartman
Bob Hale	Bob Hope
Sonny Hadley	Thurston Crane
Peaches La Fleur	Polly Walters
"Ratface" Dugan	Bill Benner
"Sure Thing" Simpson	Prentiss Davis
"Flap-Ears" Metelli	Leo Shippers
"Louie the Louse"	Bernard Jannsen
Mrs. Peabody	May Abbey
Tiny	Anne Wolfe
Louella	Jeanette Owens
Senator Musilovitch	Lew Parker
Senator Malvinsky	Robert Leonard
Senator O'Shaughnessy	Forrest Orr
Senator Del Grasso	Houston Richards
Sergeant-at-Arms	Norman Lind
First Expressman	Geoffrey Errett
Second Expressman	Karl Kohrs
Girl	Gloria Clare
First Marine	Frank Archer
Second Marine	Bruce Covert
Decorator	Houston Richards

Debutantes: Ruth Ernst, Helen Hudson, Evelyn Kelly, Marquita Nicolai, Annette Nine, Jessica Pepper, Eve Sorel

Guests: Ruth Bond, Jeanette Bradley, Dorothy Jackson, Jean Scott, Dorothy Schwank, Stella Bailey, Charlene Tucker, Nancy Lee, Althea Elder, Prudence Hayes, Peggy Oden, Mary Joan Martin, Grace Gillern, Ruth Gormley, Marguerite James, Muriel Downey, June LeRoy, Hazel Nevin, Frances Stewart, Gloria Clare, Beverly Hosier, Joanna Allen

Orchestra under the direction of Frank Tours

MUSICAL NUMBERS

Act I:

At Ye Olde Coffee Shoppe in Cheyenne	Reporters and Girls
It's a Great Life	Guests and Debutantes
Perennial Debutantes	Guests and Debutantes
Ours	Dorothy Vernon, Thurston Crane, Grace and Paul Hartman, Girls
Down in the Depths on the 90th Floor	Ethel Merman
Carry On	Thurston Crane, Reporters, Mugs
You've Got Something	Bob Hope and Ethel Merman
It's De-Lovely	Ethel Merman and Bob Hope
A Little Skipper from Heaven Above	Jimmy Durante, Mugs, Reporters
Specialty Dance	Grace and Paul Hartman
Five Hundred Million	Vivian Vance, Betty Allen, Debutantes, Guests
Ridin' High	Ethel Merman and Ensemble

Act II:

We're About to Start Big Rehearsin'	Debutantes
Hymn to Hymen	Guests
What a Great Pair We'll Be	Dorothy Vernon and Thurston Crane
You're a Bad Influence on Me	Ethel Merman
Red, Hot and Blue	Ethel Merman and Ensemble
Finale	Entire Company

Book by J. P. McEvoy; music by Arthur Schwartz; lyrics by Dorothy Fields; produced by Dwight Deere Wiman; staged by Joshua Logan; choreographed by Carl Randall; settings by Jo Mielziner; costumes by John Hambleton. Opened at the Majestic Theater, February 9, 1939. 127 performances.

Cast:

Assistant Director	Ted Gary
Second Assistant Director	Davis Cunningham
Third Assistant Director	Edward Kane
Fourth Assistant Director	Robert Shanley
Fifth Assistant Director	Dan Dailey Jr.
Sixth Assistant Director	Roger Stearns
First Girl	Edith Grant
Second Girl	Thekla Horn
Third Girl	Nancy Wiman
Wardrobe Woman	Johanne Hoven
Carpenter	David Morris
Fourth Girl	Frances Rands
Electrician	Anthony Albert
Soundman	Rennie McEvoy
Babe	Dawn Roland
Wilder	Clinton Sundberg
Cameraman	Walter Wagner
Assistant Soundman	Ambrose Costello
Fifth Girl	Phyllis Roque
Sixth Girl	Natasha Dana
Dancing Girl	Nora Kaye
Leading Man	Walter Cassel
Script Girl	Gloria Clare
Jeanette Adair	Ethel Merman
Bess	Mildred Natwick
Voice Coach	Mary Wickes
Maid	Kathryn Mayfield
Jockey	Basil Galahoff
Bill	Jimmy Durante
Darrow	Robert Ross
John Blake	Richard Carlson
Tata	Tamara Toumanova

Dawson	Richard Barbee
Photographers	Walter Cassel, Edward Kane, Davis Cunningham, Robert Shanley
Russian Consul	Russel Protopoff
French Consul	Dwight Godwin
Italian Consul	Fernando Alonso
English Consul	David Morris
German Consul	Ambrose Costello
Watchman	Ambrose Costello

Ladies and Gentlemen of the Ballet: Alicia Alonso, Peggy Conrad, Maria De Galanta, Jane Everett, Gail Grant, Marion Haynes, Thekla Horn, Johanne Hoven, Marjorie Johnstone, Nora Kaye, Maria Karniloff, Frances Rands, Audrey Reynolds, Olga Suarez, Margaret Vasilieff, Mary Jane Williams, Anthony Albert, Fernando Alonso, Paul Alvin, Sayva Andreieff, Dwight Godwin, Basil Galahoff, George Kiddon, Russel Protopoff, Richard Reed, Newcombe Rice, Jerome Robbins

Musical direction by Al Goodman

MUSICAL NUMBERS

Act I:

Places, Everybody	Company
One Brief Moment	Walter Cassel, Paul Godkin, Ensemble
This Is It	Ethel Merman, Walter Cassel, Edward Kane, Robert Shanley, Davis Cunningham
All the Time	Richard Carlson and Tamara Toumanova
Self-Made Man	Jimmy Durante
Okay for Sound	Rennie McEvoy, Dawn Roland, Ensemble
A Lady Needs a Change	Ethel Merman
Terribly Attractive	Jimmy Durante and Mildred Natwick
Just a Little Bit More	Ethel Merman
Nightclub Ballet	Tamara Toumanova, Ted Gary, Dan Dailey Jr., Ensemble
Just a Little Bit More (Reprise)	Richard Carlson

278

Act II:

As of Today	Rennie McEvoy, Frances Rands, Mary Wickes, David Morris, Kathryn Mayfield, Betty Hunter, Dan Dailey Jr., Ensemble
He's Goin' Home	Jimmy Durante and Ensemble
I'll Pay the Check	Ethel Merman
Never a Dull Moment	Dawn Roland, Ted Gary, Dan Dailey Jr., Rennie McEvoy, Ensemble
This Is It (Reprise)	Ethel Merman
Court Ballet	Tamara Toumanova, Corps de Ballet and Walter Cassel, Edward Kane, Robert Shanley, Davis Cunningham
It's All Yours	Ethel Merman and Jimmy Durante
Finale	Entire Company

DUBARRY WAS A LADY

Book by Herbert Fields and B. G. DeSylva; songs by Cole Porter; produced by B. G. DeSylva; staged by Edgar MacGregor; choreographed by Robert Alton; settings and costumes by Raoul Pene DuBois. Opened at the 46th Street Theater, December 6, 1939. 408 performances.

Cast:

Jones	Hugh Cameron
Bill Kelly	Walter Armin
Harry Norton	Charles Walters
Alice Barton	Betty Grable
Florian	Harold Cromer
Louis Blore	Bert Lahr
Vi Hennessey	Jean Moorehead
May Daly	Ethel Merman
Alex Barton	Ronald Graham
Ann Barton	Kay Sutton
Manuel Gomez	Tito Renaldo
Charley	Benny Baker
Four Internationals	Douglas Hawkins, Peter Holliday, Robert Herring, Carl Nicholas

279

Starlets of the Club Petit: Geraldine Spreckels, Betty Allen, Ann Graham, Janice Carter, Jacqueline Franc, Marguerite Benton

Dancing Girls: Stella Clauson, Nina Wayler, Marion Harvey, Tilda Getze, Nancy Knott, Jane Sproule, Helen Bennett, Edyth Turgell, Barbara Pond, Evelyn Bonefine, Ruth Bond, Patricia Knight, Adele Jergens, Frances Krell, Gloria Martin, Beverly Hosier, Gloria Arden, Marie Vannemen, Virginia Cheneval.

Dancing Boys: Gene Ashley, Boris Butleroff, Joel Friend, Russell Georgiev, Stanley Grill, Mel Kacher, Don Liberto, Tito Renaldo, Lewis Turner, Paul Thorne

Orchestra under the direction of Gene Salzer

MUSICAL NUMBERS

Act I:

Ev'ry Day a Holiday	Betty Grable, Charles Walters Ensemble
It Ain't Etiquette	Bert Lahr and Jean Moorehead
When Love Beckoned	Ethel Merman
Come On In	Ethel Merman and Ensemble
Dance	Betty Grable and Charles Walters
Dream Song	Four Internationals
Mesdames and Messieurs	Dames de la Cour
Gavotte	Betty Grable and Ensemble
But in the Morning, No!	Ethel Merman and Bert Lahr
Do I Love You	Ronald Graham and Ethel Merman
DuBarry Was a Lady	Entire Company

Act II:

Danse Tzigane	Betty Grable, Ballet
Give Him the Oo-La-La	Ethel Merman
Well, Did You Evah!	Betty Grable and Charles Walters
It Was Written in the Stars	
L'Apres Midi d'un Boeuf	Benny Baker and Harold Cromer
Katie Went to Haiti	Ethel Merman and Ensemble
Friendship	Ethel Merman and Bert Lahr
Finale	The Company

280

Book by Herbert Fields and B. G. DeSylva; songs by Cole Porter; produced by B. G. DeSylva; directed by Edgar MacGregor; choreographed by Robert Alton; settings and costumes by Raoul Pene DuBois. Opened at the 46th Street Theater, October 30, 1940. 501 performances.

Cast:

Mrs. Gonzales	Conchita
Mac	Eppy Pearson
Skat Briggs	Pat Harrington
Windy Deegan	Frank Hyers
Woozy Hogan	Rags Ragland
Chiquita	Nadine Gae
Fruit Peddler	Linda Griffith
Tim	Roger Gerry
Tom	Roy Blaine
Ted	Ted Daniels
Ty	Lipman Duckat
Hattie Maloney	Ethel Merman
Leila Tree	Phyllis Brooks
Mildred Hunter	Elaine Shepard
Kitty Belle Randolph	Ann Graham
Nick Bullett	James Dunn
Florrie	Betty Hutton
Geraldine Bullett	Joan Carroll
Vivian Budd	Arthur Treacher
First Stranger	Hal Conklin
Second Stranger	Frank DeRoss
Mike	Jack Donahue
Whitney Randolph	James Kelso

Singing Girls: Janis Carter, Ann Graham, Marguerite Benton, Vera Dean

Dancing Girls: June Allyson, Irene Austin, Jane Ball, Mimi Berry, Betsy Blair, Lucille Bremer, Nancy Chaplin, Kathlyn Coulter, Ronnie Cunningham, Marianne Crude, Doris Dowling, Vera-Ellen, Miriam Franklyn, Marguerite James, Pat Likely, Mary McDonald, Renee Russell, Audrey Westphal

Dancing Boys: Jack Baker, Cliff Ferre, Fred Ney, Harry Rogue, Jack Riley, Billy Skipper, Art Stanley, Carl Trees, Don Weismuller

Orchestra under the direction of Gene Salzer; accompanist to Miss Merman, Lew Kesler

MUSICAL NUMBERS

Act I:

Join It Right Away	Rags Ragland, Frank Hyers, Pat Harrington
Visit Panama	Ethel Merman, Ensemble
American Family	Janis Carter, Al Downing, June Allyson
My Mother Would Love You	Ethel Merman and James Dunn
I've Still Got My Health	Ethel Merman
Fresh As a Daisy	Betty Hutton, Pat Harrington, Frank Hyers
Welcome to Jerry	Singing Boys and Girls and Ensemble
Let's Be Buddies	Ethel Merman and Joan Carroll
They Ain't Done Right by Our Nell	Betty Hutton and Arthur Treacher
I'm Throwin' a Ball Tonight	Ethel Merman and Ensemble
Conga	Ethel Merman, Nadine Gae

Act II:

I Detest a Fiesta	Singing Boys and Girls and Ensemble
Who Would Have Dreamed	Janis Carter and Lipman Duckat
Make It Another Old Fashioned, Please	Ethel Merman
All I've Got to Get Now Is My Man	Betty Hutton and Ensemble
You Said It	Ethel Merman, Arthur Treacher, Rags Ragland, Pat Harrington, Frank Hyers
Let's Be Buddies (Reprise)	Ethel Merman and Joan Carroll
God Bless the Women	Rags Ragland, Pat Harrington, Frank Hyers
Finale	Entire Company

Book by Herbert and Dorothy Fields; songs by Cole Porter; produced by Michael Todd; staged by Hassard Short; book directed by Herbert Fields; dances by Jack Cole; settings by Howard Bay; costumes by Billy Livingston. Opened at the Alvin Theater, January 7, 1943. 422 performances.

Cast:

Chiquita Hart	Paula Laurence
Roger Calhoun	Jed Prouty
Harry Hart	Allen Jenkins
Blossom Hart	Ethel Merman
Staff Sgt. Rocky Fulton	Bill Johnson
Sgt. Laddie Green	Stuart Langley
Mary-Francis	Betty Garrett
Betty-Jean	Betty Bruce
Michaela	Anita Alvarez
Lois and Lucille	Barnes Twins
Lt. Col. S. D. Grubbs	Jack Hartley
Mr. Tobias Twitch	William Lynn
MP	Mervyn Vye
Corp. Burns	Bill Callahan
Sgt. Carter	Remi Martel
Melanie Walker	Frances Mercer
Burke	Walter Rinner
Mrs. Grubbs	Madeleine Clive
Gordon	Alan Fleming

Dancing Girls: Alice Anthony, May Block, Jean Coyne, Betty Deane, Patricia Dearing, Ruth Godfrey, Dolores (Dody) Goodman, Betty Heather, Margie Jackson, Jean Owens, Leslie Shannon, Ethel Sherman, Puddy Smith, Patricia Welles, Helen Wenzel, June Wieting, Nina Starkey

Dancing Boys: Stanley Catron, Bob Davis, Benny DeSio, Jerry Florio, Albert Gaeta, Aaron Gobetz, Ray Harrison, David Mann, Remi Martel, Paul Martin, Duncan Noble, Ricky Riccardi, William Vaux, Joe Viggiano, William Weber, Lou Wills Jr., Parker Wilson

Singing Boys: Jimmy Allison, Joseph Bell, Alan Fleming, Richard Harvey, Art Lambert, Buddy Irving, Bruce Lord, Paul Mario, John W. Maye, Joseph Monte, Walter Rinner, Mervyn Vye

Band: Bill Dreslin, Ted Fischer, Ken Snell, Jimmy Hanson, Wally Baron, Tony Frasetti

Orchestra conducted by William Parson

MUSICAL NUMBERS

Act I:

See That You're Born in Texas	Bill Johnson and Ensemble
When My Baby Goes to Town	Bill Johnson
Something for the Boys	Ethel Merman and Boys
When We're Home on the Range	Ethel Merman, Paula Laurence, Allen Jenkins
Could It Be You	Bill Johnson
Hey, Good Lookin'	Ethel Merman and Bill Johnson
He's a Right Guy	Ethel Merman
Assembly Line	Allen Jenkins, Betty Garrett, Betty Bruce and Girls
The Leader of a Big Time Band	Ethel Merman

Act II:

I'm in Love with a Soldier Boy	Betty Garrett, Girls and Boys
There's a Happy Land in the Sky	Ethel Merman, Paula Laurence, Allen Jenkins, William Lynn, Bill Johnson
He's a Right Guy (Reprise)	Ethel Merman
Could It Be You (Waltz Reprise)	Bill Johnson and Ensemble
By the Mississinewa	Ethel Merman and Paula Laurence
Finale	Ethel Merman and Company

1946   ANNIE GET YOUR GUN

Book by Herbert and Dorothy Fields; songs by Irving Berlin; produced by Rodgers and Hammerstein; staged by Joshua Logan; choreographed by Helen Tamiris; settings by Jo Mielziner; costumes by Lucinda Ballard. Opened at the Imperial Theater, May 16, 1946. 1147 performances.

Cast:

Little Boy	Warren Berlinger
Little Girl	Mary Ellen Glass
Charlie Davenport	Marty May
Iron Tail	Daniel Nagrin
Yellow Foot	Walter John
Mac	Cliff Dunstan

284

Cowboys	Rob Taylor, Bernard Griffin, Jack Pierce
Cowgirls	Mary Grey, Franca Baldwin
Foster Wilson	Art Barnett
Coolie	Beau Tilden
Dolly Tate	Lea Penman
Winnie Tate	Betty Anne Nyman
Tommy Keeler	Kenny Bowers
Frank Butler	Ray Middleton
Girl with Bouquet	Katrina Van Oss
Annie Oakley	Ethel Merman
Minnie	Nancy Jean Raab
Jessie	Camilla De Witt
Nellie	Marlene Cameron
Little Jake	Clifford Sales
Harry	Don Liberto
Mary	Ellen Hanley
Col. William F. Cody (Buffalo Bill)	William O'Neal
Mrs. Little Horse	Alma Ross
Mrs. Black Tooth	Elizabeth Malone
Mrs. Yellow Foot	Nellie Ranson
Trainman	John Garth III
Waiter	Leon Bibb
Porter	Clyde Turner
Riding Mistress	Lubov Roudenko
Maj. Gordon Lillie (Pawnee Bill)	George Lipton
Chief Sitting Bull	Harry Bellaver
Mabel	Mary Woodley
Louise	Ostrid Lind
Nancy	Dorothy Richards
Timothy Gardner	Jack Bryon
Andy Turner	Earl Sauvain
Clyde Smith	Victor Clarke
John	Rob Taylor
Freddie	Robert Dixon
Wild Horse	Daniel Nagrin
Pawnee's Messenger	Milton Watson
Major Domo	John Garth III
Waiters	Clyde Turner, Leon Bibb
Mr. Schuyler Adams	Don Liberto
Mrs. Schuyler Adams	Dorothy Richards
Dr. Percy Ferguson	Bernard Griffin

Mrs. Percy Ferguson	Marietta Vore
Debutante	Ruth Vrana
Mr. Ernest Henderson	Art Barnett
Mrs. Ernest Henderson	Truly Barbara
Sylvia Potter-Porter	Marjorie Crossland
Mr. Clay	Rob Taylor
Mr. Lockwood	Fred Rivett
Girl in Pink	Christina Lind
Girl in White	Mary Grey

Singers and Dancers: Truly Barbara, Ellen Hanley, Christina Lind, Ostrid Lind, Dorothy Richards, Ruth Strickland, Katrina Van Oss, Marietta Vore, Ruth Vrana, Mary Woodley, Jack Bryon, Victor Clarke, Robert Dixon, Bernard Griffin, Marvin Goodis, Vincent Henry, Don Liberto, Fred Rivett, Earl Sauvain, Rob Taylor, Franca Baldwin, Tessie Carrano, Madeleine Detry, Cuprienne Gabelman, Barbara Gaye, Evelyn Giles, Mary Grey, Harriet Roeder, Jack Beaber, John Begg, Michael Maule, Duncan Noble, Jack Pierce, Paddy Stone, Ken Whelan, Parker Wilson

Orchestra under the direction of Jay Blackton

MUSICAL NUMBERS

Act I:

Buffalo Bill	Marty May and Ensemble
I'm a Bad, Bad Man	Ray Middleton and Girls
Dance	Duncan Noble, Paddy Stone, Parker Wilson, Ensemble
Doin' What Comes Natur'lly	Ethel Merman, Nancy Jean Raab, Camilla De Witt, Marlene Cameron, Clifford Sales, Art Barnett
The Girl That I Marry	Ray Middleton
You Can't Get a Man with a Gun	Ethel Merman
There's No Business Like Show Business	William O'Neal, Mary May, Ray Middleton, Ethel Merman
They Say It's Wonderful	Ray Middleton and Ethel Merman
Moonshine Lullaby	Ethel Merman, John Garth III, Leon Bibb, Clyde Turner
I'll Share It All with You	Betty Anne Nyman and Kenny Bowers
Ballyhoo	Lubov Roudenko and Ensemble

286

There's No Business Like Show Business (Reprise)	Ethel Merman
My Defenses Are Down	Ray Middleton and Boys
Wild Horse (Ceremonial Dance)	Daniel Nagrin and Dancing Boys and Girls
I'm an Indian Too	Ethel Merman

Act II:

I Got Lost in His Arms	Ethel Merman and Ensemble
Who Do You Love, I Hope	Betty Anne Nyman
I Got the Sun in the Morning	Ethel Merman and Ensemble
Dance	Lubov Roudenko and Daniel Nagrin
They Say It's Wonderful (Reprise)	Ethel Merman and Ray Middleton
The Girl That I Marry	Ray Middleton
Anything You Can Do	Ethel Merman and Ray Middleton
There's No Business Like Show Business (Reprise)	Entire Company

1950   # CALL ME MADAM

Book by Howard Lindsay and Russel Crouse; songs by Irving Berlin; produced by Leland Hayward; staged by George Abbott; choreographed by Jerome Robbins; costumes and settings by Raoul Pene DuBois; Miss Merman's costumes by Mainbocher. Opened at the Imperial Theater, October 12, 1950. 644 performances.

Cast:

Mrs. Sally Adams	Ethel Merman
The Secretary of State	Geoffrey Lumb
Supreme Court Justice	Owen Coll
Congressman Wilkins	Pat Harrington
Henry Gibson	William David
Kenneth Gibson	Russell Nype
Senator Gallagher	Ralph Chambers
Secretary to Mrs. Adams	Jeanne Bal
Butler	William Hail
Senator Brockbank	Jay Velie
Cosmo Constantine	Paul Lukas
Pemberton Sebastian	Alan Hewitt

Clerk	Stowe Phelps
Hugo Tantinnin	E. A. Krumschmidt
Sebastian Sebastian	Henry Lascoe
Princess Maria	Galina Talva
Court Chamberlain	William David
A Maid	Lily Paget
Grand Duchess Sophie	Lilia Skala
Grand Duke Otto	Owen Coll

Principal Dancers: Tommy Rall, Muriel Bentley, Arthur Partington, Norma Kaiser

The Potato Bugs—Ollie Engebretson, Richard Fjellman

Singers: Rae Abruzzo, Jeanne Bal, Trudy DeLuz, Lydia Fredericks, Estelle Gardner, Ruth McVayne, Lily Paget, Noella Peloquin, Helene Whitney, Aristide Bartis, Nathaniel Frey, William Hail, Albert Linville, Robert Penn, Tom Reider, Joan Sheehan, Stanley Simmonds, Ray Stephens

Dancers: Shellie Farrell, Nina Frenkin, Patricia Hammerlee, Barbara Heath, Norma Kaiser, Virginia LeRoy, Kirsten Valbor, Fred Hearn, Allan Knolls, Kenneth LeRoy, Ralph Linn, Douglas Moppert, Arthur Partington, Bobby Tucker, William Weslow

Orchestra under the direction of Jay Blackton

MUSICAL NUMBERS

Act I:

Mrs. Sally Adams	The Company
The Hostess with the Mostes' on the Ball	Ethel Merman
Washington Square Dance	Ethel Merman and Company
Lichtenburg	Paul Lukas and Singers
Can You Use Any Money Today?	Ethel Merman
Marrying for Love	Paul Lukas and Ethel Merman
The Ocarina	Galina Talva, Bobby Tucker, Potato Bugs, Company
It's a Lovely Day Today	Russell Nype and Galina Talva
It's a Lovely Day Today (Reprise)	Russell Nype, Norma Kaiser, Arthur Partington, Company
The Best Thing for You Would Be Me	Ethel Merman and Paul Lukas

Act II:

Lichtenburg (Reprise)	Paul Lukas and Singers
Something to Dance About	Ethel Merman, Tommy Rall, Muriel Bentley, Norma Kaiser, Arthur Partington, Company
One upon a Time Today	Russell Nype
They Like Ike	Pat Harrington, Ralph Chambers, Jay Velie
You're Just in Love	Ethel Merman and Russell Nype
The Best Thing for You Would Be Me (Reprise)	Ethel Merman and Paul Lukas
It's a Lovely Day Today (Reprise)	Russell Nype and Galina Talva
Mrs. Sally Adams (Reprise)	The Company
Finale	Ethel Merman and Company

1 9 5 6   HAPPY HUNTING

Book by Howard Lindsay and Russel Crouse; music by Harold Karr; lyrics by Matt Dubey; produced by Jo Mielziner; staged by Abe Burrows; dances and musical numbers by Alex Romero and Bob Herget; settings by Jo Mielziner; costumes by Irene Sharaff. Opened at the Majestic Theater, December 6, 1956. 412 performances.

Cast:

Sanford Stewart Jr.	Gordon Polk
Mrs. Sanford Stewart Sr.	Olive Templeton
Joseph	Mitchell M. Gregg
Beth Livingstone	Virginia Gibson
Jack Adams	Seth Riggs
Harry Watson	Gene Wesson
Charley	Delbert Anderson
Liz Livingstone	Ethel Merman
Sam	Clifford Fearl
Joe	John Craig
Freddy	George Martin
Wes	Jim Hutchison
Mary Mills	Estelle Parsons
Dick Davis	Robert C. Held
Bob Grayson	Carl Nicholas

Maude Foley	Mary Finney
Police Sergeant	Mark Zeller
Arturo	Leon Belasco
The Duke of Granada	Fernando Lamas
Count Carlos	Renato Cibelli
Waiter	Don Weissmuller
Ship's Officer	John Leslie
Barman	Warren J. Brown
Mrs. B.	Florence Dunlap
Mrs. D.	Madeleine Clive
Mrs. L.	Kelley Stephens
Terence	Jim Hutchison
Tom	Eugene Louis
Daisy	Mary Roche
Mr. T., a Member of the Hunt	John Leslie
Mr. M., a Member of the Hunt	Jay Velie
Albert, a groom	George Martin
Margaret, a maid	Mara Landi

Singers: Peggy Acheson, Marilynn Bradley, Deedy Irwin, Jane Johnston, Jean Kraemer, Mara Landi, Betty McGuire, Estelle Parsons, Noella Peloquin, Ginny Perlowin, Mary Roche, Kelley Stephens, Helene Whitney, Delbert Anderson, Edward Becker, Warren J. Brown, David Collyer, John Craig, Jack Dabdoub, Clifford Fearl, Robert C. Held, Carl Nicholas, Seth Riggs, Charles Rule, Mark Zeller

Dancers: Betty Carr, Alice Clift, Jane Fischer, Roberta Keith, Svetlana McLee, Patti Nestor, Wendy Nickerson, Fleur Raup, Sigyn, Bob Bakanic, John Harmon, Jim Hutchison, Dick Korthaze, Eugene Louis, George Martin, Jim Moore, Lowell Purvis, Don Weissmuller, Roy Wilson

Orchestra under the direction of Jay Blackton

MUSICAL NUMBERS

Act I:

Postage Stamp Principality	Tourists and Monegasques
Don't Tell Me	Gordon Polk and Virginia Gibson
It's Good to Be Here	Ethel Merman, Estelle Parsons, Robert C. Held, Carl Nicholas
Mutual Admiration Society	Ethel Merman and Virginia Gibson
For Love or Money	Girls
Bikini Dance	Virginia Gibson

It's Like a Beautiful Woman	Fernando Lamas
Wedding-of-the-Year Blues	Mary Finney, Gene Wesson, John Craig, Clifford Fearl, George Martin, Jim Hutchison, Estelle Parsons, Robert C. Held, Carl Nicholas
Mr. Livingstone	Ethel Merman
If'n	Virginia Gibson, Gordon Polk, Passengers
This Is What I Call Love	Ethel Merman

Act II:

A New-Fangled Tango	Ethel Merman, Virginia Gibson, Leon Belasco, Guests
She's Just Another Girl	Gordon Polk
The Game of Love	Ethel Merman
Happy Hunting	Ethel Merman, Fernando Lamas, Members of the Hunt
I'm a Funny Dame	Ethel Merman
This Much I Know	Fernando Lamas
Just Another Guy	Ethel Merman
Everyone Who's "Whose Who"	Seth Riggs, Gene Wesson, Footmen
Mutual Admiration Society (Reprise)	Ethel Merman and Fernando Lamas

1959 GYPSY

Book by Arthur Laurents; music by Jule Styne; lyrics by Stephen Sondheim; produced by David Merrick and Leland Hayward; staged and choreographed by Jerome Robbins; settings by Jo Mielziner; costumes by Raoul Pene DuBois. Opened at the Broadway Theater, May 21, 1959. 702 performances.

Cast:

Uncle Jocko	Mort Marshall
George	Willie Sumner
Arnold (and his guitar)	John Borden
Balloon Girl	Jody Lane
Baby Louise	Karen Moore
Rose	Ethel Merman
Baby June	Jacqueline Mayro

Newsboys	Bobby Brownell, Gene Castle, Steve Curry, Billy Harris
Pop	Erv Harmon
Weber	Joe Silver
Herbie	Jack Klugman
Louise	Sandra Church
June	Lane Bradbury
Tulsa	Paul Wallace
Yonkers	David Winters
Angie	Ian Tucker
L.A.	Michael Parks
Kringelein	Loney Lewis
Mr. Goldstone	Mort Marshall
Farm Boys	Marvin Arnold, Ricky Coll, Don Emmons, Ian Tucker, Michael Parks, Paul Wallace, David Winters
Miss Cratchitt	Peg Murray
Hollywood Blondes	
Agnes	Marilyn Cooper
Marjorie May	Patsy Bruder
Dolores	Marilyn D'Honau
Thelma	Merle Letowt
Edna	Joan Petlack
Gail	Imelda de Martin
Pastey	Richard Porter
Tessie Tura	Maria Karnilova
Mazeppa	Faith Dane
Cigar	Loney Lewis
Electra	Chotzi Foley
Showgirls	Kathryn Albertson, Gloria Kristy, Denise McLaglen, Barbara London, Theda Nelson, Carroll Jo Towers, Marie Wallace
Maid	Marsha Rivers
Phil	Joe Silver
Bougeron-Cochon	George Zima
Cow	Willie Sumner and George Zima

Orchestra under the direction of Milton Rosenstock

Act I:

May We Entertain You	Karen Moore and Jacqueline Mayro
Some People	Ethel Merman
Small World	Ethel Merman and Jack Klugman
Mr. Goldstone, I Love You	Ethel Merman and Ensemble
Little Lamb	Sandra Church
You'll Never Get Away from Me	Ethel Merman and Jack Klugman
If Mamma Was Married	Sandra Church and Lane Bradbury
All I Need Is the Girl	Paul Wallace and Sandra Church
Everything's Coming Up Roses	Ethel Merman

Act II:

Madame Rose's Toreadorables	Sandra Church and the Toreadorables
Together, Wherever We Go	Ethel Merman, Jack Klugman, Sandra Church
You Gotta Have a Gimmick	Maria Karnilova, Faith Dane, Chotzi Foley
Small World (Reprise)	Ethel Merman
Let Me Entertain You	Sandra Church and Company
Rose's Turn	Ethel Merman

1966   ANNIE GET YOUR GUN

Book by Herbert and Dorothy Fields; songs by Irving Berlin; produced by Music Theater of Lincoln Center; directed by Jack Sydow; choreography by Danny Daniels; scenery by Paul McGuire; costumes by Frank Thompson. Opened at the New York State Theater, May 31, 1966; moved to the Broadway Theater, September 28, 1966. 78 performances.

Cast:

Little Boy	Jeffrey Scott
Little Girl	Deanna Melody
Charlie Davenport	Jerry Orbach
Dolly Tate	Benay Venuta
Iron Tail	Brynar Mehl
Yellow Foot	Gary Jendell

Mac	John Dorrin
Foster Wilson	Ronn Carroll
Frank Butler	Bruce Yarnell
The Shy Girl	Diana Banks
Annie Oakley	Ethel Merman
Little Jake	David Manning
Jessie	Jeanne Tanzy
Minnie	Holly Sherwood
Col. William F. Cody	Rufus Smith
Mrs. Little Horse	Mary Falconer
Mrs. Black Tooth	Jaclynn Villamil
Mrs. Yellow Foot	Kuniko Narai
Indian Boy	Jeffrey Scott
Conductor	Jim Lynn
Porter	Beno Foster
Waiter	David Forssen
Maj. Gordon Lillie	Jack Dabdoub
Chief Sitting Bull	Harry Bellaver
The Wild Horse	Jaime Rogers
Pawnee's Messenger	Walt Hunter
Major Domo	Ben Laney
Mr. Schyler Adams	Ronn Carroll
Mrs. Schuyler Adams	Patricia Hall
Dr. Ferguson	Marc Rowan
Mrs. Ferguson	Bobbi Baird
Mr. T. L. C. Keefer	Walt Hunter
Mr. Ernest Henderson	Grant Spalding
Mrs. Ernest Henderson	Lynn Carroll
Mrs. Sylvia Potter-Porter	Mary Falconer
Mr. Clay	John Dorrin

Singers: Bobbi Baird, Vicki Belmonte, Chrysten Carroll, Lynn Carroll, Audrey Dearden, Lynn Dovel, Mary Falconer, Patricia Hall, Florence Mercer, Susan Terry, Kenny Adams, Ronn Carroll, John Dorrin, David Forssen, Beno Foster, Walt Hunter, Ben Laney, Jim Lynn, Marc Rowan, Grant Spalding

Dancers: Diana Banks, Joanne DiVito, Rozann Ford, Barbara Hancock, Ruth Lawrence, Kuniko Narai, Eva Marie Sage, Evelyn Taylor, Jaclynn Villamil, Anne Wallace, Bjarne Buchrup, Tony Catanzaro, Frank Derbas, Ronn Forella, Marcelo Gamboa, Jeremy Ives, Gary Jendell, Daniel Joel, Brynar Mehl, Gene Myers

Orchestra under the direction of Jonathan Anderson

Act I:

Colonel Buffalo Bill	Jerry Orbach, Benay Venuta, Ensemble
I'm a Bad, Bad Man	Bruce Yarnell and Girls
Doin' What Comes Natur'lly	Ethel Merman, Ronn Carroll, Children
The Girl That I Marry	Bruce Yarnell
You Can't Get a Man with a Gun	Ethel Merman
There's No Business Like Show Business	Ethel Merman, Bruce Yarnell, Rufus Smith, Jerry Orbach
They Say It's Wonderful	Ethel Merman and Bruce Yarnell
Moonshine Lullaby	Ethel Merman, Trio, Children
Wild West Pitch Dance	Jaime Rogers and Dancers
Show Business (Reprise)	Ethel Merman
My Defenses Are Down	Bruce Yarnell and Boys
Wild Horse Ceremonial Dance	Jaime Rogers and Braves
I'm an Indian Too	Ethel Merman
Adoption Dance	Ethel Merman, Jaime Rogers, Braves
You Can't Get a Man with a Gun (Reprise)	Ethel Merman

Act II:

Lost in His Arms	Ethel Merman and Singers
There's No Business Like Show Business (Reprise)	Bruce Yarnell, Benay Venuta, Jack Dabdoub, Ronn Carroll, Patricia Hall
I Got the Sun in the Morning	Ethel Merman and Company
Old Fashioned Wedding	Ethel Merman and Bruce Yarnell
The Girl That I Marry (Reprise)	Bruce Yarnell
Anything You Can Do	Ethel Merman and Bruce Yarnell
Show Business (Reprise)	Ensemble
They Say It's Wonderful	Ethel Merman and Company

1970   HELLO, DOLLY!

Book by Michael Stewart; songs by Jerry Herman; produced by David Merrick; staged and choreographed by Lucia Victor, after the original staging and choreography of Gower Champion; settings by Oliver Smith; costumes by Freddy Wittop. Opened January 16, 1964, at the St. James Theater; Ethel Merman joined cast March 28, 1970. 2844 performances.

Cast:

Mrs. Dolly Gallagher Levi	Ethel Merman
Ernestina	Marcia Lewis
Ambrose Kemper	David Gary
Horse	Patty Pappathatos and Ellen Elias
Horace Vandergelder	Jack Goode
Ermengarde	Patricia Cope
Cornelius Hackl	Russell Nype
Barnaby Tucker	Danny Lockin
Irene Malloy	June Helmers
Minnie Fay	Georgia Engel
Mrs. Rose	Joyce Dahl
Rudolph	James Beard
Judge	George Blackwell
Court Clerk	Dick Crowley

Townspeople, waiters, etc.: Beverly Baker, Maggie Benson, Monica Carter, Joyce Dahl, Ellen Elias, Gwen Hillier, Lee Hooper, Irma Kingsley, Janice Painchaud, Patty Pappathatos, Jacqueline Payne, Pat Trott, Elise Warner, Paul Berne, George Blackwell, Ted Bloecher, Wayne Boyd, Jack Craig, Ron Crofoot, Dick Crowley, Richard Dodd, Mark East, David Evans, Ed Goldsmid, Joseph Helms, Jim Hovis, Robert L. Hultman, J. David Kirby, Sean Nolan

Orchestra under the direction of Saul Schechtman

MUSICAL NUMBERS

Act I:

I Put My Hand In	Ethel Merman and Company
It Takes a Woman	Jack Goode and the Instant Glee Club
World, Take Me Back	Ethel Merman
Put on Your Sunday Clothes	Russell Nype, Danny Lockin, Ethel Merman, David Gary, Patricia Cope
Ribbons Down My Back	June Helmers
Motherhood	Ethel Merman, Jack Goode, June Helmers, Georgia Engel, Russell Nype, Danny Lockin

Dancing	Ethel Merman, Russell Nype, Danny Lockin, Georgia Engel, June Helmers, Dancers
Love, Look in My Window	Ethel Merman
Before the Parade Passes By	Ethel Merman, Jack Goode, Company

Act II:

Elegance	June Helmers, Russell Nype, Georgia Engel, Danny Lockin
The Waiters' Gallop	James Beard and Waiters
Hello, Dolly!	Ethel Merman, James Beard, Cooks, Waiters
The Polka Contest	David Gary, Patricia Cope, June Helmers, Russell Nype, Georgia Engel, Danny Lockin, Contestants
It Only Takes a Moment	Russell Nype, June Helmers, Danny Lockin, Contestants
So Long, Dearie	Ethel Merman and Jack Goode
Hello, Dolly! (Reprise)	Ethel Merman and Jack Goode
Finale	Entire Company

Films

1930   FOLLOW THE LEADER

Paramount. Based on the Broadway musical *Manhattan Mary* by William K. Wells and George White; songs by B. G. DeSylva, Lew Brown and Ray Henderson; directed by Norman Taurog.

Cast:

Crickets	Ed Wynn
Mary Brennan	Ginger Rogers
Helen King	Ethel Merman

Stanley Smith, Lou Holtz, Lida Kane, Bobby Watson, Donald Kirke, William Halligan, Holly Hall, Preston Foster, James C. Morton

1934   WE'RE NOT DRESSING

Paramount. Screenplay by Horace Jackson, Frances Marion and George Marion Jr., based on a story by Benjamin Glazer; music and lyrics by Harry Revel and Mack Gordon.

Cast:

Stephen Jones	Bing Crosby
Doris Washington	Carole Lombard

George	George Burns
Gracie	Gracie Allen
Edith	Ethel Merman
Hubert	Leon Errol
Prince Alexander Stofani	Jay Henry
Prince Michael Stofani	Raymond Milland
Old Sailor	John Irwin
Captain	Charles Morris
First Ship's Officer	Ben Hendricks
Second Ship's Officer	Ted Oliver

KID MILLIONS

Samuel Goldwyn-UA. Written and adapted by Arthur Sheekman, Nat Perrin, Nunnally Johnson; songs by Walter Donaldson and Gus Kahn, Burton Lane and Harold Adamson, and Alfred Newman; dance ensembles by Seymour Felix.

Cast:

Eddie	Eddie Cantor
Jane Larrabee	Ann Sothern
Dot	Ethel Merman
Jerry Lane	George Murphy
Ben Ali	Jesse Block
Fanya	Eve Sully
Colonel Larrabee	Burton Churchill
Louie the Lug	Warren Hymer
Sheik Mulhulla	Paul Harvey
Khoot	Otto Hoffman
Toots	Doris Davenport
Herman	Ed Kennedy
Oscar	Stanley Fields
Adolph	John Kelly
Pop	Jack Kennedy
Stymie	Stymie Beard
Tommy	Tommy Bond
Leonard	Leonard Kilbrick
Slade	Guy Usher

STRIKE ME PINK

Samuel Goldwyn-UA. Screenplay by Frank Butler, Walter DeLeon and
Francis Martin, with additional dialogue by Philip Rapp, based on a story
by Clarence Budington Kelland; music and lyrics by Harold Arlen and
Lew Brown; directed by Norman Taurog.

Cast:

Eddie Pink	Eddie Cantor
Joyce	Ethel Merman
Claribel	Sally Eilers
Parkyakarkus	Harry Parke
Copple	William Frawley
Ma Carson	Helen Lowell
Butch	Gordon Jones
Vance	Brian Donlevy
Thrust	Jack LaRue
Sunnie	Sunnie O'Dea
Rita	Rita Rio
Killer	Edward Brophy
Chorley	Sidney H. Fields
Marsh	Don Brodie
Selby	Charles McAvoy
Miller	Stanley Blystone
Smiley	Duke York
Hardin	Charles Wilson
Pitchman	Clyde Hagar

and The Goldwyn Girls

ANYTHING GOES

Paramount. Taken from the musical comedy by Howard Lindsay and Rus-
sel Crouse; music and lyrics by Cole Porter, with additional songs by Leo
Robin, Richard A. Whiting, Frederick Hollander, Hoagy Carmichael and
Edward Heyman; directed by Lewis Milestone.

Cast:

Billy Crocker	Bing Crosby
Reno Sweeney	Ethel Merman
Rev. Dr. Moon	Charles Ruggles

Hope Harcourt	Ida Lupino
Bonnie LaTour	Grace Bradley
Sir Evelyn Oakleigh	Arthur Treacher
Elisha J. Whitney	Robert McWade
Bishop Dobson	Richard Carle
Mrs. Wentworth	Margaret Dumont
Detective	Edward Gargan
Ship's Captain	Matt Moore
Bearded Man	Rolfe Sedan

1938   HAPPY LANDING

20th Century-Fox. Screenplay by Milton Sperling and Boris Ingster; music and lyrics by Sam Parkass and Jack Yellen, Walter Bullock and Harold Spina; directed by Roy Del Ruth.

Cast:

Truly Ericksen	Sonja Henie
Jimmy Hall	Don Ameche
Herr Ericksen	Jean Hersholt
Flo Kelly	Ethel Merman
Duke Sargent	Cesar Romero
Counter Man	Billy Gilbert
Raymond Scott Quintet	Themselves
Al Mahoney	Wally Vernon
Specialists	Peters Sisters, Condos Brothers
Yonnie	El Brendel
Gypsy	Marcelle Corday
Agent	Joseph Crehan
Waiter	Eddie Conrad
Rink Manager	Ben Weldon

ALEXANDER'S RAGTIME BAND

20th Century-Fox. Screenplay by Kathryn Scola and Lamar Trotti, adaptation by Richard Sherman; music and lyrics by Irving Berlin; directed by Henry King.

Cast:

Alexander (Roger Grant)	Tyrone Power
Stella Kirby	Alice Faye
Charlie Dwyer	Don Ameche
Jerry Allen	Ethel Merman
Davey Lane	Jack Haley
Professor Heinrich	Jean Hersholt
Aunt Sophie	Helen Westley
Taxi Driver	John Carradine
Bill	Paul Hurst
Wally Vernon	Himself
Ruby	Ruth Terry
Snapper	Douglas Fowley
Louie	Chick Chandler
Corporal Collins	Eddie Collins
Stage Manager	Joseph Crehan
Eddie	Robert Gleckler
Specialty	Dixie Dunbar
Charles Dillingham	Joe King
Head Waiter	Charles Coleman
Colonel	Stanley Andrews

STRAIGHT, PLACE AND SHOW

20th Century-Fox. Screenplay by M. M. Musselman and Allen Rivkin, with additional dialogue by Lew Brown; based on the unproduced play *Saratoga Chips* by Damon Runyon and Irving Caesar; music and lyrics by Lew Brown and Lew Pollack; directed by David Butler.

Cast:

Ritz Brothers	Themselves
Denny	Richard Arlen
Linda	Ethel Merman
Barbara Drake	Phyllis Brooks
Drake	George Barbier
Braddock	Sidney Blackmer
Truck Driver	Will Stanton
Russians	Ivan Lebedeff, Gregory Gaye, Rafael Storm
Slippery Sol	Stanley Fields

Terrible Turk	Tiny Roebuck
Promoter	Ben Weldon
Detective	Ed Gargan
Referee	Pat McKee

1943   STAGE DOOR CANTEEN

Sol Lesser-American Theatre Wing-UA. Screenplay by Delmer Daves; songs by Jimmy Monaco, Richard Rodgers, Lorenz Hart, Johnny Green and Gertrude Lawrence; directed by Frank Borzage.

Cast:

Eileen	Cheryl Walker
"Dakota" Ed Smith	William W. Terry
Jean	Marjorie Riordan
"California"	Lon MacAllister
Ellen Sue	Margaret Early
"Texas"	Michael Harrison
Mamie	Dorothea Kent
"Jersey"	Fred Brady
Lillian	Marion Shockley
The Australian	Patrick O'Moore
The Captain	Louis Jean Heydt

plus some 70 guest stars, including Ethel Merman

1953   CALL ME MADAM

20th Century-Fox. Screenplay by Arthur Sheekman, based on the musical comedy by Howard Lindsay and Russel Crouse; songs by Irving Berlin; directed by Walter Lang.

Cast:

Mrs. Sally Adams	Ethel Merman
Kenneth	Donald O'Connor
Princess Maria	Vera-Ellen
Cosmo Constantine	George Sanders
Pemberton Maxwell	Billy De Wolfe
Prince Hugo	Helmut Dantine

Tantinnin	Walter Slezak
Sebastian	Steven Geray
Grand Duke	Ludwig Stossel
Grand Duchess	Lilia Skala
Senator Brockway	Charles Dingle
Senator Gallagher	Emory Parnell
Senator Wilkins	Percy Helton
Bandleader	Leon Belasco
Chamberlain	Oscar Beregi
Miccoli	Nestor Palva

1954 THERE'S NO BUSINESS LIKE SHOW BUSINESS

20th Century-Fox. Screenplay by Phoebe and Henry Ephron, based on a story by Lamar Trotti; songs by Irving Berlin; directed by Walter Lang.

Cast:

Molly Donahue	Ethel Merman
Tim Donahue	Donald O'Connor
Vicky	Marilyn Monroe
Terrance Donahue	Dan Dailey
Steve	Johnny Ray
Katy Donahue	Mitzi Gaynor
Lew Harris	Richard Eastham
Charles Gibbs	Hugh O'Brian
Eddie Dugan	Frank McHugh
Father Dineen	Rhys Williams
Marge	Lee Patrick
Helen, hatcheck girl	Eve Miller
Lillian Sawyer	Robin Raymon
Stage Manager	Lyle Talbot

1963 IT'S A MAD, MAD, MAD, MAD WORLD

Stanley Kramer-UA. Screenplay by William and Tania Rose; directed by Stanley Kramer.

305

Cast:

Capt. C. G. Culpepper	Spencer Tracy
J. Russell Finch	Milton Berle
Melville Trump	Sid Caesar
Benjy Benjamin	Buddy Hackett
Mrs. Marcus	Ethel Merman
Ding Bell	Mickey Rooney
Sylvester Marcus	Dick Shawn
Otto Meyer	Phil Silvers
J. Algernon Hawthorne	Terry-Thomas
Lennie Pike	Jonathan Winters
Monica Crump	Edie Adams
Emmeline Finch	Dorothy Provine
Smiler Grogan	Jimmy Durante
First Cab Driver	Eddie "Rochester" Anderson
Tyler Fitzgerald	Jim Backus
Airplane Pilot	Ben Blue
Police Sergeant	Alan Carney
Mrs. Haliburton	Barry Chase
Chief of Police	William Demarest
Second Cab Driver	Peter Falk
Colonel Wilberforce	Paul Ford
Dinckler	Edward Everett Horton
Jimmy, the crook	Buster Keaton

Don Knotts, Carl Reiner, the Three Stooges, Joe E. Brown, Andy Devine, Sterling Holloway, Charles McGraw, Jesse White, Lloyd Corrigan, Marvin Kaplan, Arnold Stang and Jerry Lewis

1965   **THE ART OF LOVE**

Universal. Screenplay by Carl Reiner, from a story by Richard Alan Simmons and William Sackheim; produced by Ross Hunter; directed by Norman Jewison.

Cast:

Casey	James Garner
Paul	Dick Van Dyke
Nikki	Elke Sommer
Laurie	Angie Dickinson

Madam Coco   Ethel Merman
Rodin   Carl Reiner
Carnot   Pierre Olaf
Chou Chou   Miiko Taka

INDEX

Merman, Ethel (*continued*)
and Robert Levitt, 119–25, 144–45,
156, 167–68, 182. *See also*
Levitt, Robert Daniels
London performances, 232–35
records, 74, 156, 157, 166, 186, 194,
221, 151
relationship with her parents,
10–11, 61–62, 122–23. *See
also* Zimmermann, Edward;
Zimmermann, Agnes Gardner
and Robert Six, 175–79, 182,
184–85, 187–91, 195–97, 200–01,
209–10
and William R. Smith, 111, 115–17
television appearances, 197, 223–25,
242, 244, 253–58
Anything Goes, 191
Ethel Merman on Broadway, 208
Ford Motors Jubilee, 185–86
in *Together on Broadway*, 252–62
vaudeville performances, 36–37, 39,
50–51
Merrick, David, 211–12
and *Gypsy*, 202
and *Hello, Dolly!* 218, 235, 248–49
Messina, Joe, 252
Mesta, Perle, 159–60, 165–66, 253
Middleton, Ray, 140, 149
Milland, Ray, 63
Miller, Glenn, 45
"Mr. Monotony," 163–64
"Moanin' Low," 34–35
Mok, Michael, 82
Monroe, Marilyn, 192
"Moonshine Lullaby," 139
Moore, Grace, 44
Moore, Victor
and *Anything Goes*, 69, 70–71, 72
and *Red, Hot and Blue*, 78–79
Morgan, Helen, 55
Moth and the Flame, The, 131
Mother Courage, 9
Muppets, The, 255–256
Murphy, George, 65, 189
Murphy, Julie, 65
Murray, Arthur, 186
Murrow, Edward R., 185, 188–89
Museum of the City of New York, 258
"Mutual Admiration Society," 198, 256

"My Mother Would Love You," 113
"My New Kentucky Home," 101
Myrtil, Odette, 23
"My Song," 54

Nathan, George Jean, 142
National Theater (Washington), 177–78
Natwick, Mildred, 100
NBC, 152, 169, 170, 208
Nesbitt, Fred, 189
Neubert, Martha, 10, 16, 26, 171
New York State Theater, 241
"Nice She Ain't," 204
Nichols, Lewis, 128–29
Nichols, Red, 45
Nixon, Richard, 86, 211
North, Sterling, 121
Nugent, Frank S., 92
Nype, Diantha, 14, 174, 248
Nype, Russell, 14, 97, 169, 174
in *Call Me Madam*, 162–66, 247–48
in *Hello, Dolly!* 248
and the Texas State Fair, 189

O'Connor, Donald, 184, 191–92
Odd Couple, The, 254
O'Keefe, Walter, 59
"Old Fashioned Wedding," 239
"Oldies," 157
Old Man Blues, 50, 61
Olivier, Sir Laurence, 211–12, 237
Olsen, Ole, 60
"Once Upon a Nickel," 157
"Once Upon a Time," 163
Orbach, Jerry, 240
Osterwald, Bibi, 248
"Ozarks Are Calling Me Home, The,"
82

Palace Theater, 23, 37, 39, 50, 57
Pal Joey, 180–81
Palladium (London), 232, 234, 253
Palm Erik, 252
Palmer, Bea, 36, 45
Panama Hattie, 111–14, 124, 219, 281–
282
Paramount, 61–64, 77–78, 82–83

316

Paramount Theater, 50, 78–79, 86
Parkass, Sam, 90
Parker, Fess, 208
Parker, Lew, 204
Parsons, Estelle, 198
Parsons, Louella, 87, 89, 97
Pavillon Royale (L.I.), 36
Pendleton, Austin, 257
Pene du Bois, Raoul, 106, 111–12
Peninger, Jack, 252
Perrin, Nat, 65
Persian Room, 222
Pickens, Jane, 163, 173
Pickett, Claude Gilchrist, 21
Plaza (New York), 225
Plowright, Joan, 237
"Pocket Full of Dreams," 93
Polk, Gordon, 198
Pollard, Dr. Irving, 13, 167
Porter, Cole, 9, 77, 133–34, 142, 164
  and *Anything Goes*, 69–70, 72–74, 191
  and *DuBarry Was a Lady*, 106, 108
  and Linda Porter's illness, 153–54
  and *Leave It to Me*, 106
  method of composing for EM, 136
  and *Panama Hattie*, 111, 113
  and *Red, Hot, and Blue*, 78–79, 80, 81, 82
  and *Something for the Boys*, 127, 128–29
  and television special, 255, 256, 257
Porter, Linda, 74, 80, 153–54
Poston, Tom, 208
Power, Tyrone, 91
Provine, Dorothy, 220

Quinn, Anthony, 211–12

Radio Corporation of America, 160, 166, 176
Ragland, Rags, 112, 113, 114
Rancourt, Donna, 231–32
Randall, Carl, 102
Randolph, Clemence, 135
Ray, Johnny, 192
Raye, Martha, 248
Red, Hot and Blue, 78–83, 274–76
"Red, Hot, and Blue," 81
"Red, Red Robin," 262

Reflected Glory, 197
Regan, Phil, 106
Reiner, Carl, 220, 235
Reisman, Leo, 49
Revel, Harry, 63
Rhythm at 8, 74
Richmond Club, 47, 48
"Ridin' High," 81
"Rise and Shine," 59
Ritz Theater (Elizabeth, N.J.), 36
RKO Studios, 105
Roaming, 50, 61
Robbins, Jerome, 102, 160
  and *Gypsy*, 202, 204
Robin, Leo, 78
Rockefeller, Winthrop, 75–76
Rodgers, Richard, 87, 181
  and *Annie Get Your Gun*, 139, 146–48, 240
Rogers, Eileen, 240–41
Rogers, Ginger, 38–39, 40, 50, 105, 248
Romano, Jane, 208
Roman Pools Casino (Miami), 34–35
Romberg, Sigmund, 138
Romero, Cesar, 88–90
Rooney, Mickey, 220, 221
Roosevelt, Franklin Delano, 50
Roosevelt Hospital, 15–17
Rose, Billy, 57, 62, 102, 132–33
Rose, Tania, 220
Rose, William, 220
Rose Marie, 255
Rosenberg, George, 254
Rosenstock, Milton, 211–12
"Rose's Turn," 203, 204, 205
Ross, Bob, 100
Rubin, Benny, 57
Ruggles, Charlie, 77
Russell, Rosalind, 205, 219

Sadie Thompson, 135–37, 198
Sadler, Donald, 260
"Sailor's Not a Sailor Till a Sailor's Been Tattooed, A," 192
St. Bartholomew's Church, 13, 154, 167
"Sam and Delilah," 38, 40, 48, 260, 264
Sanders, George, 184
Scandals (George White's), 29, 30, 49
  1931 edition, 53–56, 57, 269–70

319